Scientific Jury Selection

The LAW AND PUBLIC POLICY: PSYCHOLOGY AND THE SOCIAL SCIENCES series includes books in three domains:

Legal Studies—writings by legal scholars about issues of relevance to psychology and the other social sciences, or that employ social science information to advance the legal analysis;

Social Science Studies—writings by scientists from psychology and the other social sciences about issues of relevance to law and public policy; and

Forensic Studies—writings by psychologists and other mental health scientists and professionals about issues relevant to forensic mental health science and practice.

The series is guided by its editor, Bruce D. Sales, PhD, JD, University of Arizona; and coeditors, Bruce J. Winick, JD, University of Miami; Norman J. Finkel, PhD, Georgetown University; and Valerie P. Hans, PhD, University of Delaware.

* * *

Scientific Jury Selection

Joel D. Lieberman
Bruce D. Sales

AMERICAN PSYCHOLOGICAL ASSOCIATION

WASHINGTON, DC

Published by
American Psychological Association
750 First Street, NE
Washington, DC 20002
www.apa.org

To order
APA Order Department
P.O. Box 92984
Washington, DC 20090-2984
Tel: (800) 374-2721; Direct: (202) 336-5510
Fax: (202) 336-5502; TDD/TTY: (202) 336-6123
Online: www.apa.org/books/
E-mail: order@apa.org

In the U.K., Europe, Africa, and the Middle East, copies may be ordered from
American Psychological Association
3 Henrietta Street
Covent Garden, London
WC2E 8LU England

Typeset in Goudy by Stephen McDougal, Mechanicsville, MD

Printer: Data Reproductions, Auburn Hills, MI
Cover Designer: Berg Design, Albany, NY
Technical/Production Editor: Genevieve Gill

The opinions and statements published are the responsibility of the authors, and such opinions and statements do not necessarily represent the policies of the American Psychological Association.

Library of Congress Cataloging-in-Publication Data

Lieberman, Joel D.
   Scientific jury selection / by Joel D. Lieberman and Bruce D. Sales. — 1st ed.
     p. cm. — (Law and public policy)
   Includes bibliographical references and index.
   ISBN-13: 978-1-59147-427-2
   ISBN-10: 1-59147-427-2
   1. Jury selection—United States. 2. Jury selection—Psychological aspects.
3. Jury selection—Social aspects. I. Sales, Bruce Dennis. II. Title. III. Series.

   KF8979.L54 2006
   347.73'752—dc22   2006000083

British Library Cataloguing-in-Publication Data
A CIP record is available from the British Library.

Printed in the United States of America
First Edition

To Celia, for all that she is.
And to my mother and father, for all that they have done.
—*Joel D. Lieberman*

For Mary Elizabeth
—*Bruce D. Sales*

CONTENTS

Scientific Jury Selection

1

HISTORY AND OVERVIEW OF THE
SCIENTIFIC JURY SELECTION PROCESS

Over the past 3 decades, the use of social science consultants to aid attorneys in selecting jurors has grown from a novel activity performed in rare social justice-oriented cases to a full-scale industry whose practitioners are called on in almost any major litigation (Strier, 1999). This technique, commonly known as *scientific jury selection*, has become so common in major cases that it has been popularized in best-selling fiction and films (e.g., *Runaway Jury*; Grisham, 1996).

Although jury selection consultants are now more likely to advise in civil rather than criminal cases (Strier & Shestowsky, 1999), scientific jury selection originated in criminal trials in which academic researchers provided assistance to defense counsel because the researchers were concerned about the government having a disproportionate degree of power and control over the outcome of cases. Specifically, the 1972 Harrisburg Seven trial led to the development of the field of jury selection consulting and the widespread application of scientific jury selection.

HARRISBURG SEVEN TRIAL

The events surrounding the Harrisburg Seven trial inspired a group of social scientists to become involved with trial preparation. One of these critical incidents occurred when J. Edgar Hoover, then director of the FBI, asked Congress for additional funds to control antiwar protesters, including a group known as the East Coast Conspiracy to Save Lives. This group of priests, nuns, and students was led by Philip and Daniel Berrigan, both Catholic priests. The FBI had been eager to prosecute the group for years because its members were involved in many Vietnam War protests and engaged in such activities as pouring blood on draft board records and destroying selective service records with homemade napalm.

Soon after Hoover's appeal to Congress, the Department of Justice indicted Father Philip Berrigan and six other members of the group on a number of charges. The indictment accused the seven of conspiring to destroy records held by draft boards, conspiring to kidnap presidential advisor Henry Kissinger, and conspiring to blow up heating tunnels in Washington, DC. Although the draft boards named in the indictment were in Philadelphia, New York City, and Rochester, New York, the government chose to hold the trial in Harrisburg, Pennsylvania. Harrisburg was considered a conservative area, with "three Republicans for every two Democrats; an unusually low proportion of Catholics and an unusually high proportion of fundamentalist religious sects; several military installations and war-related industries; and an active Ku Klux Klan" (Schulman, Shaver, Colman, Emrich, & Christie, 1973, p. 37). The judge assigned to the trial was Federal District Judge R. Dixon Herman, a Nixon appointee, and considerable pretrial publicity surrounded the case. The government's pretrial actions led sociologist Jay Schulman and his colleagues, supporters of the antiwar movement, to believe that a jury drawn from this location would have a strong bias in favor of the prosecution, thus making it impossible to hold a fair trial. As a consequence, the Schulman group, "a coalition of social scientists, activists, and citizens," offered their services to assist the defense in creating a more impartial jury (Schulman et al., 1973, p. 39).

Before the trial began, the consulting team conducted both phone and face-to-face interviews in the Harrisburg community. This pretrial research enabled the team to identify key characteristics of survey respondents (e.g., religion, attitudes toward the government) that were related to verdict preferences. With this information, the defense team could question prospective jurors about these characteristics during the jury selection phase of the trial, traditionally known as *voir dire* (a French term meaning "to speak the truth"). In addition, the researchers developed a profile of an ideal juror. This allowed the defense team to exclude potential jurors who did not fit this profile, including those who would be particularly problematic; the specific techniques used by Schulman and his associates are described in greater detail in chapter 3.

Following voir dire, the government took 2 months to present its case. After the prosecution rested, the defense countered with the bold move of simply proclaiming the innocence of the seven defendants in its opening statement and not calling any witnesses. The jurors deliberated for 7 days before reaching the conclusion that they were hopelessly deadlocked, with 10 jurors favoring acquittal and 2 jurors favoring conviction. Despite the fact that the government spent an estimated $2 million to prosecute this case, it ended in a hung jury on all the principal charges of conspiracy. The defendants were not retried.

OTHER EARLY TRIALS USING SCIENTIFIC JURY SELECTION CONSULTANTS

Following the trial, Schulman applied his jury selection consulting methods to other cases in which he believed there was government oppression. For example, several years later he was a consultant for the defense in the Wounded Knee trials (Sayer, 1997), in which the government prosecuted Native American activists for occupying federal land and for other offenses related to the activists' behaviors. In one case, only 40% of the prospective jurors during voir dire indicated that they had followed the case in the media, even though Schulman's pretrial research showed that three quarters of the individuals in that jurisdiction had closely followed the events surrounding the case. Schulman later conducted personal interviews with the prospective jurors, and many admitted that they had intentionally lied during voir dire because they wanted to serve on the jury (Hans & Vidmar, 1986). In a related state criminal case, the trial judge dismissed the case against the defendants prior to jury selection, concluding that it would be impossible to empanel a fair jury in the South Dakota county where the trial was being held or in any other county in the state because of overwhelming bias against the defendants. The judge reached this decision after hearing testimony from Schulman about the results of his statewide survey on the attitudes of people in South Dakota toward the Wounded Knee incident and defendants.

Schulman's team included psychologist Richard Christie, who applied his research on authoritarianism to determine whether prospective jurors would be more likely to vote for conviction or acquittal (see chap. 5). Schulman and the legal team invited one of the authors of this book, psychologist–lawyer Bruce Sales, and one of his JD–PhD students David Suggs— who is now a practicing attorney—to participate in the Wounded Knee trials in South Dakota and Nebraska. They applied their research on in-court communication cues (see chap. 7) to evaluate prospective jurors during voir dire.

Some or all of the selection techniques recommended by Schulman, Christie, Sales, and Suggs were subsequently used in numerous political trials (e.g., Camden 28, Gainesville Eight, Angela Davis, other Wounded Knee cases, Attica, Mitchell–Stans conspiracy trial, etc.; Christie, 1976; Kairys, Kadane, & Lehoczky, 1975; McConahay, Mullin, & Frederick, 1977; Shapley,

1974; Strier, 1999; Zeisel & Diamond, 1976). Many of the jury selection consultants in these trials were attempting to help indigent defendants against alleged government oppression (Strier, 1999); therefore, the fees they charged were nominal (approximately $450 in the Harrisburg Seven trial). However, it was not long before jury selection methods were applied by social science consultants to civil trials with far more lucrative rewards, and in 1975 Schulman founded the first professional trial consulting firm, the National Jury Project (http://www.njp.com). This firm originally specialized in jury selection.

THE EVOLUTION OF JURY SELECTION CONSULTING AS A PROFESSIONAL INDUSTRY

The following year, Donald Vinson, a marketing professor at the University of Southern California, was contacted by the law firm of Cravath, Swaine & Moore to help in a large antitrust case brought against their client, IBM. The case involved a variety of complex technological and economic issues. Jurors often have great difficulty managing the magnitude and complexity of information presented in this type of case (Cecil, Lind, & Bermant, 1987), a situation that can lead jurors to rely on their preconceived attitudes and biases in their decision making. As a consequence, the attorneys in the case wanted to identify potential jurors' pretrial attitudes and experiences that might influence their interpretation of trial evidence. Vinson used a variety of research approaches, such as survey research (see chap. 3), focus groups, and shadow jurors (see chap. 9) to assist the attorneys. Following the presentation of the plaintiff's case, a directed verdict was delivered and IBM won the case. Considerable publicity surrounded the trial and generated a great deal of interest in the jury selection services provided by consultants with social science knowledge. Vinson's success in the case led him to leave his position at the University of Southern California and create a company known as Litigation Sciences in 1979 (D. E. Vinson, personal communication, September 2, 2005). Over the next decade, Litigation Sciences became one of the leading firms providing selection services. Vinson sold the firm in 1987 and several years later created DecisionQuest (http://www.desisionquest.com). This firm provided the consultation services for the prosecution in the O.J. Simpson criminal trial.

Aware that prosecutors' offices rarely have the financial resources necessary to retain jury selection consultants, Vinson offered the services of DecisionQuest to District Attorney Gil Garcetti and Lead Prosecutor Marcia Clark on a pro bono basis (Toobin, 1996). Vinson began his research by recruiting an ethnically diverse group of thirty individuals from Los Angeles to act as jurors and provide their reactions to the basic facts of the case. The mock jurors listened to opening statements delivered by attorneys who played the roles of prosecutors and defense lawyers. The reactions of the simulated jurors were overwhelmingly split along racial lines. African Americans clearly favored acquittal, and Whites were strongly in favor of conviction. Vinson conducted further research in Phoenix, a city with demographically comparable jurors. Yet again, African Americans indicated strong support for O.J. Simpson, with the strongest level of support coming from African American women, who also expressed a highly pejorative reaction to Marcia Clark. Jo-Ellan Dimitrius, the selection consultant for the defense team in the criminal prosecution of O.J. Simpson, independently arrived at the same conclusions, as described later in this subsection.

Although Vinson provided this information to the prosecutors, after a day and a half of jury selection he was informed that his work was no longer needed in the case and his guidelines were ignored. Instead, Marcia Clark decided to rely on her gut-level feelings that African American women would warmly accept and support her interpretation of the facts. When voir dire was complete, 12 jurors and 12 alternates had been selected. Although the initial pool of jurors summoned to the courthouse was 28.1% African American and 37.9% Caucasian, with the remaining ethnic background of jurors split among Asians, Hispanics, and other minority groups, the demographic composition of the actual jury was strikingly different. Of the 24 jurors and alternates, 15 were African American, 6 were White, and 3 were Latinos. At the beginning of the trial, the prosecution was so comfortable with the demographic makeup of the jury that they chose not to use several of the 20 peremptory challenges they were allotted to remove potential jurors from the panel (see chap. 2 for a detailed explanation of how potential jurors get challenged and excused from jury duty). The final 12-person jury was composed of 1 African American man, 8 African American women, 1 Latino man, and 2 White women. After 8 months of testimony from a multitude of witnesses, the jurors after only a few hours of deliberation acquitted O.J. Simpson of the criminal charges that he killed Nicole Brown Simpson and Ronald Goldman (Toobin, 1996).

The verdict was a major victory for the defense "Dream Team" that included Johnny Cochran, Robert Shapiro, F. Lee Bailey, Barry Scheck, and Peter Neufeld. However, during the press conference following the trial, the attorneys gave a large amount of credit for their success to Jo-Ellan Dimitrius, their selection consultant. Dimitrius, then a consultant with the firm of Forensic Technologies Incorporated (http://www.fticonsulting.com/web), had originally been hired by Shapiro to assist with jury selection.

In the months leading up to the voir dire phase of the trial, Dimitrius conducted extensive pretrial research that included community surveys (see chap. 3) and focus groups (chap. 9) and had identified pretrial opinions of individuals in downtown Los Angeles with demographically similar backgrounds to those of potential jury pool members. Like Vinson, Dimitrius's pretrial research also indicated that African American women were overwhelmingly strong supporters of O.J. Simpson (Toobin, 1996). In a memorandum entitled "General Considerations for Jury Selection" that Dimitrius provided to the defense team to aid in the selection process, she identified key attributes of the most preferred jurors, including: "Young; Less Educated; Blue Collar; African American [women]; No Prior Jury Service; Lower Income" (Toobin, 1996, p. 66). Through the strategic use of challenges to prospective jurors, the defense excluded jurors who did not match this profile, which resulted in a jury with racial and gender characteristics that reflected the demographics recommended by Dimitrius. This was in marked contrast to the prosecution, which ignored the advice of jury selection consultant Donald Vinson. As the jurors ultimately produced a verdict that was congruent with the research results of both consultants, the outcome can be argued to be a tremendous success for jury selection consulting.

Selection consultants have assisted in many other high profile trials. The most famous recent criminal cases involving consultants include the trials of Michael Jackson, Scott Peterson, Kobe Bryant, and Martha Stewart (Chawkins, 2005; Dearen, 2004; Kalajian, 2004; "Traits of the Right Juror," 2004). Consultants played a part in several major cases of the 1990s, including the trial of police officers involved in the Rodney King beating, William Kennedy Smith's rape trial, and the Menendez brothers' trial for the murders of their parents (K. Moran, 1991; "Simpson Defense Hires Trial Consultant," 1994; Wozniak, 1995). In addition, jury selection consultants have worked on many well-known civil cases, such as lawsuits against tobacco companies (Chiang, 2002), the MCI v. AT&T antitrust suit, the Dow Corning breast implant litigation, and the famed McDonald's coffee case that involved a customer who sued the hamburger chain and was originally awarded close to $3 million by the jury for burns caused by overheated coffee (Strier, 1999). In fact, the practice of jury selection consulting has become so commonplace that some attorneys maintain it is almost unthinkable that a lawyer in a major trial not use a consultant (Walker, 1995).

WHO ARE JURY SELECTION CONSULTANTS?

Originally, jury selection consultants were academic researchers interested in studying this topic or in assisting counsel because of the nature of the case. The latter group did not exclusively devote their professional lives to these consulting activities, but as the field developed during the late 1970s and 1980s it became a full-time profession for many practitioners. Some of these professionals, who eventually offered more than jury selection services, established the American Society of Trial Consultants (http://www.astcweb.org) in 1982, which has grown from a small group of about 15 members (Shartel, 1994) to an organization with over 400 members (American Society of Trial Consultants, 2004).

Although there are no specific data on the backgrounds of consultants who perform jury selection services, looking at the data relevant to the larger group of trial consultants is instructive. Trial consultants have diverse levels of overall education and areas of specialization of their highest degree. Strier and Shestowsky (1999) assessed the backgrounds of trial consultants by mailing a survey to all members of the American Society of Trial Consultants. One hundred seven consultants responded, representing a 35% response rate. The results indicated that roughly half of the consultants (51%) had a PhD, with 6% of respondents possessing both a PhD and JD degree. Thirty-two percent of respondents held a master's degree, 7% only a bachelor's degree, and 5% the juris doctor degree. In addition, 3% held a doctor of education degree, 1% held a doctor of psychology (PsyD) degree, and 1% had no college education at all. The largest percentage of trial consultants (49%) were psychologists by training. Sixteen percent had a background in communications; 11% in law, either independently or combined with a discipline other than psychology; 5% in political science; 4% in psychology and law; 4% in psychology and another specialization (not specifically reported); 3% in theater; and 13% in some other area (this includes 5% of individuals who had backgrounds in law and another specialization, reported previously for clarity).

Trial consultants' average age was reported as 45.3, with an age range from 18 to 74 years. The average amount of experience as a trial consultant was 9.6 years. Furthermore, "[a]bout 1/3 had prior professional experiences lasting 5 or more years in a field other than psychology or law. . . . This datum suggests that trial consulting has become a second career for a large portion of consultants with little or no formal background in the two traditional disciplines underlying consulting" (Strier & Shestowsky, 1999, p. 449). On the basis of these survey results, it appears that although many trial consultants possess doctorates in relevant disciplines like psychology, others who hang out a trial consultant shingle may have received minimal advanced training in scientific methodology and statistical analysis. This training, as we discuss throughout the book, is critical to jury selection consulting.

One could argue that a consultant who has extensive experience selecting jurors should be able to provide useful information to attorneys, regardless of his or her educational background. However, no one has, as yet, shown any reason why a consultant's experience-based decisions are superior to decisions made by an attorney who relies on her or his own experience (unless the attorney had minimal relevant trial experience). In addition, research on jury selection (discussed in chaps. 5 and 8) points to the importance of specificity in data collection. That is, it is important to measure how community members in the specific jurisdiction where a trial will be held respond to issues related to the trial. Such a determination requires data to be collected in a reliable and valid manner on a case-by-case basis.

Attorneys should determine the background of jury selection consultants when considering which to hire and should not assume that all trial consultants have similar backgrounds, nor focus solely on a consultant's experience. This is important because Shartel (1994) reported that interviews with several litigators revealed that the most important factor for trial lawyers in choosing a jury consultant was the consultant's experience. We do not dismiss the importance of experience; however, as we consider in detail in this book, it is important to combine experience with appropriate training, given the importance of science in jury selection consulting.

SURVEYS AND RELATED TRIAL CONSULTING SERVICES

When scientific jury selection is performed, community surveys are typically conducted in the geographic region from which the jury pool will be drawn (see chap. 3). The results of the surveys can reveal important information about the relationship of respondent characteristics (e.g., demographic information and experiences) to their attitudes and behaviors toward the case facts, litigants, and attorneys. Profiles of desirable and undesirable juror qualities are developed on the basis of this information, thus allowing attorneys to go beyond their gut-level hunches when conducting voir dire.

Community surveys can reveal useful information; however, it is essential that the information be effectively used during voir dire (see chaps. 6 and 8). After experiences, attitudes, and behaviors relevant to the trial outcome have been identified, the next step is to gain information from potential jurors to see if they possess the personal characteristics that are related to verdict propensities. During this step, care must be taken to determine whether prospective jurors respond the same way to the same or similar questions that were posed to individuals in the pretrial community survey. In addition, because potential jurors might lie about their experiences, attitudes, and behaviors, an examination of nonverbal behaviors during questioning can be used to reveal cues to deceptive responses and to determine which jurors are likely to emerge as leaders during deliberations (see chap. 7).

Although the best known aspect of trial consulting may be the selection of jurors based on community surveys (and in-court surveys of prospective jurors; see chap. 6), many professional trial consultants provide additional services to facilitate litigation based on a variety of social science research and marketing techniques (Strier, 1999), including change of venue services (chap. 3), mock jury studies (chap. 9), shadow jury studies (chap. 9), and posttrial interviews of jurors (chap. 9). These techniques allow additional data to be collected that can be used to make decisions in jury selection or to validate predictions made by the trial consultant regarding the verdict inclination of potential jurors. As a result, scientific jury selection and these other trial consulting services are inherently intertwined.

Change of Venue

The usefulness and applicability of conducting pretrial survey research in the jurisdiction where a trial will be held can go beyond identifying pretrial experiences, attitudes, and behaviors that are relevant to verdicts. Pretrial community surveys can also empirically demonstrate whether an existing bias among community members against one of the litigants, attorneys, or facts surrounding the case would indicate that selection of a fair and impartial jury is unlikely (see chap. 3). A content analysis of media coverage can also reveal the extent and source of biased attitudes in the community, as well as community awareness of such inadmissible information as failed polygraph results or pretrial settlement or plea offers. Scientifically based documentation of bias in that jurisdiction can be offered as evidence to convince a judge to change the trial location (i.e., change of venue) to one where potential jurors are less likely to be biased.

Mock Juries

Mock jury research refers to studies in which a group of individuals are hired and exposed to key elements of a case (e.g., potential opening or closing statements, witness testimony) before the information is presented in court (see chap. 9). Thus, attorneys can test their presentation style and refine trial strategies before the actual jurors are exposed to them. In addition, the consultant and attorney can determine how different types of individuals react to different presentation approaches. This information can be critical in identifying desirable potential jurors from each side's perspective, which can then be used to refine the consultant's selection recommendations to the attorney.

Shadow Juries

A shadow jury is similar to a mock jury, but shadow jurors sit in the actual courtroom and are exposed to the real trial (see chap. 9). At the end of each day, shadow jurors provide a critique of the trial to the consultants and attorneys. As a consequence, shadow jurors are able to provide feedback about their impressions of the evidence, witnesses, and attorneys based on the exact information that the real jurors are exposed to. Although shadow juries are typically a service that trial consultants provide to monitor the status of the trial, rather than as a jury selection tool, they can be used to validate jury selection predictions if the shadow jurors are matched to the actual jurors.

Posttrial Juror Interviews

At the conclusion of a trial, consultants can interview jurors about such important issues as their impressions of the evidence, their attitudes toward the parties involved (including the attorneys' presentation style), the effectiveness of the trial strategy, the jurors' general decision-making process, and the content of their deliberations. This information can be helpful for jury selection in future similar cases. In addition, posttrial interviews can be used to validate pretrial predictions regarding juror verdict inclination based on scientific jury selection.

DO ATTORNEYS NEED THE HELP
OF A JURY SELECTION CONSULTANT?

Jury selection consultants are able to provide a variety of services to attorneys, but are these services necessary? For example, shouldn't a skilled attorney be able to effectively exercise challenges during voir dire and develop a powerful strategy to persuade those selected to serve on the jury that the attorney's interpretation of facts should be adopted? Attorneys may believe they can achieve great success relying on their own judgments, but it is important to consider that although they are well trained in law, they are not trained in the scientific study of human behavior. Without information obtained from reliable research techniques, attorneys are ultimately forced to rely on their best guesses. These guesses are guided by their recollections of patterns of human behavior that are based on casual, often unintentional, observation of behavior. The deliberate observation and analysis of human behavior falls within the domain of social science disciplines such as psychology, sociology, communications, market research, psychiatry, and social work. Because these fields have developed refined techniques for the measurement of human behavior, it is possible to obtain results that have less bias, more reliability, and greater validity than observations made in the absence of formal research approaches.

Jury selection consultants would certainly point to their record of success as evidence for the superiority of their techniques over scientifically naïve attorney decision making. Attorneys who used selection consultants have claimed very high success rates since the first application of social science research to jury selection in the 1972 Harrisburg Seven trial (Hans & Vidmar, 1986). Ultimately, however, it is impossible to demonstrate that the outcome of a case, like O.J. Simpson's criminal trial, was largely due to the composition of the jury and, in that instance, driven by the defense team's adherence to (as well as the prosecution's dismissal of) the consultant's pretrial research. Couldn't the outcome have been determined by the power of the evidence for, or the effectiveness of the adversarial advocacy of, the winning side?

To determine whether selection consultants can improve attorney performance, particularly during voir dire, it is critical to know whether verdicts (jury behavior) can be predicted from demographic and personality factors or other identifiable pretrial attitudes or observed behaviors. There has been considerable social science research investigating the relationship between attitudes and behavior. Some social scientists have argued that background factors (demographics and attitudes) only explain a small amount of verdict variance (i.e., what explains the verdict; see chaps. 4, 5, and 8). Other research has shown that the inclusion of information about prospective jurors' general and case-specific attitudes will enhance predictive accuracy in the selection process. The extent to which it is possible to increase the accuracy of predictions about pretrial bias and verdict inclination and whether that enhanced accuracy makes it worth employing selection consultants is discussed throughout this book.

GOALS AND ORGANIZATION OF THIS BOOK

Given the importance of jury selection consultants to the modern practice of law, this book is designed to be informative for psychologists, other professionals interested in this type of consulting (e.g., sociologists, communication experts, market researchers, and psychiatrists), and attorneys. We provide a thorough review of the most common techniques consultants use to select jurors, accompanied by a critical evaluation of the effectiveness of these methods. This critique is based on an examination of relevant social science literature on jury selection consulting and on jury decision making when it has relevance to the selection phase of the trial.

To set the stage, chapter 2 provides an overview of the voir dire process, including the use of voir dire for purposes other than jury selection, such as educating jurors, enhancing impartiality, and ingratiation. A major focus of the chapter is on reviewing social science research that has attempted to determine the impact of jury selection on trial outcome.

Chapter 3 then takes a more detailed look at the use of community surveys to obtain information regarding attitudes held by the population of individuals from whom the jury will be drawn. This information can be used in identifying favorable and unfavorable types of jurors and for making more effective arguments for a change in venue. We also discuss the process of conducting community surveys to provide readers with an understanding of the methodological issues consultants must consider so that reliable and valid data can be collected.

The following two chapters, chapters 4 and 5, discuss demographic, personality, and attitudinal factors related to verdict outcome. These chapters begin with a discussion of traditional attorney beliefs regarding the influence of background characteristics, followed by a review of research studies that have investigated the connection between these characteristics and trial outcome.

Chapter 6 focuses on the application of social science findings to the process of questioning jurors in the courtroom. Issues such as who should do the questioning (the judge or the attorneys), the need for expanded questioning to reveal underlying biases, the style of questioning, the need for private questioning of jurors during voir dire, and the use of pretrial questionnaires for venire members are discussed. Many of these issues reflect approaches that are typically not used in voir dire because of time constraints but that could be used at the judge's discretion. As empirical research has indicated that these techniques often produce more useful responses from jurors, we discuss how research may be used to argue for the use of these procedures during voir dire.

In chapter 7 we review the practice of making in-court observations of the nonverbal behavior of prospective jurors and how nonverbal behavior (paralinguistic cues or speech patterns and kinesic cues or body movements) can potentially reveal subtle cues regarding jurors' attitudes or deceptive statements. We present a method of making systematic observations of nonverbal behavior in court, discuss the need for theoretically guided observations of behavior, and discuss the strengths and limitations of this approach.

The overall effectiveness of scientific jury selection is addressed in chapter 8 and includes a critical review of the relevant empirical research. We also discuss the techniques used in scientific jury selection that may limit its effectiveness, and the need for identifying systematic ways of combining the various scientific jury selection techniques that do exist.

In chapter 9, we discuss how additional trial consultant activities, such as conducting mock juries, shadow juries, and posttrial interviews can be used to validate information obtained in pretrial community surveys and in-court observations, develop and test case themes directed to specific types of jurors, and provide information that can refine the jury selection. In this chapter we also review how jurors may rely on their commonsense notions of justice to arrive at verdicts (Finkel, 1995), particularly when presented with complex information during the trial or judicial instructions that are poorly worded and difficult to understand. We discuss the importance of identifying jurors' commonsense beliefs about justice during voir dire to better understand how these beliefs may affect trial outcome and guide jury selection decisions.

Following the preceding chapters' discussions of the way scientific jury selection is conducted and its likely effectiveness, chapter 10 considers the potential ethical and professional issues raised by the use of selection consultants. We evaluate potential solutions to those problems that may improve the quality of scientific jury selection and mitigate injustices that the use of consulting services may present.

Finally, chapter 11 focuses on approaches to improve scientific jury selection. This chapter first considers the application of theoretical models, rarely applied in today's work, to better predict jury behavior and inform jury selection decisions. We also discuss innovative statistical and methodological approaches that may produce better information to improve selection decisions and may potentially identify the types of cases in which scientific jury selection will be most useful.

The ultimate goal of this book is to familiarize readers with various consultant activities that are related to jury selection and to discuss research that has evaluated the effectiveness of those activities. As a result, psychologists, other social scientists, and practicing jury selection consultants who read the book should have a better understanding of the current state of research relevant to scientific jury selection and of areas in which new research needs to be conducted to advance the field. In addition, attorneys who read the book should be better able to decide whether to hire selection consultants to assist in future litigation, and if they do, what types of services these consultants should provide. We hope that this will lead to more widespread and creative collaborations between academic researchers, consultants, and attorneys and that more effective approaches for eliminating biased jurors can be developed.

2

THE PURPOSE AND EFFECTIVENESS OF VOIR DIRE

The Sixth Amendment of the U.S. Constitution guarantees criminal defendants the right to a fair trial by an impartial jury drawn from the state and district where the crime was committed. The Seventh Amendment makes similar guarantees for civil litigation. Thus, there is a burden on the legal system to impanel impartial jurors. The principal technique for achieving this end is the process of voir dire.

The goal of voir dire is to determine whether members of the venire (i.e., the larger pool selected for jury duty from which the actual jurors for a trial are chosen) are qualified to serve as jurors and to identify any biases that may interfere with their ability to be impartial triers of fact (also referred to as prejudiced or substantially prejudiced jurors; see, e.g., *Brooks v. Zahn*, 1991). Voir dire typically lasts several hours, but can take several months in rare cases, particularly those in which there has been intense pretrial publicity (Kovera, Dickinson, & Cutler, 2003). Many, perhaps most, attorneys place an enormous amount of importance on voir dire. It has been argued that "[t]here is no aspect of a criminal trial more important to the ultimate outcome than the jury selection process" (Mogill & Nixon, 1986), although as we discuss later in the book, some social scientists dispute that position.

Before critically examining the literature relevant to evaluating scientific jury selection in the rest of the book, this chapter reviews essential factual information concerning the jury selection process. We begin by providing a brief overview of the historical development of voir dire and the two main approaches to selecting the venire. We then consider the bases for challenging and excusing venire members (i.e., the challenge for cause and the peremptory challenge). As the exercise of these challenges implicitly raises the issue of the purposes of voir dire (i.e., the attorney conducts voir dire and exercises challenges with a specific purpose or purposes in mind), we next consider these purposes and follow with a discussion of attorney effectiveness in the absence of scientific jury selection.

HISTORICAL DEVELOPMENT OF VOIR DIRE

Voir dire has been used for several hundred years and in the United States can be traced to the 1760 Massachusetts Jury Selection Law (MacGutman, 1972). At the time, juries were selected from pools of individuals at town meetings, and one result of the passage of the Selection Law was that defendants began to use the meetings to question members of the pool about their relevant biases.

Attorneys and judges have long been concerned with the impact of attitudes on jurors' impartiality. This concern was articulated as early as the trial of Aaron Burr, when the trial judge in that case, Chief Justice John Marshall, noted,

> Why do personal prejudices constitute a just cause of challenge? Solely because the individual who is under their influence is presumed to have a bias on his mind which will prevent an impartial decision of the case, according to the testimony. He may declare that notwithstanding these prejudices he is determined to listen to the evidence, and be governed by it, but the law will not trust him. . . . He will listen with more favor to that testimony which confirms, than to that which would change his opinion. (*United States v. Burr*, 1807, ¶ 2)

Key-Man System

The potential that a jury pool would contain many members who hold similar biases was substantial for most of the history of the legal system in the United States because of the way individuals were selected for jury duty. For many years, a *key-man system* was used, a system in which prominent community members submitted names of potential jurors to an officer of the court. The prominent members naturally tended to be from a demographically constrained group (i.e., White, male, educated, etc.; see Broeder, 1965, for a good description of the problems inherent with drawing a jury pool using the key-man system). In the late nineteenth century, the Supreme Court ruled that "cognizable groups" (e.g., racial or religious) could not be excluded from jury duty (*Strauder v. West Virginia*, 1879). Cognizable groups are composed of those the community perceives as a group because its members are distinctive in the attitudes and experiences they share, and the "group's absence from the jury may have an impact in the specific case before the court" (Hans & Vidmar, 1982, p. 44). Women were not considered a cognizable group and were excluded from jury duty until 1898, when Utah became the first state to allow women to serve. Even after legal obstacles preventing women from serving on juries were removed, systematic obstacles remained. For example, for women to serve as jurors, they needed to go to the courthouse and register. This requirement did not apply to men. In addition, in Missouri, if a woman did not want to serve on a jury, all she had to do was sign her name at an appropriate place on her jury questionnaire, as all women were offered an automatic exemption from jury service. As a result, only about 15% of Kansas City jurors were female until the exemption was eliminated (Wrightsman, Greene, Nietzel, & Fortune, 2002). In a similar way, racial minority group members historically did not serve on juries in large numbers (or at all) for many years. Thus, homogeneous juries continued for many decades.

Increasing Community Representation—Jury Selection Acts

The potential for a strong degree of bias remained in jury pools until 1968, when Congress passed the federal Jury Selection and Service Act (JSSA) in an attempt to make jury pools truly representative of the local community where a given trial would be held. The JSSA explicitly stated that juries be "selected at random from a fair cross section of the community" and that no citizens be excluded from jury service on account of "race, color, religion, sex, national origin, or economic status" (Sections 1861–1862). As a result of the act, the key-man system was replaced with the use of public lists to identify prospective jurors in a given community.

The requirement that jurors be drawn from a representative cross section of the community is based on policy assumptions that doing so will improve the fact-finding ability and legitimacy of trial juries (Hans & Vidmar, 1982). These assumptions are based on the principles that (a) a representative jury will be better able to problem solve because it will be composed of individuals with a greater diversity of perspectives, (b) various randomly distributed biases will be cancelled out because the individual jurors have different backgrounds, and (c) the presence of minority jurors will inhibit the expression of biases held by majority group members (Hans &Vidmar, 1982). If a jury is not representative and is instead composed of individuals drawn from a narrow segment of society, then the verdicts produced may be perceived as less acceptable, particularly to excluded groups who have not been able to fully participate in the legal process.

To achieve representativeness under the JSSA, voter registration lists were initially used to obtain a community sample. It is unfortunate that these lists did not provide for a representative cross section of the community, because certain groups tend to be underrepresented (e.g., ethnic and racial minorities, low income individuals, young people, transient people, etc.; Hans & Vidmar, 1982). In 1970, the Uniform Jury Selection and Service Act (UJSSA) was drafted with the goal of increasing diversity among jurors. This act states that voter lists must be supplemented with other lists that may be more successful at identifying underrepresented jurors. These lists include utility customers, income and property tax payers, owners of registered vehicles, and driver licensees.

In 1983, the American Bar Association attempted to continue reforms to the jury selection process initiated by the JSSA and the UJSSA by encouraging the use of source lists in jury selection. This would ensure that any individual whose name appears on a variety of lists (such as those mentioned under the UJSSA) has an equal chance of being selected for jury service. Over half the states now use source lists rather than only voter registration lists ("Development in the Law," 1997). However, a number of states continue to use the key-man system that allows jury commissioners and town civil servants to exercise discretion over which source they will draw from when impaneling venire persons (Bureau of Justice Statistics, 1998).

IDENTIFYING AND ELIMINATING PROSPECTIVE JURORS

If a person is so biased that no information presented in the trial will overcome his or her prejudgment of the case, then he or she may be excluded from the jury as a matter of law through what is known as a challenge for cause (discussed in detail later in this chapter). To eliminate a prospective juror this way, it must be demonstrated that the bias is significant enough to interfere with the juror's ability to act impartially (*Flowers v. Flowers*, 1965). Thus, jurors who do not clearly express a strong bias may end up serving on juries. During trials, judges deliver a variety of cautionary and other procedural instructions to limit the influence of bias that the remaining jurors may possess. It is unfortunate that, as MacGutman (1972) has noted,

> . . . the rules of evidence can only partly limit the extent to which a juror's bias affects his deliberation. The tests which the law furnishes to the jury for weighing evidence are crude and imperfect and provide few internal checks on jury prejudice. There is a critical area in every case where a juror must rely on his own experience to reach a decision. If bias permeates a juror's thinking, it may distort the importance of evidence consistent with it. . . . Bias may, therefore, be a fact of singular importance in the case. (pp. 303–304)

If there is an assumption that life experiences create a subjective lens through which jurors view the evidence, causing different jurors to view the same evidence in very different ways, it becomes imperative to identify and eliminate the most biased prospective jurors. Voir dire provides a mechanism for achieving this goal.

Although voir dire is often referred to as *jury selection*, this label is a misnomer. Attorneys cannot create a jury by selecting the individuals they want. Lawyers have no power to say, "I want juror number 16 to serve." Rather, as noted in the next two sections, voir dire allows a judge and attorneys to remove biased prospective jurors within the constraints of the law. As a result, *juror exclusion* is a far more accurate term for this process. Typically, the judge in federal cases and the judge and attorneys in many state cases ask the jurors questions to elicit sufficient information to help judges and attorneys decide which jurors to eliminate. During this process, jurors can be excluded in one of two ways: a challenge for cause or a peremptory challenge.

Challenge for Cause

Challenges for cause are used when it can be demonstrated that a juror is ineligible to serve on a jury because he or she does not meet a specific statutory requirement. For example, a challenge for cause would be exercised if a juror was biased to the extent that he or she could not be impartial, was a nonresident of the local jurisdiction or not a U.S. citizen, did not speak English (New Mexico is the only current exception; *State ex rel. Martinez v. Third Judicial District Court*, reprinted as an appendix in *State v. Singleton*, 2001), has a mental or physical disability that would interfere with his or her ability to serve on a jury, had recently served on a jury, had previous felony convictions, had a relationship with one of the parties or their attorneys involved in the case, or met other occupational or age restrictions listed in the law (Treger, 1992).

There are no limits placed on the number of challenges for cause that may be exercised during voir dire. However, when an attorney attempts to remove a juror with a challenge for cause, the judge is the ultimate arbitrator of the decision. Judges may also remove a prospective juror for *cause sua sponte* (on his or her volition).

Although there are no limits on the number of jurors attorneys can challenge for cause, there are two reasons judges do not often grant these challenges when bias is alleged. First, if a juror admits bias, the judge may feel that such sentiments are not substantial enough to interfere with that person's ability to appropriately carry out his or her duties. Second, when jurors indicate they have formed a pretrial opinion about the case, they still may indicate that they can set aside this opinion and be impartial.

Judges are not always correct, unfortunately, in their confidence in jurors' ability to set aside bias. For example, jurors may indicate that they can be open-minded, even if that is not truly the case. Moran and Cutler (1991) investigated the impact of pretrial publicity in highly publicized trials in southern Illinois and in Miami. In both trials there was a positive relationship between pretrial knowledge of details about the case and perceptions that the defendants were culpable. However, there was no relationship between knowledge of case details and respondents' indications that they could be fair and impartial. Further, many respondents reported that they would be unable to set aside case-relevant news stories, but still claimed they could be impartial. Jurors may be unaware that they possess such biases or that they cannot set them aside. In addition, some jurors may simply lie during voir dire (Broeder, 1959; Seltzer, Venuti, & Lopes, 1991).

Courts have acknowledged that jurors may not be aware of the preconceptions they have about a case or whether they are qualified to serve on a jury (Mogill & Nixon, 1986). For example, in *United States v. Dellinger* (1972), the Seventh Circuit Court of Appeals noted, "We do not believe that a prospective juror is so alert to his own prejudices. Thus it is essential to explore the backgrounds and attitudes of the jurors to some extent in order to discover actual bias, or cause" (p. 367). Further, jurors may be deceptive because they may not want to publicly admit they hold certain biases or because they are hoping that the admission of biases they do not really hold may provide a means for getting out of jury duty. In either case, it may be quite difficult to remove jurors that are partial to one side with a challenge for cause.

An alternative problem to jurors misrepresenting their attitudes and experiences during voir dire questioning is jurors simply failing to respond to voir dire questions. That is, if voir dire is conducted by questioning prospective jurors in groups and jurors respond by raising their hands, jurors may simply remain silent during questioning (Treger, 1992). Attorneys and judges may be inclined to follow up with individual questioning of jurors who have responded affirmatively to questions, but it is difficult to know what to make of jurors who have not responded to any of the questions. Mize (2003), a practicing judge on the District of Columbia Superior Court, recommended questioning silent jurors outside the presence of the other jurors, so that all jurors were questioned individually. Although this process takes more time, Mize maintained that it would be worth the extra effort if it uncovered biases. In private questioning, 28% of silent jurors in criminal and civil cases revealed information they were unwilling to admit to in open court, leading to a number of jurors being struck by challenges for cause. In Mize's trials, silent jurors admitted such experiences as participation in a narcotics anonymous program on a narcotics case, being in an automobile accident a month before being called for an automobile accident case, knowing the defendant from church, and even being the defendant's fiancée! As these examples show, there may be a real need to question silent jurors. However, if a judge is unwilling to spend the time to further interview unresponsive jurors, jury selection consultants may prove useful at identifying potentially biased jurors. As we discuss in the next chapter, pretrial surveys may be useful for developing profiles of jurors likely to hold case relevant biases. In addition, there is reason to believe that the body language of jurors may reveal hidden biases (see chap. 7 for discussion of this issue).

Peremptory Challenge

Courts have long recognized that it may be difficult to demonstrate that a prospective juror is biased to such a degree that he or she should be eliminated under a challenge for cause. For example, an attorney may have strong suspicions that a juror is biased, but that juror may not have made any statements that would clearly support that suspicion. As a result, attorneys can also exclude jurors using peremptory challenges. With this challenge, an attorney is not required to provide a justification to the court for removing a juror. The attorney must only inform the judge that he or she would like to exclude a specific juror.

Unlike the unlimited number of challenges for cause that may be exercised, each side is given a limited number of peremptory challenges. The total number of peremptory challenges allocated to each side is dependent upon the jurisdiction, type of trial (civil or criminal), and seriousness of the case, but typically, more peremptory challenges are provided in criminal cases than in civil. In addition, the judge will grant the parties the same number of peremptory challenges in civil cases. In criminal cases, the defendant will typically receive the same or a greater number than what is allocated to the prosecution. For example, in civil trials held in states such as Florida and Missouri, both the plaintiff and defendant are allowed three peremptory challenges (Kovera et al., 2003; see Bureau of Justice Statistics, 1998 for a list of all state and federal peremptory challenge–voir dire procedures). In felony criminal cases tried in federal court, 6 peremptory challenges are provided to the prosecution and 10 to the defense; however, more can be awarded depending on the circumstances of the case (Bureau of Justice Statistics, 1998). When there is a large degree of pretrial publicity surrounding a case, the number of peremptory challenges allotted to each side is generally increased. Thus, in the criminal trial of O.J. Simpson, the prosecution was awarded 20 peremptory challenges (Wrightsman et al., 2002).

Peremptory challenges are necessary because jurors may not reveal sufficient bias during voir dire to merit excusal under a causal challenge. As already noted, even if bias is revealed, jurors may report that they are capable of putting their biases aside and considering the evidence in a fair and impartial manner, thus satisfying the courts' requirements. Typically, such an assurance is all that is required. However, building on our discussion in the prior subsection on causal challenges, there are a variety of reasons why pledges of impartiality made by jurors may be insufficient (Patterson & Neufer, 1997).

First, jurors may be unaware of their biases. Social psychological research has found that individuals may not be consciously aware of attitudes that influence their behavior (Nisbett & Ross, 1980). It is unfortunate that the influence of stereotypic beliefs (referred to as heuristics) on behavior increases when individuals are under cognitive demands from such factors as time pressure, exhaustion, or requirements to make complex judgments about information (Bodenhausen, 1990; Bodenhausen & Lichtenstein, 1987; Gilbert & Hixon, 1991; Kruglanski & Freund, 1983). Jurors may also distort their reports of past experiences and attitudes because they do not accurately recall information from memory, or because they do not want to reveal information that would be socially undesirable. When voir dire is conducted in a group setting, jurors may feel pressure to conform to the predominant responses of the group (Asch, 1955). In addition, despite promises of impartiality, preexisting beliefs relevant to aspects of the case may cause jurors to search for information that supports their belief system (i.e., engage in a confirmatory information search; Swann & Read, 1981) or to distort information that contradicts their belief system (i.e., engage in belief perseverance; Anderson, Lepper, & Ross, 1980). Finally, research on the effects of pretrial publicity has shown that jurors are unable to ignore pretrial information they have been exposed to, despite judicial instructions to do so (Lieberman & Arndt, 2000).

Given that jurors walk into the courtroom with a myriad of different backgrounds, personality factors, and cognitive biases, it is not surprising that jurors, in their first ballot verdict preferences, disagree about two thirds of the time (Zeisel & Diamond, 1976). Thus, because individual differences may produce verdict differences, and because the U.S. population is heterogeneous, peremptory challenges may be necessary to produce an impartial jury (Zeisel & Diamond, 1976).

Historically, attorneys have been allowed wide latitude in their motivations for excluding potential jurors under peremptory challenges. In *Swain v. Alabama* (1965), Justice White noted that these challenges can be based on "sudden impressions and unaccountable prejudices" including "the race, religion, nationality, occupation or affiliations of people summoned for jury duty" (pp. 220–221). Although attorneys do not have to state a reason for excluding a juror when exercising a peremptory challenge, in the past 2 decades there have been certain limits placed on the criteria attorneys are allowed to use when excluding jurors. First, the United States Supreme Court in *Batson v. Kentucky* (1986) and its progeny (*Edmonson v. Leesville Concrete Co., Inc.*, 1991; *Miller-El v. Dretke*, 2005; *State v. McCollum*, 1992) ruled that attorneys in both criminal and civil trials could no longer use peremptory challenges to remove potential jurors on the basis of race. In addition, in *J.E.B. v. Alabama ex rel.* (1994), the Supreme Court ruled that jurors could not be excluded on the basis of gender. If an opposing counsel believes the *Batson* or *J.E.B* rulings are being violated, he or she can attempt to convince the judge that discriminatory strikes have been made. If the judge finds that the argument has merit, the judge can ask the attorney who made the peremptory challenges to defend the logic behind his or her decision (but see discussion of research by Baldus, Woodworth, Zuckerman, Weiner, & Broffitt, 2001, later in this chapter regarding the effects of the *Batson* and *J.E.B.* rulings on attorney behavior).

Thus, a selection consultant assisting with voir dire must be able to provide an attorney with information that indicates certain types of individuals are likely to be biased and should be interviewed in greater detail to establish if they are indeed biased. If sufficient grounds are found, the attorney can argue for a causal challenge. If the requisite level of bias cannot be established to the judge's satisfaction for the causal challenge, then the attorney can exercise a peremptory challenge. Finally, if attorneys wish to avoid revealing their pretrial information, they can rely on peremptory challenges and reduce their questioning of prospective jurors.

PURPOSES OF VOIR DIRE

Voir dire serves three primary purposes, which are to determine whether prospective jurors (a) are eligible to serve based on legal restrictions, (b) will be able to consider in an impartial manner the information presented to them during the trial, and (c) will be able to render a verdict based on the evidence of the trial rather than on extralegal factors. Determining these issues will allow the attorney to obtain sufficient information about prospective jurors to intelligently guide causal and peremptory challenge decisions.

It is unfortunate that the purposes of voir dire are not always achieved, particularly when carried out by judges who limit their questioning to asking jurors, "Can you be fair?" (Hafemeister, Sales, & Suggs, 1984). It is relatively easy for the juror to respond in a way that is acceptable to the court, even though they may actually possess attitudes that are potentially prejudicial. To overcome the possibility that jurors may not reveal their intentional or unconscious biases, questioning often goes beyond the purposes of determining whether a juror meets the legal and statutory requirements to serve and instead focuses on other factors that may be related to more subtle biases that could affect the verdict decision. For this purpose, jurors may be questioned about such factors as demographic characteristics (such as race, religion, marital status, number of children, occupation), attitudes toward aspects of the legal system (such as a presumption of innocence and burden of proof), or attitudes toward aspects of the case (e.g., litigants, attorneys, case facts, controlling law). Depending on the case, this latter category of questions could focus on such topics as knowledge of parties or attorneys, personal involvement in prior lawsuits, prior experiences as a juror, attitudes toward the death penalty, attitudes toward racial minorities, activities and hobbies (e.g., gun enthusiast), books and magazines read (e.g., paramilitary magazines; ultraconservative or ultraliberal magazines), and television viewing habits.

This line of voir dire questioning is based on the presumption that attitudes and life experiences affect verdict decisions. Courts recognize, and there is empirical research to show, that the evidence presented during the trial will not necessarily be viewed without bias. As a result, in the vast majority of trials jurors enter the deliberation room with differing opinions regarding the conclusions that can be drawn from the evidence (Zeisel & Diamond, 1976); these conclusions can reflect jurors' preexisting biases.

Peremptory challenges are permissible because it is assumed that jurors enter the courtroom with biases they may not be able to put aside. By eliminating the most heavily biased (and unfavorable) jurors on each side, the remaining jurors are theoretically able to be impartial. Although the remaining jurors are still likely to have a diversity of views, this diversity should result in some jurors being favorably predisposed to each of the parties involved, with the expectation that the biases will neutralize each other and, following structured discussion deliberation, the appropriate verdict will be rendered (Fukurai, Butler, & Krooth, 1993).

In certain circumstances, a community may hold such extremely partial views against one of the parties involved that it becomes impossible for an attorney to eliminate all extremely biased jurors during voir dire with the limited number of available peremptory challenges. If an attorney suspects she or he is facing this type of case, a consultant may be able to demonstrate that the prevailing viewpoint in the community is so pervasively biased that it is impossible for an impartial jury to be seated (see chap. 3). This information could then be used to argue for a change of venue motion or to have an increase in the number of peremptory challenges allocated.

The remainder of this chapter and the next several chapters of this book are devoted to discussing the effectiveness of attorneys and jury selection consultants at achieving the primary voir dire goals that are relevant to peremptory challenges: determining which jurors will be able to impartially consider and deliberate about the facts of the case and extracting useful information from voir dire to guide peremptory challenges. Although our focus is on the exercise of peremptory challenges, this information can be useful for causal challenges as well. For example, an attorney may convince a judge that potential bias in a juror warrants that he or she should be questioned more extensively or even privately, or that the bias in a prospective juror rises to the level prohibited by law (i.e., overwhelming bias). In most cases, attorneys will not be able to convince the judge that this level of bias exists in a prospective juror unless the juror admits to it. Thus, the attorney will be forced to use a peremptory challenge to exclude the juror. In addition, as discussed in the next four sections, voir dire can be used by attorneys for other purposes that are not necessarily judicially sanctioned.

Education

Voir dire can be used to educate jurors about central issues in the case or about relevant law that they must ultimately apply (McNulty, 2000). For example, there is considerable social science research that indicates jurors have a poor comprehension of judicial instructions given to them that explain the laws relevant to the case at hand (Lieberman & Sales, 1997). One solution is to use voir dire to clarify some of the legal issues that jurors will have to contend with if the judge allows for a discussion of legal concepts during this phase of the trial (Penrod & Cutler, 1987). Despite the fact that voir dire can be used for the purpose of education, it does not mean such use is judicially sanctioned. Rather, courts have ruled that voir dire may not be used by either party to preeducate or indoctrinate prospective jurors to a particular theory or defense, nor to impanel jurors with particular predispositions (e.g., *People v. Lanter*, 1992).

Ingratiation

Voir dire can also serve as an opportunity for attorneys to develop a rapport with venire members and ingratiate themselves in the process (Hafemeister et al., 1984; Levine, 2001; Weaver, 1993). Attorneys may be excessively courteous to the panel members, use humor, express polite concern for the health of older panel members, or try to make it known that they have similarities of one sort or another with jurors. Although ingratiation attempts might indeed build a rapport between attorneys and jurors, such behavior might also backfire if jurors think the attorney is using an obvious ploy (Suggs & Sales, 1978a).

In the process of ingratiation, an attorney may even attempt to make a "grandstand" play (Suggs & Sales, 1978a). This may be accomplished by an attorney announcing his or her faith in the jury system and in the particular current panel and declining the opportunity to question prospective jurors during voir dire (Field, 1965). To our knowledge, there have not been empirical attempts to evaluate the effectiveness of this approach; however, this technique might also backfire, leading the jurors to think that a lawyer is careless about his or her case (Belli, 1982). In chapter 9, we discuss how trial consultants can use mock juries to evaluate different variations of an attorney's interaction with jurors and whether methods of ingratiation are successful.

Enhancing Impartiality

Research on persuasion and attitude change has shown that individuals who make public commitments to behave in a certain manner are more likely to ultimately behave in that way (Kiesler, 1971). Penrod and Linz (1986) suggested that if an attorney knows that a client's past felony conviction will become known during the trial, the defense lawyer may want jurors to pub-licly pledge to follow the judge's limiting instructions that indicate the le-gally acceptable ways such information can be used (i.e., to determine the credibility of statements made by the defendant, as opposed to the legally impermissible manner of using such information as an indication of guilt in the current trial). As limiting instructions have been shown to be generally ineffective on their own (Lieberman & Arndt, 2000), it may be useful to obtain this type of public commitment.

Enhancing Trial Satisfaction

An additional benefit of voir dire is that it allows trial participants to feel that by being able to select the individuals who will ultimately judge the facts of the case, they have a greater degree of control over the proceedings. This feeling of control may lead to a greater sense of procedural fairness (i.e., that the trial process is fair; Lind & Tyler, 1988; Thibault & Walker, 1975) and to greater satisfaction with the trial process.

DOES JURY SELECTION MATTER?

Is voir dire a critical part of the trial process? Much of this book is devoted to answering this question. It is inherently obvious that at some level jury selection must matter. Jurors sit next to each other for the duration of the trial and are exposed to exactly the same evidence presented in exactly the same manner. However, following the presentation of evidence, jurors retreat to the deliberation room where they take an initial verdict vote. As already noted, it is rare that a unanimous decision emerges on that initial vote (Kalven & Zeisel, 1966). Rather, there is almost always some disagree-ment among jurors. As they have all been exposed to the same evidence, those disagreements must stem from preexisting differences in jurors' back-grounds or beliefs that have affected how they have interpreted the evidence (Diamond, 1990). Some trial attorneys go further and argue that "experi-enced trial lawyers agree that the jury selection process is the single most important aspect of the trial proceedings. . . . In fact, once the last person on the jury is seated, the trial is essentially won or lost" (Covington, 1985, pp. 575–576). For this reason, jury selection consultants seek to measure how personality characteristics, demographic factors, and personal experiences will affect the outcome of a trial.

A number of empirical studies investigated the influence of voir dire on trial outcome. Whereas some studies provide support for the belief that voir dire is very important to the trial outcome, other studies cast doubt on this conclusion.

Research Demonstrating That Voir Dire Has an Important Effect on Trial Outcome

Several studies support the belief that voir dire has an important effect on trial outcome. There are, unfortunately, methodological limitations associated with some of these studies.

Padawer-Singer, Singer, and Singer (1974) conducted a study examining the effectiveness of voir dire at reducing the prejudicial effects of pretrial publicity. Mock jurors were presented with a trial that contained mostly circumstantial evidence that was ambiguous as to the defendant's guilt or innocence. All the jurors read newspaper reports about case facts that were admissible in trial. However, half the jurors were exposed to additional pretrial publicity that indicated the defendant had a criminal background and had allegedly retracted a confession. Juries were chosen by either randomly selecting individuals without any voir dire questioning or by conducting a voir dire examination. Voir dire was conducted by two attorneys, the first from the Legal Aid Society and the second from the district attorney's office. Jurors were then exposed to an audiotape based on the transcript of the real trial that the pretrial publicity had drawn from. Juries composed of individuals exposed to the pretrial publicity rendered more guilty verdicts. However, jurors who were selected via voir dire rendered fewer guilty verdicts (60%) than jurors selected at random (78%). Voir dire jurors displayed fewer opinion changes during deliberation and a greater tendency to follow the law, even if this meant adhering to an unfair law or releasing a defendant "whom one knows is guilty because of insufficient evidence." In addition, jurors selected with voir dire expressed more favorable attitudes toward protecting the rights of the accused and toward mitigating factors such as mental illness.

This study provides some evidence that attorneys are able to conduct effective voir dire examinations without the use of consultants. However, confidence in these findings is diminished by a number of factors. First, as the authors did not report statistical tests it is somewhat difficult to interpret the group difference findings. Second, the authors did not report any results for the group of jurors struck during voir dire. A better test of the effectiveness of voir dire would involve presenting excluded jurors with trial materials and having them render verdicts. Third, the study involved testing the effects of pretrial publicity. It may be easier to identify juror biases caused by this kind of clear-cut information than prejudicial attitudes formed in other ways. It is relatively simple to ask if jurors have been exposed to this type of publicity, and in the context of a jury simulation study, jurors may not be motivated to lie. This may not be true in other types of cases in which the biases and causes of those biases are more subtle (e.g., preexisting attitudes about certain groups of people) and when prospective jurors can more easily avoid admitting to their predispositions prior to the case. Finally, it is unclear whether the two lawyers who conducted voir dire in this study were especially skilled at conducting it or how other attorneys would have performed.

In another study, Diamond and Zeisel (1974) conducted a courtroom experiment in a series of federal court cases in which multiple juries were exposed to the same trial. In each trial, the verdict of the actual jury was compared with the verdicts of both an experimental jury composed of jurors who had been peremptorily challenged and dismissed and a second experimental jury composed of jurors who had been randomly selected from the jury pool. All three juries sat in the courtroom, heard the same trial testimony, and deliberated before reaching a verdict. The results indicated that the verdicts of the real juries were different from those of the experimental juries. Five of the 10 real juries rendered guilty verdicts, compared with 8 of the challenged juries, and all 10 randomly drawn juries favored conviction. A questionnaire delivered to the judge in each case indicated that judges supported the verdict trend of the experimental juries, with judges in 9 of the 10 cases favoring conviction.

When Diamond and Zeisel (1974) examined the verdict preferences of the peremptorily excused jurors, they found that attorneys were able to successfully eliminate prospective jurors who were biased against their side. In 7 of the 10 trials, defense attorneys eliminated more jurors who favored conviction. In two cases, equal numbers of conviction-prone and acquittal-prone jurors were excused, and in only one case did defense attorneys eliminate more acquittal-oriented than conviction-oriented jurors. Prosecutors were also effective at eliminating biased jurors. In five trials, the prosecutors eliminated more jurors who favored acquittal than those who favored conviction. In two cases, an equal number of friendly and unfriendly jurors were excused, and in three cases the prosecutors mistakenly excused more jurors who were inclined to convict than jurors who were prone to acquit.

Diamond and Zeisel (1974) also gave questionnaires to attorneys immediately after voir dire to assess the reasons for excusing each juror. The researchers then compared those reasons with the predeliberation verdict choices of excused jurors. Attorneys were most likely to exclude jurors on the basis of demeanor, followed by occupation, residence, gender, and race. Further analysis of the data indicates that challenges based on race were the most accurate (89% correct), followed by demeanor (76%), residence (70%), age (67%), occupation (62%), and gender (44%). This study was done prior to the United States Supreme Court decisions prohibiting exclusion of prospective jurors on the basis of their race (*Batson v. Kentucky*, 1986; *Miller-El v. Dretke*, 2005) or gender (*J.E.B. v. Alabama*, 1994).

These results suggest that voir dire influences the trial outcome, and that attorneys are often able to effectively exercise their peremptory challenges. However, it is important to consider that these results are based on a limited sample (only 10 trials). It may have been the case that the attorneys in these trials were particularly skillful, or perhaps the defense attorneys were simply better lawyers than the prosecutors, thus producing the pattern of results obtained. In addition, although peremptory challenges were successfully used, the attorneys relied heavily on race, which was a very accurate predictor of verdicts for excused jurors. As attorneys are no longer able to use peremptory challenges to remove jurors on the basis of race, one would expect lower levels of challenge effectiveness if the study was conducted today, assuming attorneys and courts adhere to the restrictions placed on voir dire strategies as a result of these decisions.

However, an analysis of peremptory challenges in capital murder trials held in Philadelphia between 1981 and 1997 conducted by Baldus et al. (2001) indicated that opposing counsel rarely raised *Batson* or *J.E.B.* claims, and when charges of discriminatory peremptory strike strategies were made, they were usually not successful (at least in Philadelphia courts). Further, Baldus et al. concluded that the Supreme Court decisions in *Batson* (and subsequent race-related challenge decisions) and *J.E.B.* had had almost no impact on attorney behavior, and that peremptory challenges continued to be made on the basis of race and gender.

In addition, Baldus et al. (2001) found that prosecutors were more effective than defense attorneys at using peremptory strikes to eliminate undesirable jurors in capital murder trials. Baldus et al. noted that one reason for the superior performance of prosecutors may have been that they were focused on excluding fewer types of jurors than were defense attorneys. The more concentrated approach of prosecutors made it easier to eliminate most, if not all, jurors in the specific groups they targeted (e.g., young Black males and Black females). However, because defense attorneys focused on eliminating a greater variety of jurors (e.g., older non-Black men, middle-aged non-Black men, and older non-Black women), they were not able to remove most jurors in the categories they targeted with their limited number of peremptory challenges.

Further, Baldus et al. (2001) found that in cases in which the prosecution made a "high effort" to eliminate Black jurors (defined as cases in which the strike rate for Black venire members in a particular trial was above the median rate[1] across all trials), Black defendants were sentenced to death at a rate 24 percentage points greater than White defendants (39% vs. 15%, respectively). However when prosecutors made a "low effort" to eliminate Black jurors (cases in which the strike rate was below the median rate), the frequency of death sentencing for Black defendants was slightly lower than White defendants (27% vs. 31%, respectively). Thus, research by Baldus et al. indicates that a focused effort to use voir dire challenges to eliminate Blacks from serving on juries has an important discriminatory effect on the verdict in trials of Black defendants.

---

[1]A *median* is a statistical term used to indicate the midpoint between the highest and lowest score in a distribution. Medians are reported when there is potential for mean (average) scores to be strongly affected by extreme scores at either end of the distribution.

Research Casting Doubt on the Effectiveness of Voir Dire

There are other studies that question the effectiveness of attorney conducted voir dire. But as was the case in several of the supportive studies previously discussed, these studies also have methodological limitations.

Zeisel and Diamond (1978) used more complex methodology and analyses than reported in their earlier research (Diamond & Zeisel, 1974) to study the effects of peremptory challenges. Their results cast doubt on attorneys' ability to effectively use peremptory challenges. They compared the verdicts of actual trial juries with reconstructed "juries without challenges" (Zeisel & Diamond, 1978, p. 500) that consisted of the first 12 jurors who entered the jury box (a combination of actual jurors and peremptorily excused jurors) to ascertain the effects of attorney challenges. The data indicated that in 7 of the 12 trials the effect of attorney challenges was minimal and did not affect the verdict. In three cases there was a moderately strong verdict effect. In only two of the remaining five cases was there a large verdict shift, which was possibly caused by peremptory challenges.

In addition, attorneys' performance in the Zeisel and Diamond (1978) study was markedly inconsistent. Prosecutors, for example, made just about the same number of effective challenges as ineffective ones (i.e., challenges that backfired because the removed jurors were actually conviction-prone). This is problematic because a central purpose of peremptory challenges is to provide attorneys with an additional tool to eliminate biased jurors who may not have publicly admitted their judgment propensities. For this tool to be effective, attorneys on both sides must be competent in ferreting out cues of subtle bias in prospective jurors and in exercising peremptory challenges against those jurors. Inconsistent attorney voir dire performance can certainly obstruct a defendant's right to a fair trial. Zeisel and Diamond note that one way of overcoming the unwanted effects of attorneys' inconsistent voir dire performance would be to expand the scope of questioning to obtain more information from jurors. Presumably, if attorneys are better informed regarding the backgrounds and attitudes of jurors, they should be able to more effectively exercise peremptory challenges.

However, there are problems with accepting Zeisel and Diamond's (1978) results at face value. The results were based on a small sample of 12 trials which, as noted earlier, is too small a number from which to generalize. There were also a number of other limitations in their methodology, such as basing much of their analysis on assumptions and estimations, rather than on clear observations of juror behavior (e.g., in two cases in which it was not possible to obtain the predeliberation votes of the jurors, the initial distribution was estimated based on the length of time the jury deliberated; see Fulero & Penrod, 1990, for a discussion of these limitations).

Johnson and Haney (1994) have also argued the need for expanded voir dire conducted by attorneys rather than by the judge. Johnson and Haney came to this conclusion after finding that almost half of the individuals who were retained as jurors in a study of voir dire in felony cases admitted that they were unable to put aside their "personal beliefs, feelings, and life experiences" (p. 499) during the trial. This suggests that it may be difficult for attorneys to effectively identify and eliminate biased jurors using the standard information available during voir dire and indicates a need for additional sources of information. However, it is important to note that their findings were based on a relatively small sample of 15 jurors who agreed to answer questions following the conclusion of a trial.

Broeder (1965) conducted one of the earliest studies examining attorney effectiveness in voir dire. As part of the study, he conducted posttrial interviews with attorneys and jurors in a federal court. Participants were questioned about jurors' backgrounds and attitudes, as well as factors that they took into consideration for verdict decisions. Broeder found that "[v]oir dire was grossly ineffective" (p. 505) at identifying unfavorable jurors, and as a result, attorneys were unsuccessful at eliminating these unfavorable jurors. Part of the reason for the attorneys' problem was that the jurors frequently concealed information intentionally and unconsciously failed to reveal important information about themselves. His findings also showed that in many instances attorneys did not attempt to seek pertinent information from jurors and frequently did not use all of the peremptory challenges available to them.

Attorneys chose to use voir dire for indoctrinating jurors on aspects of the case more than for searching for bias. Attorneys spent only 20% of voir dire time questioning prospective jurors about prejudicial experiences or biased attitudes they may hold, whereas attorneys spent 80% of their time indoctrinating jurors. Indoctrination included discussing negative evidence that might be presented in the case, educating jurors on points of law, and trying to ingratiate themselves to the jurors. In a similar manner, Balch, Griffiths, Hall, and Winfree (1976) found that a minority (36%) of voir dire statements made by attorneys and judges focused on personal characteristics of jurors, whereas 43% of statements focused on instructing jurors regarding various matters.

Although the prior two studies are fairly old, a more recent study (Johnson & Haney, 1994) that also examined the voir dire process in actual cases assessed attorney effectiveness at eliminating biased jurors using a Criminal Justice Attitudes questionnaire (CJA) that was based on Boehm's (1968) Legal Attitudes questionnaire (see chap. 5 for a review of Boehm's measure). The CJA provides a means for determining whether prospective jurors hold a proprosecution or prodefense bias. The CJA scores of jurors who were retained were compared with individuals peremptorily excused by the prosecution and defense. Analysis of the CJA scores indicated that the attorneys were somewhat successful in their challenges. Jurors excused by the defense were more proprosecution than those excused by the prosecution, and jurors excused by the prosecution were more prodefense than those excused by the defense.

Although these results would appear to be an endorsement of attorney effectiveness, that conclusion must be tempered by consideration of additional findings. Overall, jurors who had been excused via peremptory challenges did not have more extreme CJA scores than did individuals retained as jurors. Some of the retained jurors had very high or very low CJA scores. In addition, when the CJA scores of retained jurors were compared with a group composed of the first 12 jurors questioned during voir dire for each trial and with a group of individuals randomly drawn from the venire (representing juries that could have been drawn if voir dire had not been conducted), there was not a significant difference in CJA scores. Thus, as Johnson and Haney (1994) noted,

> although voir dire was "effective" in the sense that each side eliminated persons likely to be biased against their position or point of view, the overall result was a jury that did not differ much from one that would have been selected randomly or by accepting the first 12 names called to the box. (p. 498)

However, some degree of caution should also be exercised in interpreting these findings because only four trials were examined by Johnson and Haney, and the skill level of the attorneys in each trial may have affected the results in such a relatively small sample of cases.

In a series of studies, Olczak, Kaplan, and Penrod (1991) also examined attorneys' intuitive approaches to identifying favorable and unfavorable jurors during voir dire. Attorneys were asked to report what type of juror characteristics they would try to identify and use in their voir dire judgments. Participants then were given a transcript of a criminal trial (either murder or rape) and asked to rate the jurors in terms of the degree to which they were likely biased against the defendant. Attorneys also rated jurors on a number of personality dimensions. The results indicated that attorneys appeared to use relatively simplistic voir dire strategies, relying on only a few demographic factors (e.g., intelligence, age, appearance, occupation) and personality factors (e.g., general attitudes toward crime and the police, exposure to pretrial publicity, history of victimization) in that process. Although there was some degree of consensus among the attorneys regarding which factors were important, there was also considerable variability. In a second study, Olczak et al. demonstrated that the strategies used by attorneys were not substantially different from those used by college students, who had similar performance levels. This general finding was replicated in a third study comparing the performance of experienced attorneys to that of law students at predicting the verdicts of mock jurors who had previously rendered verdicts in a manslaughter case. Once again, experienced attorneys did not outperform the student comparison group. Both groups had difficulty accurately predicting the verdicts of mock jurors.[2]

Other researchers have obtained similar findings. For example, Hayden, Senna, and Siegel (1978) examined the categories of information most frequently used by prosecutors. They presented a group of prosecutors with two hypothetical cases and asked them to conduct a simulated voir dire by requesting information on jurors. The prosecutors were then given a list of 17 categories of information about jurors and allowed to select one category at a time. After reviewing the information in that category an attorney could either make a decision about the acceptability of the juror or seek an additional category of information. Decisions regarding the acceptability of a juror were typically made after reviewing approximately seven categories of information. The category that prosecutors were most likely to seek information about was jurors' age, followed by occupation, demeanor, gender, appearance, and residence. The attorneys were also significantly more likely to request information regarding a juror's race when the defendant was described as being Black. However, as Fulero and Penrod (1990) noted, caution should be exercised when interpreting these findings, because only two cases were presented to the attorneys. It is likely that the categories of interest may vary depending on the characteristics of a specific case (see chap. 4). In addition, the sample size was small, with only 20 prosecutors (and no defense attorneys) randomly selected for participation in the study.

Using a similar methodology, Penrod (as cited in Fulero & Penrod, 1990) investigated the jury selection strategies of 19 prosecutors and defense attorneys. The attorneys were first interviewed about their typical jury selection strategies and relevant background factors. The attorneys were then presented with a set of profiles for 32 jurors and asked to indicate the amount of potential bias in favor of the defense and prosecution for each juror in two separate cases (a murder and a rape case). Intelligence was the characteristic attorneys were most interested in. The attorneys reported that they most frequently asked about juror attitudes toward the specific crime at hand, general attitudes regarding the police, exposure to pretrial publicity, and previ-

---

[2]Finkelstein and Levin (1997) used a mathematical model based on actual trial data to estimate the percentage of attorney challenges that are clear choices, as well as those involving guesswork. The results indicated that only about 20% of attorneys' choices are *clear* (defined as a challenge where multiple lawyers would generally agree on the juror's bias), whereas about 80% were based on guesswork. Although these estimated percentages do not necessarily conflict with the findings of other studies reported in this section, the results are somewhat difficult to interpret because they are based on a number of assumptions such as "that no two lawyers would reach opposite conclusions about the bias of jurors who are clear choices, and that their guesses would be randomly distributed among the other jurors" (p. 277). In addition, Finkelstein and Levin based their mathematical estimates on the behavior of attorneys in federal criminal trials. However, in federal trials the judge typically does the voir dire questioning and the attorney's role is quite limited. As a result, attorneys' ability to gather information on which to base challenges is less than in many state courts, which should increase the frequency of making guesses regarding juror bias, compared with jurisdictions that allow attorney-conducted voir dire.

ous experiences the jurors may have had as crime victims. In addition, the attorneys were asked to sort the jurors in terms of perceived juror similarity. Four characteristics emerged as predictive of similarity ratings: attitudes toward legal technicalities, gender, ideological orientation, and age. These characteristics were also indicative of juror bias. Occupation was the characteristic that attorneys remembered most about the jurors, and attorneys with more experience placed greater emphasis on the importance of this characteristic. However, there was considerable variation among the attorneys in terms of the factors about the jurors they felt were important, and none of the variables that attorneys focused on accounted for more than 3% of the verdict variance in either of the two cases (described in Penrod & Linz, 1986).

Hawrish and Tate (1974–1975) presented 43 attorneys with a list of simulated jurors and asked them to accept or reject each juror from a defense standpoint. The jurors were described in terms of a variety of factors, including age, sex, occupation, and appearance. Attorneys indicated the level of acceptability of each juror in different criminal trials (fraud, rape, issuing a false prospectus [fraudulent inducement relating to shareholders and creditors], and murder). Hawrish and Tate reported that defense-oriented attorneys believed males are more acceptable jurors across different criminal trials, most strongly in the rape trial. Age was also a significant selection criterion for attorneys across the different trials. Older jurors (over age 60) were the least desirable. It is interesting to note that socioeconomic status was a significant factor, but only in the fraud trial. However, as the study involved attorneys looking at the profiles of jurors but not actually questioning them, it is not clear how strongly these characteristics would affect an attorney's actual voir dire challenges. Appearance, which was operationalized as clothing style, was a significant factor only in the false prospectus trial, in which attorneys indicated they had lower preferences for prospective jurors dressed in countercultural attire.

CONCLUSION

The studies discussed in the previous section present a mixed picture as to attorney effectiveness at conducting voir dire. Several studies indicate that attorneys are somewhat effective (Baldus et al., 2001; Diamond & Zeisel, 1974; Padawer-Singer et al., 1974). However, a more common finding is that attorneys often fail to exclude unfavorable jurors, and that attorneys often do not do much better than chance at correctly identifying biased jurors (Fulero & Penrod, 1990; Kovera et al., 2003; Olczak et al., 1991; Zeisel & Diamond, 1978). This has led some social scientists to conclude that techniques used by attorneys during jury selection are not very effective and often have minimal impact on the jury's verdict (Hans & Vidmar, 1982; Kovera et al., 2003). Although attorneys may feel comfortable in their ability to predict human behavior, "[l]awyer confidence (and experience) is not generally related to accuracy in selecting jurors" (Vidmar, 1999, p. 268). Famed attorney Alan Dershowitz has remarked, "Lawyers' instincts are often the least trustworthy basis on which to pick jurors. All those neat rules of thumb, but no feedback. Ten years of accumulated experiences may be ten years of being wrong" (as cited in Hunt, 1982, p. 82).

The issue then arises as to whether scientific jury selection as practiced by consultants can provide an added benefit to attorneys. Presumably, an attorney who was relatively unsuccessful at excluding biased jurors would stand to benefit greatly from any additional information he or she could get regarding the predispositions of venire members. Scientific jury selection methods may also be useful to skilled attorneys if the methods allow for greater prediction than what they are able to do on their own.

To know whether scientific jury selection adds incremental value to attorney-conducted voir dire, it is necessary to consider its theoretical underpinnings and the empirical research on its use and impact. The next three chapters start this critical analysis of the scientific techniques. As scientific approaches to jury selection often involve identifying background characteristics that may be related to verdicts, these three chapters first introduce what scientific jury selection comprises, and then examine the relationship between specific demographic, personality, and attitudinal factors and juror decisions.

3

COMMUNITY SURVEYS

As noted in chapter 1, the scientific approach to jury selection involves the use of community surveys for a variety of purposes (Nietzel, Dillehay, & Abbott, 1999). Surveys are used to identify bias in a community, which can justify a change of venue motion or form the basis for a challenge to the composition of a jury pool (Kairys, Schulman, & Harring, 1975). Community surveys are used in the development of demographically based profiles of prospective jurors who would be more prone to agree with the attorney's case, feel sympathy for one of the litigants, or just be a fair juror. Surveys are also used to develop trial strategy and case themes to which particular types of jurors will respond. For example, the survey is used to probe which facts and issues prospective jurors are likely to attend to and find most persuasive, and how jurors will perceive the litigants. The assumption is that with this information attorneys may be better able to provide the judge with more effective guidelines for issues to probe during voir dire in jurisdictions where attorneys are not allowed to question jurors themselves.[1]

---

[1]Survey results can be used by consultants for purposes other than jury selection. For example, consultants can conduct the surveys and use the results as legal evidence when presenting as an expert witness. Results from such surveys have been used on a wide variety of topics, such as trademark infringement and unfair competition lawsuits to prove that consumers are or would likely be confused as to the source of goods or products (English & Sales, 2005).

Typically, there are five parts to a community survey. In one part, basic demographic factors are measured. Other parts include a brief summary of the case and presentation of key evidence, along with questions designed to measure experience with and attitudes toward the evidence. Questions concerning other case-specific attitudes are also included as experience with and attitudes toward the legal system are assessed. Finally, beliefs about defendant responsibility (i.e., guilt, negligence) are measured.

The first part of this chapter reviews several of the most widely used applications of community surveys in scientific jury selection. The second part discusses key issues involved with conducting community surveys. We reserve our discussion of the proven effectiveness of these surveys until chapter 8.

USING SURVEYS TO IDENTIFY UNDESIRABLE JURORS

Surveys are a fundamental part of scientific jury selection because they allow a jury selection consultant to learn the pretrial verdict inclinations of community members. By analyzing respondents' responses about trial-related issues (e.g., litigant and case characteristics) and relating them to the demographic characteristics and experiences of the respondents, the consultant can identify the qualities that make potential jurors either more or less desirable for each side. As a consequence, attorneys can go beyond professional hunches when deciding what types of individuals to question extensively (if allowed by the judge) and to challenge during voir dire.

For example, consider the use of the community survey by Jay Schulman and the other selection consultants in the now famous Harrisburg Seven case (see chap. 1). Although his approach has been refined over the years, it provides a good illustration of the use of a community survey as well as the strength and weakness of relying on the resulting data to guide attorney decision making. Schulman and his colleagues began their work by conducting a phone survey of registered voters in the area around Harrisburg, Pennsylvania, the same population from which the venire (jury pool) would be drawn. A sample of 840 respondents were interviewed and care was taken to insure that the demographic characteristics (age, gender, race, education, marital status, and occupation) of the sample proportionally matched the characteristics of the existing jury panel. Respondents were asked about a number of general issues believed to be relevant to the outcome of the case. In addition, 252 people in the original group of 840 were later contacted and given a second more in-depth interview in person, rather than over the phone.

During the face-to-face interviews, respondents were asked about the type and extent of media contact they had (i.e., their choice of newspapers, magazines, and television exposure); their knowledge about the defendants and their case; their selection of the greatest Americans in the past 10 to 15 years; their trust in the government; the ages and activities of their children; their religious attitudes and commitments; their hobbies and leisure activities; and any organizational memberships they had. Other questions assessed a variety of specific attitudes potentially related to the trial (e.g., "People should support their country even when they feel strongly that the federal authorities are wrong," or "If the authorities go to the trouble of bringing someone to trial in a court, the person is almost always guilty" [Schulman, Shaver, Colman, Emrich, & Christie, 1973, p. 40]). Finally, respondents were asked to respond to a scale of acceptable antiwar activities, where participants were asked to agree and disagree with seven statements ranging from, "Accept what the government is doing and keep quiet about one's feelings," to "Become part of a revolutionary group which attempts to stop the government from carrying on the war by bombing buildings or kidnapping officials" (Schulman et al., 1973, p. 40).

The results of the phone survey indicated that religion was related to all relevant attitudes, and that Episcopalians, Presbyterians, Methodists, and Fundamentalists were prosecution oriented and should be excluded by the defense attorneys during voir dire. This information was critically important because the attorneys originally had been reluctant to ask about religion. In addition to specific religious beliefs, higher education and greater contact with the local news media were associated with conservative attitudes. This finding was surprising to the research team because higher education is generally associated with more liberal attitudes. Later, this counterintuitive finding was explained when the researchers discovered that after returning from college, liberal well-educated people tended to move away from conservatively oriented Harrisburg.

According to the research team's findings, an ideal juror for the defense was a female Democrat with no religious preference and a white-collar or skilled blue-collar job. In addition, a preferable juror would have sympathy for the defendants' attitudes toward the Vietnam War, tolerate nonviolent resistance to government polices, and indicate that they would adhere to a presumption of innocence on the part of the defendants. The defense followed these guidelines to strategically exclude potential jurors during voir dire with the use of peremptory challenges. The judge provided the defense with 28 peremptory challenges, whereas the prosecution was only allotted 6.

The trial began at the end of January 1972, and the prosecution took 2 months to present its evidence. After presenting 64 witnesses, William Lynch, the chief prosecutor, rested the government's case. The following day, lead defense attorney and former attorney general Ramsey Clark unexpectedly announced in his opening statement that "the defendants continue to proclaim their innocence—and the defense rests" (as cited in Schulman et al., 1973, p. 38). The jury deliberated for 7 days before acknowledging that it was a hung jury. On the three principal charges of conspiracy, 10 jurors favored acquittal, while only 2 voted guilty. On the basis of pretrial research, both guilt-oriented jurors should have been excluded during voir dire. The attorneys stopped questioning the first of these two jurors as soon as they learned that she had four sons who were conscientious objectors. Had questioning continued, the lawyers might have gotten her to reveal that she strongly disagreed with her sons' opinions about the war and military service. The second juror simply lied about his attitudes during voir dire. He claimed he could not dislike people like the defendants because his own sons looked like hippies, and that church people should do more to oppose the war. However, as soon as deliberations started he proclaimed them guilty by the will of God and refused to discuss the evidence.

Attorneys rely on a survey not only to identify the voting propensities of individual jurors but also to elicit responses that can be used in successful challenges for cause and to request an extended voir dire of prospective jurors (Nietzel & Dillehay, 1983; the importance of conducting an extended voir dire is discussed in detail in chap. 6). In addition, a survey is used to identify the types of jurors that are more likely to be exposed to and influenced by prejudicial information. If the percentage of the surveyed respondents is high, the attorney can use this information in a pretrial motion to argue for a greater number of peremptory challenges. Particular attention can then be paid to these types of individuals during voir dire, with the knowledge that there will be sufficient peremptories to exclude those who are biased.

The basic techniques developed by Schulman are still in use today. Community survey data is used to develop profiles of desirable and undesirable jurors. However, when this data is used to guide jury selection, it is predicated on the assumption that specified attitudes are predictive of subsequent behavior. The merits of this assumption are discussed in detail in chapter 8.

CHANGE OF VENUE

Community surveys are also used to provide evidence in a change of venue motion. Widespread community hostility toward a defendant can threaten the fairness of jurors and juries. Where this occurs, the only solution may be to move the location of the trial to a jurisdiction where community bias will not jeopardize the fairness of the trial. Known as a *change of venue*, this is an appropriate remedy when there is a "reasonable likelihood of prejudice" in a community (*Sheppard v. Maxwell*, 1966).

A number of factors can produce a reasonable likelihood of community bias, including the nature of the case, the defendants or victims, the existing community values, the composition of the community, and pretrial publicity (Nietzel et al., 1999). Although most of these factors will be discussed later in this book (see chaps. 4 and 5), the threat of pretrial publicity is particularly relevant to change of venue motions. Courts are generally reluctant to change the venue of a trial because of the expense and inconvenience involved and the preference to hold a trial in the jurisdiction where the crime was committed. But the Sixth Amendment to the U.S. Constitution guarantees defendants the right to a trial by an impartial jury, which in some cases may only be achieved by moving the location of the trial. This is particularly important in today's society, in which the pervasiveness of the media and the Constitution's First Amendment right to freedom of the press can effectively damage a defendant's right to a fair trial in the location where a crime was committed.

Although the proliferation of cable news channels and the Internet as a source for information and news has certainly contributed to the problem of pretrial publicity, courts have had to deal with the conflict between the First and Sixth Amendments as far back as the treason trial of Aaron Burr in 1807. In that case, Burr argued that he could not receive a fair trial because community opinion was biased against him as a result of a series of inflammatory newspaper articles. In a decision by the United States Supreme Court, Chief Justice John Marshall, writing the majority opinion, noted that there was no legal requirement that a jury be free of "any prepossessions whatever respecting the guilt or innocence of the accused," although jurors could be disqualified if they "have deliberately formed and delivered an opinion on the guilt of the prisoner as not being in a state of mind to fairly weigh the testimony" (*United States v. Burr*, 1807).

Courts have subsequently followed the basic principle regarding pretrial publicity outlined by Marshall. For example, in *Murphy v. Florida* (1975), Murphy argued that intensive publicity surrounding his prior convictions denied him his right to a fair trial. The Supreme Court concluded that it is not essential that jurors be completely unaware of a defendant's history, if that information would not interfere with their ability to be impartial jurors. However, exposure to inadmissible information that is highly probative regarding the specific case may conflict with Sixth Amendment guarantees. For example, in *Rideau v. Louisiana* (1963), Rideau's death sentence was reversed because at least three members of the jury had seen a local television station's repeated broadcast of the defendant confessing to the offenses he was charged with, and a defense request for a change of venue had been denied.

Social science research has also demonstrated that pretrial publicity can be damaging to defendants (for a review, see Lieberman & Arndt, 2000). A number of studies found that individuals who have been exposed to media crime stories develop a proprosecution bias (Constanti & King, 1980; Freedman & Burke, 1996; Moran & Cutler, 1991; Simon & Eimermann, 1971). For example, Moran and Cutler (1991) examined the effects of pretrial publicity on perceptions of defendants in two highly publicized trials. Greater pretrial knowledge regarding facts of the case was positively related to believed culpability of defendants. It is interesting to note that awareness of case details and the likelihood of a respondent reporting that he or she could be fair and impartial were not related. Further, respondents who stated they felt they could be impartial also admitted that it would be difficult for them to ignore case-relevant media reports they had been exposed to. Thus, though potential jurors may be aware that they have been exposed to damaging publicity about a defendant, they still claim impartiality when in fact they have already developed a prejudicial opinion of the defendant.

Once jurors have been exposed to pretrial publicity it becomes quite difficult to eliminate its biasing effects (Steblay, Besirevic, Fulero, & Jimenez-Lorente, 1999), in both criminal and civil cases (Bornstein, Whisenhunt, Nemeth, & Dunaway, 2002). A variety of remedies have been used to deal with the problem of pretrial publicity, including removing biased prospective jurors during voir dire, delaying the start of the trial with a continuance, and delivering judicial admonitions to ignore the publicity. These remedies, however, are typically ineffective. For example, admonitions to ignore pretrial publicity usually do not reduce the biasing effects of the publicity. In fact, admonitions to disregard information can sometimes backfire, leading to greater use of the inadmissible information (Broeder, 1959; Cox & Tanford, 1989). The preferred method for courts to manage prejudicial pretrial publicity is to use voir dire to identify and remove biased individuals. Research unfortunately also indicates that voir dire is not an effective remedy (Dexter, Cutler, & Moran, 1992; Freedman, Martin, & Mota, 1998). It is difficult for attorneys to tell who has been influenced by publicity if the jurors do not admit it. Further, even if jurors admit to being exposed to pretrial publicity but maintain that they can be objective when considering the facts of the case, it is very difficult for them to actually do so.

In cases where there is extensive pretrial publicity that biases community attitudes, a change of venue may be granted. Two issues that the courts and attorneys must be concerned with are how widespread is the information, and how much of an impact has it had on the community? Selection consultants can demonstrate the prevalence, nature, and impact of pretrial publicity through content analysis[2] of media stories and through the use of surveys of community attitudes toward the litigant, issues in the trials, and related issues.

In particular, the consultant can attempt to identify categories of information that the American Bar Association (1983) has stated should not be publicly disseminated because it can be considered highly prejudicial to a defendant. These categories include opinions regarding the guilt or inno-

---

[2]A *content analysis* refers to the methodological technique of systematically looking for trends in social artifacts (i.e., items that are produced by humans). Typically, although not exclusively, social artifacts are recorded materials, which includes newspaper articles and recorded television broadcasts. Thus, a researcher could conduct a content analysis by examining news stories for negative (and inadmissible) information about the defendant or other parties involved with the case.

cence of the accused; comments regarding the strength of the evidence; prior record information; details about the character or reputation of the accused; pretrial confessions, statements, or refusal to make a statement; refusal of the defendant to submit to relevant tests or exams, or test or exam performance; or a plea of guilt to the offense or to a lesser offense.

Studebaker, Robbennolt, Pathak-Sharma, and Penrod (2000) provided an excellent example of using a content analysis for a change of venue motion in a review of work they conducted for the Oklahoma City federal building bombing trial of Timothy McVeigh. The content analysis involved a comparison of newspaper stories in Oklahoma City with articles in other potential trial locations in Oklahoma (Lawton and Tulsa) and in Denver, Colorado. The research team sampled articles from a newspaper in each city for 264 days (the period of time from the day after the bombing to a date several weeks before the change of venue hearing). Articles were analyzed for references to many of the categories mentioned in the American Bar Association guidelines noted previously, as well as for the amount of emotional publicity (e.g., statements regarding the emotional suffering of victims) and for other relevant categories of information, such as statements about motives for committing crimes or statements about the death penalty.

In addition to quantifying the number of articles with potentially prejudicial references, Studebaker et al. (2000) also measured the amount of space devoted to each article (number of paragraphs and physical space) and the importance of the articles. Importance was measured by identifying the physical placement of the article (e.g., front page or not; above or below the fold; side of the page and size) and such factors as headline font and inclusion and content of photographs. Photograph content included categories such as pictures of the buildings, victims, and rescuers, as well as photos of the accused (Timothy McVeigh and Terry Nichols) both in and out of custody. The results indicated large differences in the content and nature of news articles among the cities, with far greater coverage and prejudicial information reported in the Oklahoma City newspaper. The research was presented in a change of venue motion that successfully led to the relocation of the trial to Denver.

Although a content analysis of media stories about a trial is useful for demonstrating the amount of publicity the media has reported, it cannot assess whether individuals in the community have actually seen the reports or what effect it has had on them. This is a major concern because courts have long held that exposure to publicity is not enough to infringe on a defendant's right to a fair trial. The issue is whether the publicity has affected the potential jury pool to the extent that it would be impossible to impanel an impartial jury. A community survey can address this issue and is the preferred technique for demonstrating the existence of a reasonable likelihood of such significant bias that it is unlikely an impartial jury could be drawn (Nietzel et al., 1999; but see Posey & Dahl, 2002, for a discussion of ethical issues related to conducting change of venue surveys). In the Timothy McVeigh trial, Studebaker et al. (2000) supplemented the content analysis data with results from a public opinion survey conducted in the cities from which the newspaper articles were drawn. The survey results indicated that there was a considerable amount of prejudgment regarding the guilt of Timothy McVeigh. In addition, the survey showed "respondents in the Oklahoma venues were more likely to report being absolutely confident of McVeigh's guilt than were respondents in Denver" (p. 331).

When a change of venue survey is conducted, it should consist of questions that address whether participants (a) have heard of the criminal or civil issue or are aware of relevant litigants, lawyers, or witnesses in the case; (b) have heard of specific facts central to the case, key issues that would be prejudicial to the case, or sources of that information (i.e., newspapers, television, radio, Internet);[3] and (c) have reached conclusions about the case (e.g., how much evidence is there against the defendant and do you think the main suspect is guilty?) and about the appropriate type of penalty if the defendant is guilty. Finally, the survey should include questions regarding basic demographic information. For an excellent example of a change of venue survey, see Nietzel et al. (1999). Although an experienced survey researcher will be skilled at constructing survey questions, he or she may not be aware of the law or facts that may be relevant to the case and, therefore, to the survey questions. In a similar way, the attorney may be extremely knowledgeable about the case but unaware of the nuances of constructing reliable survey questions. As a consequence, an attorney should work with the consultant to develop the questionnaire (Cotsirilos & Philipsborn, 1986).

PROCEDURE FOR CONDUCTING COMMUNITY SURVEYS

The process of conducting a survey is generally the same, regardless of its purpose. For example, if one wanted to conduct a survey for change of venue or for jury selection purposes, the questions on the survey and the technique used to collect data from respondents would be very similar. Thus, in the rest of this chapter we focus on issues related to the methodology of conducting a survey, and in subsequent chapters we elaborate on the application of the data collected in community surveys.

As we discuss in the following sections, to gather useful survey data the survey instrument (the questionnaire) must be carefully written and effective sampling of the local community must be done. After the data is col-

---

[3]It may be helpful to ask about the specific media sources respondents have been exposed to, such as the identity of the specific newspapers, television channels, radio stations, or Web sites that have been viewed. This is important because different media outlets may provide different styles of coverage regarding elements of the case or trial participants. For example, the tabloid style of media used by *The New York Post* newspaper may lead to coverage that is different from that of *The New York Times*.

lected, it must be entered into a computer and statistical analyses of the data performed. Finally, the data must be interpreted. As a result, it is imperative that this process be conducted by a social scientist with appropriate training in survey research. Failure to effectively conduct any of these stages can produce invalid data. For example, misleading data may be generated that could potentially undermine the development of an effective jury selection strategy.

Survey Preparation

The development of a useful survey begins with adequate preparation. If proper techniques are not used in the design and implementation of the community survey, results that are not reliable or not valid are likely to be obtained. Proper methodology should be used so that the responses provided by the sample are an accurate reflection of the opinions and experiences of the community from which they are drawn. Nietzel et al. (1999) reported that a 2-month preparation time is typically desirable. However, they note that if the demands of the trial schedule dictate a shorter time interval, survey research can still be effectively conducted. In fact, it is possible to survey small homogeneous communities and analyze the data within several days (discussed in the "Sample Size" section).

As early as possible, the consultant should meet with the legal team to discuss the trial strategy the attorneys plan to pursue and try to identify the likely strategy that opposing counsel will follow. The identification of key themes regarding the case, as well as relevant characteristics of the defendant and witnesses, will allow for the development of a refined survey instrument (Nietzel et al., 1999).

The questions on the survey must be relevant to any fact that needs to be proven (Pollock, 1977). For example, it is important to measure not only whether jurors have been exposed to media stories and the source of those stories but also the specific evidentiary-related information the sample has been exposed to. As Pollock noted,

> the poll should determine whether the respondents think they can give a fair trial of the accused; whether they have been influenced, and how much, by what they have seen, heard, or read about the case; and most important, exactly what respondents do know about the facts of the case from what they have seen, read, and heard. Even if the change of venue is denied, counsel will have obtained much useful information for voir dire, and may have grounds for reversal on appeal if the poll shows a reasonable likelihood that no fair trial was possible. (pp. 280–281)

Care must be taken to avoid leading and suggestive questions (Pollock, 1977). The questions must be in-depth and go beyond measuring respondents' affective reaction to the defendant or other key figures in a case (Arnold

& Gold, 1978–1979). Furthermore, it is not sufficient to measure opinions regarding guilt or liability and whether respondents would be capable of giving the defendant a fair trial. The survey should also measure what evidentiary factors respondents have been exposed to in the media (Pollock, 1977) and their awareness of potentially inadmissible evidence (such as incriminating statements made by the defendant that are ruled inadmissible during the trial; Cotsirilos & Phillipsborn, 1986). The survey may also include a free association task when respondents articulate what comes to mind when presented with the names of a defendant or other key parties in a case (Penrod, Groscup, & O'Neil, 2004). These results may be useful in determining positive and negative affect associated with the defendant.

The goal of the survey should ultimately be to identify if there is bias in the community and if so, which specific community subgroups (e.g., deeply religious people over the age of 50) are likely to have that bias and what element of the case is likely to trigger it. This information can be used to support a change of venue motion if the bias is of such magnitude that it is unlikely a fair jury can be selected. If the change of venue motion will not succeed, then the survey can aid the attorneys in using their challenges against jurors who are likely to be biased against their client or their case (see chaps. 2 and 6).

Methods for Conducting Surveys

Traditionally, survey research is conducted using self-administered questionnaires, face-to-face interviews, or telephone interviews. When self-administered questionnaires are used, a respondent fills out answers him- or herself and either hands or mails the questionnaire back to the interviewer. With face-to-face interviews, an interviewer will ask the respondent questions in person. Telephone interviews are, of course, conducted over the phone. Each method has strengths and limitations (Dillman, 1993). For example, self-administered questionnaires are typically more cost efficient but produce lower response rates than other techniques. In-person interviews have much higher response rates and provide an opportunity to pursue open-ended questions or complex questions in greater depth. In addition, an interviewer can easily clarify questions that are confusing to the respondent. However, in-person interviews can be quite expensive and time consuming. Telephone interviews provide a good alternative to self-administered questionnaires and in-person interviews because an adequate response rate can be achieved for a reasonably economical price. Also, with phone interviews the time period required to collect the data can be quite short, and changes to the survey or clarification of questions can be easily made if necessary. Finally, when houses are called on a random basis, it is much easier to collect data in an anonymous or confidential way than is possible with mail or face-to-face surveys. As a result, in most surveys conducted for jury selection or change of venue purposes telephone interviews are used (for an extensive review of these methods, see Dillman, 1993).

In recent years, we have seen the development of electronic surveys using the Internet (Dillman, 1999; Gosling, Vazire, Srivastava, & John, 2004; Kraut et al., 2004). Comparisons of Internet data collection methods to traditional paper-and-pencil measures (e.g., Gosling et al., 2004) have indicated that both approaches produce findings consistent with each other, and that Internet data gathering produces samples that are relatively diverse in terms of age, gender, and socioeconomic status.

Electronic surveys can be conducted either through e-mails or survey Web sites (see Studebaker et al., 2002, for a detailed discussion of both approaches within the context of an Internet study on pretrial publicity effects). With an e-mail survey, respondents are sent a questionnaire to which they respond by typing in the body of the message and e-mailing it back to the researcher. The main advantage of the e-mail approach is that it is easier for researchers to administer than the Web site method.

In an alternate way, a Web site can be set up, and respondents can reply to questions online using pull-down menus, check boxes, open-ended text boxes, and other techniques. A major advantage of this approach is that responses are automatically put into a database by the computer, eliminating potential data entry errors and speeding up the data analysis portion of the study. A Web-based approach to collecting data also offers tremendous potential for consultants to conduct surveys that are relevant to the legal cases. This is because the Internet not only allows for the transmission of printed material but also of audio, graphic, and video information. For example, a consultant concerned about the impact of the physical appearance of a defendant could easily scan in a photograph and adjust the appearance (hairstyle, dress, facial hair, etc.) through the use of photo-editing software. The computer could then randomly choose one of the photographs to present to respondents as they complete the Web survey. Another possibility is that multiple versions of opening statements could be videotaped using a digital video camera and shown over the Internet for comparison. The potential for this type of research will grow as more homes gain access to the Internet with high-speed connections and electronic information transmission capacity improves.

It is unfortunate that this approach requires detailed programming knowledge and may necessitate a Web designer consultant. The initial development of such a Web site will also be more time consuming than the other survey techniques. The largest limitation of this technique, however, is obtaining a representative sample. Only computer users will be able to respond using this technique and that population will likely be wealthier and more youthful than the general population of a given community.

Sampling Issues

A key issue in survey research is which type of sampling technique will be used. It is essential that the sample is representative of the appropriate population (i.e., individuals who are eligible to serve on the jury in that particular case). The consultant should begin by identifying local requirements for juror eligibility, because it is critical that the sample is drawn from the jury eligible participants. Individuals who are contacted as part of the survey but who are ineligible for jury service (e.g., foreign nationals) must be excluded from the data. In addition, respondents who might be witnesses or other trial participants should be excluded (Nietzel et al., 1999). Schulman (1973) argued that the most accurate information is obtained when the sample is drawn from individuals who have previously served on juries held in the same district as the current case, assuming there have not been substantial changes to the procedure for selecting the jury pool. People who have previously served as jurors in that jurisdiction are most likely to share characteristics with jurors. The obvious problem with this recommendation is that potential jurors who have not previously served remain an unknown entity to the consultants and attorneys. This may be important if the lack of prior juror service leads the novice jurors to hold different attitudes or reach different decisions. Without survey information to explore this issue, the consultant is providing incomplete information to the attorney.

Two common sampling methods are random sampling and stratified sampling. *Random sampling*—randomly sampling from the population—is the simplest sampling technique. For example, the consultant could draw a random sample of phone numbers for telephone interviewing from the voter registration list, which is likely to be the most efficient sampling approach in terms of time and cost. If the voter registration list is too costly, lists of randomly generated phone numbers can be purchased relatively inexpensively from market research firms. If a consultant does not wish to purchase any list, he or she can use a sample created by random numbers. One way to do this is to generate a list of all three-digit prefixes in use in the area that will be surveyed and then randomly select a series of four digits. The combination of the three-digit prefix and the random four digits will produce a random phone number. A random numbers table, found in most statistics textbooks, can be used to generate the random four-digit numbers. Another approach involving a random numbers table is to use the table to identify the page, column, and number of entries from the top (or bottom) of the page to be called in a residential telephone listing. One limitation to this approach is that unlisted numbers will not appear. However, this problem can be easily overcome using the Plus 1 method (Nietzel et al., 1999). The Plus 1 method simply involves adding the value of one to the number obtained in the telephone directory, which will ensure that unlisted numbers are not systematically excluded.

It should be noted that this procedure will produce a random selection of phone numbers, not individuals. Whoever is most likely to answer a phone in a given household will be most likely to respond to the survey. As a consequence, household members who stay home frequently (e.g., to raise children) will be overrepresented in the sample (Dillman, 1993).

An alternative to random sampling is *stratified sampling*. In this method a population is broken down into relevant subgroups (e.g., by racial–ethnic background, political affiliation, age, etc.) and the sample is stratified to match the population. Thus, after the appropriate proportions of relevant characteristics have been identified within a population, individuals from the population who possess these characteristics are randomly sampled until enough individuals have been selected to match the appropriate population proportions. For example, if a community is 60% Caucasian, 20% Hispanic, 10% African American, 5% Asian, and 5% other racial–ethnic groups and a 500-person sample is drawn from the community, a stratified sample will contain 300 Caucasians, 100 Hispanics, 50 African Americans, 25 Asians, and 25 members of other racial–ethnic groups. The advantage of this technique over simple random sampling is that it protects against the possibility of having a disproportionate number of a particular type of individual in the sample. This may be a particular concern when a subgroup is relatively small and may not be represented in a randomly drawn sample. This technique is more complicated than simple random sampling and is thus more time consuming and expensive to conduct. In addition, a sample must be quite large if a population is stratified on multiple variables, adding to the challenge of using this sampling technique. However, as a general rule, stratified sampling is preferable to ensure subgroup representation, which is a particular concern when a community survey is used for scientific jury selection purposes.

Sample Size

The determination of sample size is often an educated guess on the part of the researcher. A sample should be small enough to allow for a fast and efficient collection and analysis of data, but large enough that one can generalize the response to the population of interest. As a rule of thumb, the larger the sample size the greater the confidence one can have in the generalizability of the results. The available time and resources, however, will put restrictions on a consultant's ability to generate a large sample.

Although some researchers have indicated that a sample of approximately 400 respondents is typically used in community surveys (Nietzel & Dillehay, 1986), it is difficult to put a precise number on an appropriate sample size, because the unique characteristics of each study will impact sample size. For example, an important consideration in sample size is the homogeneity of the population of interest (Shutt, 2004). A smaller sample is acceptable when it is drawn from a relatively homogenous population, such as a rural county where many of the residents share basic demographic characteristics such as race, religion, political affiliation, etc. If the population is heterogeneous, such as in a metropolitan area where there is great diversity in the backgrounds and attitudes of the residents, a larger sample is required.

In addition, the goal of the research will affect sample size. If the consultant plans on analyzing the responses of multiple subgroups in a sample and using many variables to predict behavior (e.g., when classes of individuals who would be undesirable jurors need to be identified), a large sample size is necessary. In that case, the size of the subgroups is a more important consideration than the initial size of the sample (Levy & Lemeshow, 1999). If the consultant plans to use only a few variables to describe a population, however, a smaller sample will suffice (Shutt, 2004). For example, if only a few variables are under consideration, as in a change of venue survey in which a sample of residents from the county where a trial will be held are compared with samples drawn from other counties, Nietzel et al. (1999) noted that a sample size of 30 to 60 respondents per county may be adequate.

A final consideration is that a large sample size cannot compensate for a poor sampling procedure. This was clearly illustrated in the 1936 presidential election. *Literary Digest*, a popular news magazine at the time, conducted a poll to determine which candidate people were likely to vote for in the upcoming election that pitted the incumbent, Franklin Roosevelt, against the Republican challenger Alf Landon (Babbie, 1998). *Literary Digest* contacted 10 million United States citizens in a postcard mail survey. An enormous sample of over two million individuals responded to the poll and indicated a solid and decisive victory for Mr. Landon. However, the results of the actual election were quite different. Landon only carried 2 states and received 8 electoral votes, compared with 523 electoral votes for Roosevelt. This tremendous error in results was the product of poor sampling. Respondents were selected from telephone books and automobile registration lists. The result of such a sample during the Depression was an overrepresentation of wealthy individuals (Babbie, 1998). Thus, the representativeness of a sample should always be a paramount consideration.

Questionnaire Length

The survey should be as short as possible. When telephone interviews are conducted, they should last no more than 10 to 15 minutes (Nietzel et al., 1999). When interviews go beyond this time frame, respondents quickly become disinterested and may put less thought into their responses or terminate the interview altogether.

Use of Bogus Publicity Items

When respondents are asked if they have heard specific news items, there is a possibility that individuals will indicate they are familiar with the incident when in fact they have not heard the news stories. Hence, reported rates of media awareness may be overestimates. As a result, bogus publicity items are frequently included in change of venue surveys to assess the validity of the data (Moran & Cutler, 1997). If only a small percentage of respondents claim to recognize a bogus item or items, one can have confidence in the accuracy of the responses. As the percentage gets larger, the validity of the survey becomes suspect (Moran & Cutler, 1997). Haney reported that awareness rates of bogus items can be quite high, with as many as one third of respondents claiming knowledge of the phony item (as cited in Moran & Cutler, 1997).

One method of interpreting the responses to bogus items is to adjust the rates of actual publicity awareness downward. Thus, if 78% of respondents reported awareness of actual items, and 23% reported awareness of a bogus item, then awareness of the actual item would be adjusted downward to 55% (Moran & Cutler, 1997). However, on closer consideration it is unclear exactly what should be made of respondents who indicate they have previously heard stories about the bogus items. Awareness rates of bogus items are not fixed and absolute numbers, but will largely depend on the bogus item's plausibility (Moran & Cutler, 1997). Hence, in the absence of the development of standard items with expected rates, the bogus items should not be used for correcting actual awareness rates. In addition, although a person may indicate she or he has heard a bogus item, as Haney reported this does not mean this individual has not been exposed to the actual item (as cited in Moran & Cutler, 1997). Excluding this type of respondent from the sample may produce an underestimate of bias in the community.

Moran and Cutler (1997) empirically examined the effects of bogus publicity items on the relationship between awareness of pretrial publicity and perceptions of guilt and self-reported impartiality. Responses of an entire sample of individuals questioned about exposure to pretrial publicity items were compared with a subsample of respondents restricted to those who appropriately denied seeing bogus media items. Excluding respondents who indicated they had viewed bogus publicity did not significantly affect the results of the survey. A significant relationship between awareness of publicity and perceptions of defendants' guilt was obtained for both the full sample and the subsample of respondents, and in both groups the relationship between awareness of publicity and ability to be impartial was nonsignificant. Thus, it does not appear that including participants who respond affirmatively to bogus items appreciably affects the critical relationship between publicity awareness and pretrial bias.

Comparison of Results

To effectively demonstrate the impact of pretrial publicity on community bias, it may be useful to report two comparisons of the data: (a) a comparison of the responses of those who have heard media stories with those who have not and (b) a comparison of rates of exposure to news stories in the venue where the trial is scheduled with the rates of exposure in a different venue. These types of comparisons should create a more compelling case regarding the existence of community bias and the advantage of holding the trial in another jurisdiction. In addition, it is helpful to conduct a survey twice (Cotsirilos & Phillipsborn, 1986). The first survey should measure initial community knowledge of the case as soon as the attorney becomes involved with the case. A second survey should be conducted closer to the start of the trial to measure whether community awareness and sentiment has changed. This comparison may be useful in showing that community members have become quite knowledgeable of the case, presumably because of continued extensive media coverage, and that initial negative reactions to the case have not dissipated over time. For example, an examination of media coverage and community awareness in the high-profile trial in New York of Lizzie Grubman, who while intoxicated backed her car into a crowd waiting outside a nightclub, indicated that perceptions of Ms. Grubman became more negative over time (Penrod et al., 2004; see also Studebaker & Penrod, 2005). As a consequence, if only an initial survey measure of community sentiment were conducted in her case, it might paint a more favorable picture than actually existed at the time of the trial. Thus, the point when a selection consultant is brought in to work with the defense team may be critical to the information obtained by the consultant.

Reliable Interviewers

In the early years of jury selection consulting, the work was driven by concerns that the government was abusing its power (e.g., the Harrisburg Seven and Wounded Knee trials) and work was done on a pro bono basis, with volunteer interviewers commonly used (e.g., Schulman, 1973). Although jury selection–trial consulting is now a profit-oriented enterprise, volunteer interviewers may still occasionally be used by consultants. It is unfortunate that volunteers may be less reliable than paid interviewers because they may not have a commitment to the research and may not be willing to spend the time to be trained properly. The result is that they will lack the expertise needed to adequately perform their job (e.g., being inconsistent in the way they interview different respondents). This can ultimately produce survey results of low reliability and little value (Berman & Sales, 1977).

Data Analysis

After the data is collected it will need to be analyzed. Although meaningful information may be gained by examining the data using relatively simple statistics, it will typically be necessary to use advanced statistical skills to extract maximum information from the data. This often occurs because a combination of factors, rather than a single factor, is what may be necessary to predict verdict inclination. For example, although women in general may not be more conviction prone given pretrial information they have heard in the media, White females with incomes over $100,000 may be conviction prone. Thus, the identification of the optimal juror or the characteristics associated with the most damaging type of juror for one side may require the combination of multiple factors (variables) to predict the outcome of interest (verdict inclination).

The statistical technique of multiple regression is often necessary to examine the relative contributions of various factors on a behavior. *Multiple regression* is a technique that allows researchers to identify the strength of relationships between several predictor (independent) variables and the dependent variable. For example, a worker's salary (dependent variable) may be predicted from a set of independent variables such as job type, educational experience, length of employment, and other factors identified by a researcher. A multiple regression would show the strength of the relationship between these predictor variables and the worker's salary variable.

Other exploratory data analysis techniques, such as factor analysis, may also be necessary to clearly see useful connections in the data. *Factor analysis* is a technique that allows researchers to identify the interrelationships between a set of variables. After subsets of variables that are strongly related to each other have been identified, logical reasoning is applied to clearly describe a concept that the variables are measuring. For example, a factor analysis on a juror bias survey (e.g., Kassin & Wrightsman, 1983) may reveal that responses to some questions are strongly related (such as whether it is acceptable to vote to convict a defendant if one is 90% sure of the defendant's guilt, whether a defendant should be convicted if only 11 of 12 jurors vote guilty, and whether too many people are wrongfully imprisoned). The interrelated nature of these questions may be described by the application of the abstract concept of reasonable doubt (an entity that is not directly measurable). In addition to identifying relationships among variables and allowing indirect concepts to be measured, the factor analysis technique also allows unrelated variables to be identified and eliminated. This information may be needed to keep pretrial surveys short and may be useful when attorneys are limited to asking only one or two key questions about a concept during voir dire.

The consultant may also want to check the quality (reliability) and validity of the questionnaire he or she administers (see generally, Babbie, 1998). Not surprisingly, for pretrial research to be truly useful, it is essential that these techniques be used by qualified individuals. The data analysis skills necessary are often taught in advanced graduate courses in the social science fields. As a result, it is critical that attorneys use consultants who have adequate backgrounds in these areas. Simply because someone calls him- or herself a jury selection consultant does not guarantee that he or she possesses the skills necessary to effectively analyze collected data.

CONCLUSION

Developing a survey requires skills and experiences that go far beyond simply writing questions down on paper. Creating a survey is almost like creating a work of art, in which one must consider every stroke. The particular words used, the construction of the sentences, the order of the questions, and certainly the particular respondents who are selected will affect (sometimes dramatically) the information obtained. The skills involved in survey design and implementation can only be developed through extensive training. As a consequence, an attorney must turn to an individual trained to collect this type of information and should seek selection consultants with backgrounds in fields that rely heavily on survey research, such as psychology, sociology, communications, political science, or market research. We return in greater detail to the problems selection consultants face in conducting proper surveys and the relationship between attitudes and behavior in chapter 8. However, in the next chapter we consider the importance of respondents' demographic information on community surveys in the scientific jury selection process.

4

THE INFLUENCE OF
DEMOGRAPHIC FACTORS

For centuries, lawyers in the United Sates have been relying on their own beliefs about who would be a favorable or unfavorable juror to guide their decisions during voir dire. These beliefs may be based on their intuitions or on guidelines they learned from such sources as trial advocacy texts, senior attorneys, or law school. Identifying specific demographics that are predictive of verdict orientations is an important result of community surveys. This assumes that there is an empirically identifiable and reliable relationship between demographics and verdict inclination. This chapter begins by examining the advice that has been offered to attorneys on using demographic characteristics to predict juror behavior in criminal and civil trials. We then discuss the research that has been carried out to evaluate the relationship between these characteristics and verdicts (see also Bonazzoli, 1998, and Fulero & Penrod, 1990, for excellent reviews on this topic).

THE LEGAL TRADITION OF USING
DEMOGRAPHIC FACTORS IN JURY SELECTION

Since at least the nineteenth century, legal literature has been replete with recommendations as to the characteristics of desirable and undesirable jurors (Donovan, 1887, as cited in Fulero & Penrod, 1990), with the suggestions typically being couched in terms that generalize across entire groups of people. For example, Melvin Belli (1982) felt that married people made better jurors for criminal defendants because they are more forgiving. Clarence Darrow (1936) argued that wealthy jurors are conviction prone, except when the defendant is on trial for a white-collar crime. Other suggestions have been more outlandish, such as to avoid jurors whose profession starts with the letter p, thereby excluding "pimps, prostitutes, preachers, plumbers, procurers, psychologists, physicians, psychiatrists, printers, painters, philosophers, professors, phonys, parachutists, pipe-smokers, or part-time anything" (Bryan, 1971, p. 28). However, an even larger group of people might be excluded by following Wishman's (1986) suggestion to avoid any juror whose face one does not like, because "chances are he doesn't like yours either" (pp. 72–73). Apparently, a preference for certain baseball teams has even been used to guide jury selection decisions. During the 1950s in New York (at least before 1957, when two New York baseball teams migrated to California), there was a belief in the legal community that defense attorneys should reject Yankee fans and prosecutors should eliminate Brooklyn Dodger fans. New York Giants fans were acceptable to both sides because they were considered "the only reasonable people in town" (DiPerna, 1984, p. 151). Assuming such guidelines were accurate, one would expect Brooklyn to have been a haven for criminals, where law breakers had no fear of being convicted in a jury trial. However, court records prior to 1957 indicate that many convictions did actually occur in this borough.

A variety of factors have been identified as predictive of verdicts, including: ethnicity–race, gender, wealth and social status, occupation, age, religion, marital status, demeanor, and appearance (Belli, 1982; Fulero & Penrod, 1990). Generally, the view adopted by authors of legal texts is that individuals who are good criminal defense jurors are also good civil plaintiff jurors, whereas people who make good jurors for the prosecution are also desirable to the defense in a civil case. The assumption is that prosecution–civil defense types are more conservative in their attitudes.

These recommendations logically need tempering because they are based on large generalizations and do not take into account specific types of legal decisions that jurors may have to make. For example, Goodman, Loftus, and Greene (1990) noted that "a juror favorably disposed to a party on the issue of liability will not necessarily be favorably disposed to that party on the issue of damages" (p. 306). They also noted that "a review of advice commonly offered to lawyers on how to conduct voir dire in civil cases shows that it . . . tends to focus on issues related to proof of liability, not matters related to the determination of damages" (p. 306).

Mauet (1992) reported that the most popular approach to jury selection is probably reliance on beliefs and attitudes to predict verdict, with the best predictors of beliefs and attitudes likely to be age, education, employment history, residence history, marital and family history, hobbies and interests, reading and television, organizations, and related life experiences. He also asserted that although "every case needs to be individually analyzed to determine the kind of jurors you want and don't want, certain generalizations are probably true" (p. 25).

Unfortunately, it is hard to rely on Mauet's (1992) assertions because attorneys provide conflicting advice about whether specific demographic or attitudinal factors are the most useful predictors of verdicts. For example, Hayden, Senna, and Siegel (1978) report that attorneys are most interested in juror age, occupation, demeanor, gender, appearance, and residence. However, Penrod (as cited in Fulero & Penrod, 1990) reports that attorneys are concerned with attitudes toward legal technicalities, gender, ideological orientation, and age.

What does the empirical research tell us about this topic? Wiener and Stolle (1997) examined the influence of demographic and attitudinal variables on jury decision making in a murder case with a potential capital punishment sentence. In addition, the researchers examined attorneys' (specifically, Missouri public defenders') beliefs as to which variables were influential, to determine if attorneys were able to identify critical factors. The results indicated attorneys believed that more factors were influential than actually were. For example, in trying to distinguish which jurors would vote guilty or not guilty, attorneys indicated that marital status; race; political ideology; and attitudes toward African Americans, handgun control, and illegal drugs were all influential, when none of these factors differentiated between jurors' verdicts or correlated with the certainty of the jurors in their verdicts. Attorneys not only identified irrelevant factors but in some cases omitted relevant factors. For example, attorneys tended not to identify as a predictive variable whether jurors had children, but this factor did distinguish between those favoring life imprisonment or death. These results indicate that if attorneys rely on their hunches about what to ask on a pretrial survey or base questions on previous pretrial surveys that may contain items that have never been empirically validated, they run the risk of including irrelevant factors and omitting relevant ones.

RESEARCH ON THE EFFECTS OF DEMOGRAPHIC CHARACTERISTICS ON VERDICTS AND DAMAGES

There is research that addresses the effectiveness of demographic factors in predicting juror verdict decisions and damage awards. This research, as shown in the following section, has revealed inconsistent findings across specific demographic characteristics.

Occupation

Occupation appears to be one of the most commonly articulated demographic factors used to guide jury selection, with legal writers having generated an almost inexhaustible list of occupations that are predictive of verdicts. Perhaps there is such focus on occupation because it is a demographic characteristic that individuals choose. Unlike gender, race, age, and to a large extent, religion, occupation is a characteristic that one chooses or that develops over time as a result of life experiences. As a consequence, attorneys may view it as having greater predictive value. In addition, because there are so many occupations, attorneys may feel that there is a great deal of homogeneity among the members of a specific occupation, producing a far more cohesive and clear-cut characteristic than would be generated by broader variables such as gender or race–ethnicity.

Some legal authors (e.g., Cornelius, 1932) recommended excluding jurors with the same occupation as the opposing party in civil trials. Other writers had more specific recommendations. For example, some (e.g., Appleman, 1952) argued that farmers had a tendency to be generous when rendering civil damages, whereas others argued the reverse (i.e., that farmers were desirable civil defense jurors; Belli, 1982). The logic, although inconsistently articulated across legal authors, appears to be that the characteristics of one's profession will affect decision making (Mossman, 1973): "Cabinetmakers and accountants, the adage went, should be avoided because they require everything in a case to fit together neatly. Carpenters, on the other hand, were said to be more likely to accept the defendant's case, because they are accustomed to making do with available materials" (p. 78). In a similar vein, some authors (Cartwright, 1977; Jacobs, 1983) stated that individuals who are experienced with injury and suffering will be bad jurors for civil plaintiffs because they have become accustomed to suffering and will not be shocked by it. Although nurses may claim to be concerned about people who have experienced injuries, they will actually be intolerant of pain and suffering because of their occupation, as will people who work in social welfare services (Jacobs, 1983). Advice about police also exists. Using this same logic, some authors indicated that police would not be sympathetic to a plaintiff's pain and suffering (Cartwright, 1977); others disagree (Appleman, 1952). Using a different analytic approach, Bailey (1974) suggested that criminal defense attorneys should generally reject jurors with an authoritarian-oriented occupation (e.g., law enforcement or military), except when the defendant is a military veteran (a position supported by research on authoritarianism, see chap. 5). It has also been argued that jurors with occupations that expose them to a variety of aspects of life (e.g., artists, writers, and actors) are less likely to be shocked by the details of a crime, and as a result, are more preferable defense jurors in criminal cases (Bailey & Rothblatt, 1971). In addition, a 1986 training video used by Philadelphia prosecutors in capital murder trials (discussed in Baldus, Woodworth, Zuckerman, Weiner, & Broffitt, 2001) says that prosecutors should exclude jurors whose occupations require high intelligence or critical analysis, such as "doctors, lawyers, law students, social workers, and teachers (unless they are 'fed up' with their Black students)" (p. 43). This, of course, assumes the defendant is Black.

Finally, some writers provided long lists of acceptable jurors, such as Lane (1984), who suggested the following:

> . . . artists, musicians, actors, laborers, carpenters, mechanics, salespersons, office workers and writers as good civil plaintiff jurors. Good civil defense jurors include bankers, bank employees, members of management, low salaried white-collar workers, retired police officers, military men, school teachers, clergymen's wives, utility company employees, insurance representatives or adjusters, farmers, accountants, engineers, professional people in general, tool and die makers, cabinet makers, corporate executives, superintendents, and former court officials. (as cited in Fulero & Penrod, 1990, p. 235)

Criminal Trial Research

Despite the myriad of strategies for selecting jurors on the basis of occupation, there is little research that shows occupation is independently related to verdict. It has been shown that higher socioeconomic status (measured by education and occupation) led jurors to be more likely to vote guilty (Adler, 1973; Reed, 1965). However, others reported that occupation did not significantly affect verdicts (e.g., Bridgeman & Marlowe, 1979; Simon, 1967).

Civil Trial Research

There are relatively few studies that have shown occupation to be an important determinant of civil trial decision making. One study (Denove & Imwinkelried, 1995) reported that occupation was not a significant predictor of liability decisions, but was predictive of the amount of damages awarded when examined in conjunction with the jurors' income level. White-collar workers awarded lower damage awards than blue-collar workers for emotional injuries, but this pattern was reversed for physical injuries. Occupation also was shown to be predictive of damage awards when median damage awards (as opposed to mean awards) were examined, with white-collar professionals awarding larger damages (Goodman et al., 1990). Gender exerted important interactive effects in this study. As Bonazzoli (1998) noted,

> [f]emales employed as general professionals, technical professionals, business professionals or managers–supervisors awarded higher damages than females employed as clerical workers or craftworkers–laborers. Among males, those employed as general professionals were significantly more likely than those employed as technical professionals to award [larger] amounts. (p. 282)

Additional Considerations Regarding Juror Occupation

Given the importance placed on occupation as a juror selection strategy, it is surprising that so few studies have shown occupation to be related to jury verdicts. This may be the result of the fact that there is little relationship, or because of the way many jury research studies are conducted. Most mock jury studies use experimental designs, which typically have relatively small sample sizes. With small samples (that often range from 15–20 participants per condition) it may be hard to have enough participants to reflect the wide range of possible occupations. In addition, it may be almost impossible to get jurors who have high status occupations (e.g., doctors, lawyers, and other professionals) to participate, given the demands of their jobs. A variant of this dilemma applies to convincing anyone who works full time to find the available time to participate in simulated research. Finally, jury studies often use college students as participants, so it may be difficult to obtain much occupational variability with such participants. These concerns permeate the literature reviewed in this chapter, with the exception of the influence of gender, and for our purposes we will not discuss them again.

Finally, a number of researchers have noted that occupation may be an important determinant of verdict decisions in a more indirect way (e.g., Bonazzoli, 1998; Hastie, Penrod, & Pennington, 1983). Jurors with high status occupations are more likely to be chosen as foreperson. In addition, high-status occupation jurors are likely to emerge as opinion leaders during deliberations and influence others toward a particular verdict (Kassin & Wrightsman, 1988; Kerr, Harmon, & Graves, 1982). Low-status individuals tend to be less influential on others and more susceptible to conformity pressures (Driskell & Mullen, 1990; Milgram, 1974). As a consequence, an attorney may be well-advised to use peremptory challenges to exclude high-status occupation jurors if such individuals appear to be initially predisposed to favor the opposing side. There may be less need to use peremptory challenges to exclude unfavorable low-status jurors.

Socioeconomic Status–Income–Education

Socioeconomic status is a variable that usually combines income, education level, and occupational prestige. These factors are inherently tied together, as a person's wealth is often a function of their occupation. Although attorney beliefs have often focused on characteristics associated with occupation, beliefs have been articulated regarding the other aspects of this concept, in particular the influence of income level. Clarence Darrow (1936) cautioned defense attorneys to avoid wealthy jurors because they were conviction prone, except in cases where the defendant was accused of white-collar crime. For civil cases, it has been argued that wealthy individuals will be on the side of the plaintiff, because they are less reluctant to pay large awards (Belli, 1982), and that individuals at the lower end of the economic scale may be favorable for the defense (Biskind, 1954; Harrington & Dempsey, 1969).

Criminal Trial Research

Socioeconomic status has been shown to be correlated with verdicts (Hastie et al., 1983; Visher, 1987). Although it has been found that higher socioeconomic status is associated with a greater conviction rate (Adler, 1973; Reed, 1965), alternative findings have also been presented. For example, Moran and Comfort (1982) found that high income jurors tended to acquit defendants in actual criminal trials studies, whereas low income male jurors tended to convict defendants. The effects of socioeconomic status were not found for female participants in Moran and Comfort's study. Simon (1967), however, found that mock juror occupation and income level were not significantly related to verdicts in insanity cases.

The independent effects of education (a component of socioeconomic status) on verdicts are also inconsistent. Some research has shown that less educated people are more conviction prone (Goodman & Loftus, 1987; Mills & Bohannon, 1980a; Moran, Cutler, & Loftus, 1990; Wiener & Stolle, 1997). Simon (1967), however, found that college-educated jurors were more conviction prone than those with less than a high school education. Reed (1965) similarly found that when education was used along with occupation level to identity a juror's socioeconomic status, higher status was related to a greater degree of being conviction prone. This relationship between higher education and conviction proneness is also supported by Field (1978a), who found that higher education correlated with more positive attitudes toward rape punishment, and these attitudes correlated with longer sentencing decisions. However, some research has shown that education is unrelated to verdict (Bridgeman & Marlowe, 1979; Hepburn, 1980; Moran & Comfort, 1982).

Civil Trial Research

Research has shown that low socioeconomic status is related to proplaintiff liability decisions (Bornstein & Rajki, 1994) and damage awards (Darden, DeConinck, Babin, & Griffin, 1991). However, when education is examined separately, the findings appear to be more inconsistent. For example, Goodman et al. (1990) found that less educated jurors were more defense oriented in terms of awarding lower damages than jurors with a college education. However, Diamond, Saks, and Landsman (1998) found that less educated jurors were more likely to find for a plaintiff (as were low-income jurors). Bornstein and Rajki (1994) found that education was not related to damage awards, even though less educated jurors were more plaintiff oriented in their liability decisions. Given these conflicting findings, it is not surprising that other researchers found education to be unrelated to liability decisions and damage awards (Denove & Imwinkelried, 1995; Reed, 1965).

Age

A number of conflicting attorney guidelines have been articulated regarding the use of juror age as a selection criterion. Appleman (1952) suggested that defense attorneys exclude older jurors, but Adkins (1968–1969) felt that the elderly are more lenient (although not always in criminal cases). It has been demonstrated that prosecutors were more likely to peremptorily challenge younger jurors (between 30 and 34 years old), whereas defense attorneys were more likely to challenge somewhat older jurors (between 40 and 44).

Jordan (1980) felt that older jurors in civil trials were more likely to render a verdict for the plaintiff, whereas Lane (1984) argued that jurors over the age of 55 were more favorable to defendants in civil cases. Although Jordan and Lane both appear to agree that the older jurors tend to award lower damages, Lane presented a more complicated picture and suggested that the relationship between age and verdict in civil trials is nonlinear. Jurors under 30 are typically favorable to defendants, as are jurors over 55; this may be due to young jurors' inexperience in life. However, jurors in the 30 to 55 age range are plaintiff-oriented in nature, because they are better able to appreciate the serious effects a permanent injury has on a victim.

Criminal Trial Research

Some studies demonstrated that age relates to verdict choice in criminal trials, with older people typically being more conviction prone (Hepburn, 1980; Mills & Bohannon, 1980a; Wiener & Stolle, 1997). However, other studies failed to find a relationship between age and verdict (Moran & Comfort, 1982; Simon, 1967). In addition, it has been shown that the influence of age on verdict may depend on the crime. Mills and Bohannon found that in rape cases, older jurors were more conviction prone, but were less conviction prone in murder cases.

Civil Trial Research

The effects of age on civil trial decision making are mixed. Some research has shown that middle-aged jurors are more plaintiff-oriented than either younger or older jurors in liability decisions (Denove & Imwinkelried, 1995), and that older jurors are more likely to believe there are too many illegitimate lawsuits and that damage awards are too high (Hans & Lofquist, 1994). It is interesting to note that Denove and Imwinkelried found that even though younger jurors were defense-oriented in liability decisions, they were also more likely to award larger damages than older jurors after a guilty verdict. Green (1968) reported a curvilinear relationship, with participants in the 30 to 44 age range being more plaintiff-oriented than jurors who were younger or older. However, other research has indicated that age is not related to verdict or the amount of damages awarded (Diamond et al., 1998; Goodman et al., 1990; Reed, 1965).

Gender

The use of gender as a selection criterion has produced a myriad of views (see Fulero & Penrod, 1990). For example, Darrow (1936) believed that attorneys representing criminal defendants should avoid female jurors. However, contradictory advice has also been offered by Belli (1982), and Katz (1968–1969), who suggested that women are desirable jurors from the perspective of criminal defendants, with the exception being if the defendant is an attractive woman. In addition, well-known attorney F. Lee Bailey (Bailey & Rothblatt, 1971) advised that if a witness against a defendant is female, the attorney should choose women for the jury because women are "somewhat distrustful" of other women. However, Brenner (1989) argued that young women should be avoided as jurors if the case involves a defendant being tried for rape. Hawrish and Tate (1974–1975) found that Canadian defense attorneys preferred male jurors in cases of fraud, rape, homicide, and misrepresentation.

A variety of viewpoints have also been articulated for civil trials. For example, Biskind (1954) argued that women should be avoided when seeking large damage awards. Wagner (1989) added the caveat that this opinion was particularly true for suburban housewives. Many attorneys have commented on the interaction between the gender of the plaintiff and juror. For example, Wagner cautioned attorneys representing male plaintiffs to be careful when selecting females with a feminist orientation. Heyl (1952) advocated that plaintiffs' attorneys should select male jurors if the plaintiff is female, but defense attorneys should select women if the plaintiff is male. As was true for criminal trials, Wagner noted that women have a tendency to dislike other women who are attractive or successful and should be avoided when representing an attractive female plaintiff. Lane (1984) reported that female jurors are desirable when the plaintiff is a woman. However, some attorneys have argued that women are not always predisposed to be hostile to other women, and that older women are sympathetic to female plaintiffs (Lane, 1984; Wagner, 1989). There appears to be a general belief that women are sympathetic to children when they are plaintiffs (Heyl, 1952; Lane, 1984). It should be noted that despite these beliefs, Van Dyke (1977) found that there was no difference in the number of peremptory challenges used to remove men as opposed to women from trials in New Mexico. However, in an examination of peremptory strike patterns in Philadelphia capital murder cases, Baldus et al. (2001) found that prosecutors felt that Black female jurors were particularly dangerous and attempted to routinely remove Black women from serving. The strategy of eliminating females is now prohibited by the Supreme Court ruling barring the use of gender as a criterion for making peremptory strike decisions (*J.E.B. v. Alabama*, 1994; see also *Batson v. Kentucky*, 1986).

Criminal Trial Research

Some researchers found that juror gender is unrelated to verdicts. For example, Simon (1967) found no relation between gender and mock juror decisions in insanity cases. Bridgeman and Marlowe (1979) examined the relationship between demographic characteristics and verdicts among 65 jurors who had previously served on criminal trials, and they also found no relationship between gender and verdict. However, as the vast majority (82%) of defendants in these cases were found guilty, the minimum variability of verdicts may have made it difficult to detect any differences. In addition, statistical tests were not reported by the authors, making in-depth interpretation of the results more difficult. Similar nonsignificant findings have been obtained by other researchers (e.g., Cowan, Thompson, & Ellsworth, 1984; Hastie et al., 1983).

Other researchers reported a relationship between gender and verdict. Cutler, Moran, and Narby (1992) found that gender was correlated with verdicts for mock jurors in an insanity defense case, with females more likely to convict than males. Similar findings were obtained in a trial involving a drug trafficking charge (Moran et al., 1990), child sexual abuse cases (Bottoms & Goodman, 1994; Kovera, Gresham, Borgida, Gray, & Regan, 1997), and in rape cases (Brekke & Borgida, 1988; see also Kovera, McAuliff, & Hebert, 1999). Wiener and Stolle (1997) reported that older men were more certain of their not guilty verdicts, whereas women were more certain of their guilty verdicts. However, the research is not consistent in the relationship between gender and verdict. Some research supports the conclusion that women are more likely to acquit than their male counterparts. For example, in cases involving women accused of killing men who had repeatedly battered them, female jurors were less conviction prone than their male counterparts (Schuller, 1992; Schuller & Hastings, 1996). Similar findings have been obtained in death penalty studies (Fitzgerald & Ellsworth, 1984; Thompson, Cowan, Ellsworth, & Harrington, 1984).

Some research suggests that race interacts with gender, with Black females being more conviction-prone than Black males, but no gender differences emerge for white jurors (Mills & Bohannon, 1980a). Mills and Bohannon also found that the effect of gender was dependent to some degree on case type. The authors examined juror verdicts in actual murder, rape, and robbery trials. However, only in robbery trials did gender have an independent effect, with females being more conviction prone than males.

Moran and Comfort (1982) examined actual trial jurors and also found that the effects of gender are not necessarily straightforward. They argued that gender is a moderator of personality factors, which in turn affect verdicts. For example, guilty verdicts were associated with stronger beliefs in a *just world* (a general belief that people get what they deserve in life, discussed in more detail in chap. 5) for women but not for men. Women who served on juries that convicted also felt less alienated and had higher authoritarianism (discussed in chap. 5) scores. With males, however, there was a relationship between guilty verdicts and lower income, more children, and lower social desirability scores. Moran and Comfort based these conclusions on surveys that were completed by actual jurors some time after they finished jury duty. Unfortunately, there was a low response rate (22.7%) in their study, but as the general conclusions of the study are consistent with other research, this limitation may not be too significant.

It is interesting to note that Hahn and Clayton (1996) found that juror gender interacted with attorney gender, with attorneys being more successful when presenting their case (either an assault or robbery case) to mock jurors of the same sex. In addition, male attorneys were most successful when they presented their case to male jurors using an aggressive presentation style. Female jurors were not influenced by presentation style.

Civil Trial Research

The effects of juror gender have also been examined in a number of studies that focused on civil trials. The results of those studies reinforce the notion that gender is not a strong or reliable verdict predictor. Green (1968) found that gender did not have a significant effect on liability judgments or damage awards in a case involving a child who was harmed after falling in a pool. Goodman et al. (1990) found that gender did not have a significant effect on jurors' awards, regardless of the type of wrongful death case jurors were presented with (product liability, automobile negligence, and medical malpractice). And Bornstein and Rajki (1994) reported that gender did not significantly predict verdicts in a number of product liability cases (although juror race and education were related to verdicts).

Denove and Imwinkelried (1995), however, did find gender to be marginally related to liability verdicts, but not to damage awards. The effect of gender on liability judgments was stronger when other variables were taken into account. For example, in a personal injury case, financially well-off males were more defense-oriented than other groups. In a similar way, females who worked in white-collar jobs awarded larger damage awards than male white-collar workers. Diamond et al. (1998) also found that women were more likely than men to find a defendant liable. Goodman et al. (1990) found gender to interact with several variables. For example, female jurors without a college education awarded lower damages than males with low levels of education, whereas well-educated female jurors with at least some college background awarded greater damage awards than their well-educated male counterparts.

Although there has been less research on civil trial judgments, there is no reason to believe that the influence of gender should be any stronger than what has been shown in criminal trial research. On the basis of the results of both interviews with jurors in actual trials and mock jury simulations, gender does not appear to be a particularly useful or reliable predictor of verdicts, and it is not possible to make gross generalizations regarding its influence.

Additional Considerations Regarding Juror Gender

Although gender may not be a strong predictor of verdicts, research has shown that men are more likely to adopt a task-oriented leadership role during deliberations, whereas women are more likely to adopt a socioemotional role. Task oriented leaders are better able to drive a group to achieving a goal and in the process are more likely to offer opinions. Socioemotional leaders are more likely to express support with a position and are better at reducing conflict in groups (potentially created by task-oriented leaders). Males also speak more frequently than females in deliberation. As a result, although gender may not directly influence verdict, it may increase the likelihood that a particular position will be expressed during deliberations (Kovera, Dickinson, & Cutler, 2003).

Ethnicity–Race

Ethnicity–race is one of the most commonly articulated characteristics in jury selection writings by lawyers. These ethnically based assertions were probably driven in part by the flood of immigration that occurred in the United States during the latter part of the 19th century and early part of the 20th century. The initial stereotypes about these immigrants held by those already living in the United States who were not part of these incoming ethnic groups may have been perpetuated (Cartwright, 1977; Lane, 1984; Wagner, 1989).

Many beliefs regarding the effects of ethnicity are based on assumptions about the degree of emotionality of different groups. These beliefs are more commonly used to predict the behavior in civil, rather than in criminal, trials. There is a general belief in the legal community that in personal injury trials the plaintiff will benefit from emotionally oriented jurors, and the defendant will benefit from rationally oriented jurors (Belli, 1982; Mauet, 1992; Sannito & McGovern, 1993; Simon, 1980; Vinson, 1993). This is based on the assumption that the greater the amount of feeling or empathy evoked in the juror, the more sympathy he or she will feel toward the victim (the plaintiff; Sannito & McGovern, 1993). In addition, emotional processing should increase the ability of jurors to imagine the injury and the pain and suffering it has produced (Darrow, 1936; Sannito & McGovern, 1993). Conversely, individuals who engage in rational processing should be responsive to law-and-order arguments and against windfall damages (Mauet, 1992).

Goldstein (1935) ranked the following groups on emotionalism from high to low: Irish, Jewish, Italian, French, Spanish, Slavic, and Nordic (English, Scandinavians, Germans). Similar sentiments were expressed by Clarence Darrow, who strongly recommended that plaintiffs' attorneys in civil cases select Irish jurors. Darrow asserted,

> You should be aware that he is emotional, kindly and sympathetic. If he is chosen as a juror his imagination will place him [at the scene of the injury]; really, he is trying himself. You would be guilty of malpractice if you got rid of him except for the strongest reasons. (Darrow, 1936, p. 36)

More recently, Hispanics and African Americans have been added to the list of proplaintiff individuals (Lane, 1984; Wagner, 1989). Obviously, these suggestions are tempered when the ethnic group of the juror is in conflict with the ethnic group of a litigant. Wagner has noted that attention should be paid to the existence of historical conflicts between different ethnic groups, because tensions between such groups may spill over into the courtroom. For example, if an attorney is representing a Jewish plaintiff, Arabs may make undesirable jurors.

There is empirical evidence that attorneys' beliefs regarding ethnicity–race guide their behavior. Van Dyke (1977) found that prosecutors in New Mexico were most likely to use their peremptory challenges to remove non-Anglo-European jurors, whereas defense attorneys were most likely to challenge White jurors. As previously mentioned, attorneys' historical tendency to make race-based peremptory challenges led to the Supreme Court's prohibition of this practice in the *Batson v. Kentucky* (1986) decision (and in the subsequent relevant cases of *Edmonson v. Leesville Concrete Co., Inc.*, 1991; *Miller-El v. Dretke*, 2005; *State v. McCollum*, 1992). Despite these rulings by the Court, race appears to be a factor that is still used by attorneys. Rose (1999) found that in 13 post-Batson cases in a North Carolina county, Black jurors were disproportionately excluded by prosecutors. The population of the county where the trials took place was 37% Black and the proportion of Blacks in the venires was slightly less at 32%, yet 60% of the prosecutions' struck jurors were Black. However, 87% of defense attorneys' strikes were against White jurors, leading to a slight overrepresentation of Blacks on juries.

Similar conclusions were reached by Baldus et al. (2001) who found that peremptory challenges based on race (and gender) were widespread by both prosecutors and defense attorneys, and that the Supreme Court rulings have had very little impact on attorneys' behavior. Baldus et al. examined capital murder trials held in Philadelphia between 1981 and 1997. They reported that "[i]n the Philadelphia system, prosecutors appear to have been guided for many years by a jury selection model . . . [that] emphasizes the importance of voir dire and the overarching goal of seating jurors who are 'conviction prone'" (p. 42). This approach is outlined in a 1986 training video made for Philadelphia prosecutors. The training tape emphasizes that the worst jurors for prosecutors who are trying a case against a Black defendant are Blacks who live in low-income areas, and in particular young Black women. However, the training tape claims that older Black men are actually good jurors for the prosecution (because they grew up in a different time period and as a result have a different respect for the law). Baldus et al. speculated that the tendency for attorneys to continue to use race (and gender) as selection criteria despite the *Batson* and *J.E.B.* rulings may reflect the strong beliefs attorneys have regarding the importance of these factors on jury decisions.

Criminal Trial Research

Broeder (1959) found that jurors with a German or British heritage were more prosecution oriented, whereas individuals with Italian or Slavic backgrounds were more defense-oriented. He also found that Blacks were more defense oriented than Whites. Simon (1967) found Blacks to be acquittal prone in insanity cases (but race accounted for less than 5% of verdict variance), although Mills and Bohannon (1980a) found that Blacks were more conviction prone. This effect was largely driven by Black women being more conviction prone than Black men or Whites of either gender. Cutler, Moran, and Narby (1992) reported that race and verdicts were correlated in an insanity defense case, with Hispanics being more conviction prone than non-Hispanics. In a survey of 1,400 jury eligible respondents, Williams and McShane (1990) found that Black and Hispanic jurors were less likely than White jurors to recommend a sentence of death. However, Baldus et al. (2001; discussed in greater detail in chap. 2, this volume) reported that in actual cases where prosecutors used their peremptory challenges to exclude many Blacks from serving on juries, there was a greater likelihood of sentencing a Black defendant to death compared with a White defendant. Significant correlations between race and verdict have been obtained by other researchers as well (e.g., Visher, 1987). However, Hepburn (1980) found race to be unrelated to verdict for mock jurors in a murder case.

Similarity and the Black Sheep Effect

Some attorneys maintain that a fundamental principle of jury selection is that prospective jurors relate to those with similar characteristics, backgrounds, or experiences (Blue, 2001). Some research supports this assertion and demonstrates that jurors are more lenient to defendants who share their background and more punitive toward defendants with different backgrounds, particularly for racial characteristics. The general finding in the literature is that White jurors are more punitive toward Black defendants than they are toward White defendants (Baldus, Woodworth, & Pulaski, 1990; King, 1993). Ugwuegbo (1979) demonstrated that similarity effects are also operational among Black jurors in a mock jury study involving a rape case in which the race of the defendant, victim, and jurors were varied. White jurors were most punitive when the defendant was Black and the victim was White, whereas

Black jurors were most punitive when the defendant was White and the victim was Black.

There have been exceptions to the similarity rule (Nietzel & Dillehay, 1986). For example, Hagen (1974) and Nickerson, Mayo, and Smith (1986) reported no consistent findings regarding the tendency for White jurors to be more punitive toward Black defendants. Further, in a meta-analysis of 29 studies, Mazzella and Feingold (1994) found no overall effects of defendant race on mock juror judgments. However, race did interact with the severity of the crime, in that Black defendants were more likely to receive greater punishment from jurors when they were charged with more serious crimes. The interactive effect of race with other factors is apparent in a number of other studies. Johnson, Whitestone, Jackson, and Gatto (1995) found that mock jurors (who were primarily White) were more punitive toward a Black defendant compared with a White defendant when they were presented with incriminating inadmissible evidence. However, when the incriminating evidence was admissible, or omitted in a control condition, racial prejudice was not exhibited. Other research showed that discrimination against Black defendants appeared to be more pronounced among participants with poor comprehension of judicial instructions (Lynch & Haney, 2000).

Kerr, Hymes, Anderson, and Weathers (1995) found that in cases in which evidence against a defendant was weak, basic similarity effects were found for mock jurors. That is, White jurors were more lenient to White defendants and Black jurors were more lenient to Blacks. However, when the evidence against the defendant was strong *and the majority of jurors were White*, Black jurors were *more punitive* than White jurors to Black defendants. Kerr et al. termed this phenomenon the *black sheep effect*. The black sheep effect did not occur when Blacks composed the majority of individuals on the jury. This may indicate that similarity effects are secondary to self-presentation concerns. If jurors think that their affiliation with the defendant will lead them to be viewed negatively by other jurors, they may be overly punitive toward the defendant (see also Nietzel & Dillehay, 1986). This possibility highlights the notion that attorneys should be cautious before relying on simple rules of thumb in voir dire strategies.

Sommers and Ellsworth (2000, 2001) identified another important exception to racial prejudice findings obtained in experimental research. In several studies they showed that contrary to intuitive beliefs, White jurors are *more* likely to find a Black defendant guilty in interracial trials where racial issues are *not* emphasized. Sommers and Ellsworth explain these counterintuitive findings by suggesting that in trials where racial issues are made salient by the nature of the trial itself or by trial testimony, White jurors may become aware of the possibility of behaving in ways that could be perceived as prejudicial, and they may modify their behavior to display current egalitarian norms.

Civil Trial Research

Few studies have examined the relationship between ethnicity–race and civil decisions (Bonazzoli, 1998). Bornstein and Rajki (1994) found that minority mock jurors (mostly Black) were more likely to find defendants liable, but race was not related to damage awards. Denove and Imwinkelried (1995) supported Bornstein and Rajki's findings regarding liability judgments, but found that Black jurors tended to award greater damages than White jurors. Hispanic jurors behaved similarly to White jurors in terms of liability judgments, but were more generous than White jurors regarding damages. However, Diamond et al. (1998) found that minority jurors were less likely to find liability in a product liability case than were nonminority jurors.

Additional Considerations Regarding Juror Ethnicity

For the folklore-based assumptions (i.e., those derived from custom without consideration of scientific accuracy) to be predictive of jury behavior, two assumptions must be accurate. First, individuals within a given ethnic group must be more or less emotionally oriented than members of other groups. Second, emotional processing must lead to proplaintiff verdicts in civil cases.

Research has provided some support for the first assumption. A number of studies showed a link between ethnicity and emotions. For example, Consedine and Magai (2002) found that African Americans and Jamaicans reported greater joy and less negative affect than European Americans or Russian–Ukrainian immigrants. Vrana and Rollock (2002) similarly found that Blacks expressed more positive emotions and fewer negative emotions than Whites, and that Blacks, in particular Black men, exhibited higher blood pressure in emotional contexts than Whites. Asian Americans, in particular Japanese Americans, and Indians have been shown to have lower levels of positive emotions and higher levels of negative emotion than Europeans and Hispanics (Scollon, Diener, Oishi, & Biswas-Diener, 2004). Matsumoto (1993) also reported differences in self-reported emotional expressions of European American, Black, Asian, and Hispanic participants; McConatha, Lightner, and Deaner (1994) found Americans to be more inhibited regarding emotional expression than British participants. However, overall there has been surprisingly little research conducted in this area, and more work is needed (particularly with a specific legal focus) to firmly establish a link between ethnicity and emotional reactions to trial testimony and exhibits.

In addition, there is little empirical research on the second assumption regarding the effects of emotional processing on verdicts despite the amount of attention paid to it in the legal literature. The studies that have examined emotional influences have focused on using situational manipulations to activate emotional information processing, rather than relying on individual ethnic differences. For example, Whalen and Blanchard (1982) found that the presentation of emotionally arousing color photographs led to greater damage awards on the part of mock jurors for severely injured plaintiffs when a defendant's behavior was highly negligent. Kassin and Garfield (1991) found that exposing mock jurors to a videotape of close-ups of a bloodied young man who had been stabbed to death and left lying in the street led participants to set lower standards of proof necessary for conviction. Kramer, Kerr, and Carroll (1990) found that mock juries were unable to ignore emotionally arousing pretrial publicity, and Edwards and Bryan (1997) reported that emotionally arousing evidence had a significantly greater effect on participants' verdicts when it was ruled inadmissible than when it was allowed by a judge. On a surface level, it appears that attorneys may be correct in their assumption that emotional information processing is beneficial to plaintiffs and detrimental toward defendants. Although the predictions of attorneys are often focused on jurors' likely behavior in civil cases, this research was conducted in the context of criminal, rather than civil, cases.

However, the effects of emotional processing may not be as straightforward as presented in the research described previously, at least in civil cases. A study on jury decision making that examined the effects of processing information in either a rational or experiential (emotional) mode indicated that the effects of processing mode interact with other extralegal factors (in that case, defendant appearance; Lieberman, 2002). Mock jurors were given a transcript of a personal injury trial involving an automobile accident and asked to award damages. The participants were also given a photograph of either a physically attractive or unattractive defendant. Processing mode was manipulated through the use of either emotionally or rationally oriented language and by presenting a photograph of the accident victim lying on the ground in a pool of blood or a photograph of the intersection where the accident took place. The results indicated that when participants were in a rational mode, defendant appearance did not have an effect on their verdict. However, when participants were in an emotionally oriented (experiential) mode, they were more lenient to the attractive defendant and more punitive to the unattractive defendant. Thus, from a plaintiff's perspective, having emotionally oriented jurors is not beneficial when the defendant is attractive, which is contrary to the simplistic emotionally oriented guidelines repeatedly asserted in legal texts.

Religion

As noted previously, it has been suggested that Jewish people make good defense jurors in civil cases (Goldstein, 1935; Sams, 1969, as cited in Frederick, 1984). This belief may be particularly strong in death penalty cases, at least for some in the legal community. For example, John Quatman, a prosecutor in Alameda County, California, recently said that the trial judge (Stanley Golde) in a capital case he prosecuted told him Jews should be excluded because "no Jew would vote to send a defendant to the gas chamber" (Murphy, 2005, p. A1). This belief apparently exerted a strong influence during jury selection in many cases in Alameda County. A review of jury selection procedures in 25 capital trials held in Alameda County from 1984 to 1994 (conducted in part by the Habeas Corpus Resource Center) found that non-Jews were excluded at a rate of 49.97%, whereas Jews and people with Jewish surnames were excluded at a rate of 93.10% (Murphy, 2005). Darrow (1936) extended religious-based predictions beyond Jews to include Unitarians, Congregationalists, Universalists, and agnostics as preferable jurors for the defense. Presbyterians, Baptists, and Lutherans were considered to be prosecution-oriented jurors. However, Appleman (1952) felt that religious background was not a useful predictor of verdicts.

Criminal Trial Research

The research is consistent in reporting that there are no effects for either religious preference or church attendance on juror decisions in actual criminal trials (Reed, 1965), or in simulated studies using mock jurors (Hepburn, 1980; Simon, 1967).

Civil Trial Research

Hans and Lofquist (1994) found that Protestants were more likely to believe that there were too many frivolous lawsuits and exorbitant damage awards than non-Protestants. However, Reed (1965) found no relationship between religious preference and civil jury decisions.

Marital Status

From a criminal defense perspective, married jurors are argued to be preferable to single jurors, especially when the defendant is young (Bailey & Rothblatt, 1985; Belli, 1982); in a civil case, married people are thought to be better jurors for the plaintiff (Belli, 1982). The logic is that married jurors are more experienced in life and will be more sympathetic than single people to young people making mistakes and to "excuse the derelictions of contributory and comparative negligence civilly and minor failures of moral rectitude criminally than the unmarried prospective juror" (Belli, 1982, p. 442). Mauet (1992) noted that middle-aged jurors with stable marriages are typically preferred by prosecutors. This prediction is consistent with those just noted in that married couples who are very protective of the family would be hostile to adult defendants because these types of individuals threaten all families. Mauet also inexplicably predicted that middle-aged jurors with stable marriages would be supportive of civil defendants. Finally, he argued that single and young persons or young married couples are preferred by plaintiffs and criminal defense lawyers because such individuals are more receptive to emotional appeals.

Criminal Trial Research

Reed (1965) found marital status did not affect juror decisions in actual criminal trials, but Hastie et al. (1983) found a significant correlation between martial status and verdict preferences among representative mock jurors who viewed a homicide trial. In this study, married people were more inclined to convict on more serious crimes (e.g., first degree murder) than were nonmarried people.

Civil Trial Research

We did not find any research that focused on this factor.

Additional Demographic Characteristics

In addition to the factors mentioned previously, other characteristics of juror backgrounds have been examined. For example, in terms of political attitudes, conservatives have been shown to be more conviction-prone in insanity defense cases (Cutler et al., 1992), whereas independents are less likely to convict in murder cases (Wiener & Stolle, 1997). Republicans tend to express greater support for the death penalty than Democrats, and support for the death penalty has been shown to be associated with conviction-proneness (attitudes toward the death penalty are discussed in greater detail in the next chapter).

A variety of personal experiences have also been shown to relate to verdict. For example, Hastie et al. (1983) found a relationship between verdict preferences and prior jury service in criminal and civil cases. Individuals with a history of military service have been shown to be more conviction prone (Hepburn, 1980). However, the effect of these experiences on verdicts tends to be relatively weak.

OVERALL STRENGTH OF DEMOGRAPHIC FACTORS

The research described in this chapter has generally shown demographics to be unreliable predictors of juror behavior. Not surprising, the studies that have investigated the strength of demographic influences on juror decision making have shown that these characteristics accounted for only a minimal amount of verdict variance. For example, Baldwin and McConville (1980) examined the behavior of almost 4,000 jurors in 326 actual juries in England. The results indicated that verdicts were not affected by variability in jurors' age, gender, and occupation. Further, Hastie et al. (1983) examined the backgrounds and verdict inclinations of over 800 individuals who were representative of actual jurors recruited from jury pools in the Boston area. They found that education, political orientation, occupation, age, gender, and previous trial experience accounted for less than 2% of verdict variance. The low level of variance accounted for by demographic factors is fairly consistent across research studies, and even when characteristics are combined, the total variance accounted for remains low (5.4%, Diamond et al., 1998; 10%–16% in Mills & Bohannon, 1980a; 10.7% in Moran & Comfort, 1982; 2% in Visher, 1987; less than 5% in Simon, 1967). In addition, the amount of variance accounted for by juror characteristics appears to vary on a case-by-case basis (Diamond, 1990; Mills & Bohannon, 1980a; Moran, Cutler, & DeLisa, 1994; Penrod, 1990).

Demographics also have little predictive value for jury awards. In a study of juror decision making in civil trials, Wissler, Hart, and Saks (1999) found that demographic factors of gender, state of residence, and rural–urban location of residence accounted for only 2% of juror awards. It is interesting to note that when judges, plaintiff's attorneys, and defense attorneys were asked to complete the same experimental materials as the jurors, there was almost no difference in the amount of variance accounted for by demographic factors (2% vs. 4%, 1%, and 4%). Perceptions of the severity of injury to the plaintiff in terms of physical pain, mental suffering, disability, and disfigurement had a far more powerful influence on award decisions, with 23% to 58% of variance of the different groups accounted for by these factors. An important implication of this finding is that strength of evidence is a critical factor in predicting verdicts. We explore this issue further in chapter 8.

Persistence of Juror Mythology

Although many attorneys are interested in demographic characteristics (e.g., age, occupation, demeanor, gender, appearance, and race) that create a profile for desirable jurors (Fulero & Penrod, 1990), most of these factors have minimal or no predictive value for verdicts. And, unfortunately, despite the fact that demographic factors do not appear to provide useful rules of thumb that are applicable across a wide range of cases, general beliefs regarding the effects of such characteristics have been around for years and continue to be passed down to new generations of attorneys. The issue then arises as to why such unreliable strategies continue to be used.

One reason may be that it is difficult for attorneys to assess the accuracy of their selection strategies. Simply observing the verdict that the trial jury returns provides little information regarding the relative influence of jury selection strategies as opposed to the impact of evidence strength and attorney litigation strategy and presentation style. For example, an attorney might be inclined to attribute an unsuccessful trial outcome to numerous external factors, such as his or her belief that a witness did a poor job of testifying or the judge's exclusion of certain evidence, rather than to an unsuccessful jury selection strategy. There is little chance voir dire strategies can be validated by an attorney because the attorney is unable to determine which verdict the challenged jurors would have rendered.

A better approach is to conduct a community survey (see chap. 3) to identify key factors in a particular case that predict verdict preferences and include those factors on a refined pretrial survey. The pretrial survey responses can be followed up with additional questions during voir dire. In addition, as Wiener and Stolle (1997) noted,

> [p]erhaps the most significant contribution that juror surveys may make to voir dire is to reduce the number of criteria available in memory to attorneys when forming peremptory challenges. Armed with the results of such surveys, attorneys may be more able to detect true juror bias . . . and avoid overinterpreting juror attributes. (p. 243)

Relationship Between Demographics and Personality Factors

Another problem that can result from attorneys' relying on their intuitions rather than on data resulting from a community survey is that in the former approach, attorneys are relying on what social psychologists term *implicit personality theories* (Bruner & Tagiuri, 1954; Schneider, 1973; Sedikides & Anderson, 1994). This refers to individuals having a natural tendency to associate certain types of individuals with specific traits and behaviors. Thus, a network of associations is formed, and when an observer learns that an individual possesses one trait they easily associate it to the other related traits. This process allows humans to be cognitively efficient, because they can gather a wide range of information about individuals by simply learning one or two traits. For example, hearing that a particular person is a "liberal" or "conservative" brings to mind a wide range of associations regarding likely attitudes and behaviors.

Of course, the problem with relying on implicit personality theories or stereotypes is that beliefs regarding entire classes of people may be unfounded. Even if our personality theories are relatively accurate for members of a group in general, they will not hold for all individuals within a group. That is the major limitation for attorneys. An attorney who uses peremptory challenges to craft a jury largely composed of blue-collar workers is not interested in the decision-making behavior of blue-collar workers in general. He or she is interested in how specific blue-collar workers will react to the specific set of facts presented to them during the trial. It is in these highly specific situations when attorneys' jury selection theories may be ineffective.

CONCLUSION

Although for many years attorneys have recommended voir dire strategies based on demographic characteristics, demographic factors are not reliable predictors of verdicts. Some studies have shown that demographic characteristics do not predict verdicts at all. When specific demographic factors do predict verdicts, the factors are not consistent across studies (or even across different types of trials within a study) and are generally weak (Baldwin & McConville, 1980; Hepburn, 1980).

Attorneys are concerned with demographic characteristics because of the belief that these factors predict verdicts. Of course, demographic factors on their own do not lead individuals to arrive at specific verdicts. Rather, the assumption is that demographic factors are predictive of personality and attitudinal factors and these factors lead one to be more or less likely to accept different interpretations of the facts of a case. If individuals possess personality characteristics and attitudes that are related to verdicts, they may be predisposed to "develop a cognitive justification that inoculates the belief against disconfirming data" (Wiener & Stolle, 1997, p. 226). As a result, it is important to identify the relationship between personality, attitudes, and verdicts, which we address in the next chapter.

5

THE INFLUENCE OF
PERSONALITY AND ATTITUDES

As noted in chapter 4, individuals can be relatively easily classified on the basis of demographic characteristics such as gender, religion, income, age, and even race-ethnicity. Although such distinctions reveal a person's group membership in different categories, they tell very little about the specific person. For example, classifying an individual as female lumps her in with approximately half the people on the planet, a group containing about 3.2 billion members. It is clear that there is enormous diversity among the members of this and other demographic groups and because such diversity exists, it is extremely difficult to predict the behavior of specific members of the group.

If one wants to know how a particular person will behave in a given situation, more diagnostic information is necessary regarding individual differences, which may come in the form of personality or attitudinal differences. Although the terms *personality* and *attitudes* are often used relatively interchangeably, social psychologists generally refer to personality as consistent patterns of behavior, thoughts, or feelings that distinguish people from each other (e.g., extraversion vs. introversion, agreeableness vs. antagonism, neuroticism vs. emotional stability). Attitudes refer to evaluative judgments toward something or someone (e.g., support or opposition for the death penalty, abortion, or gun control). From a jury selection standpoint, both personality characteristics and attitudinal beliefs may be relevant to verdict decisions and thus are sought out in pretrial surveys. As is the case with demographic information, one needs to determine if personality and attitudes have been empirically demonstrated to predict verdicts.

The study of personality and attitudes has been a large focus in psychology for decades, and many different personality dimensions have been applied to jury decision-making research (e.g., Boyll, 1991; Graziano, Panter, & Tanaka, 1990). This chapter critically reviews personality characteristics and attitudes relevant to jury decision making, including general personality factors (e.g., authoritarianism, legal authoritarianism, Juror Bias Scale, dogmatism, locus of control, just world beliefs) and attitudes toward specific case elements (e.g., attitudes toward tort reform and legal claims, attitudes toward the death penalty, attitudes toward psychiatrists).

PERSONALITY CHARACTERISTICS AND ATTITUDES RELEVANT TO JURY DECISION MAKING

Research has identified a number of relatively broad personality characteristics (e.g., authoritarianism, defined below) that have some predictive ability regarding legal decision making. More recently, researchers studying jury decision making have focused on identifying specific attitudes that have greater relevance for legal decisions (e.g., attitudes toward tort reform—the law redressing personal or business injuries, the death penalty, and legal issues such as reasonable doubt). In this section, we discuss the relationship between these various personality characteristics, attitudes, and juror decisions.

Authoritarianism

Authoritarianism is a concept that has received a great deal of social science research attention over the past half century. Originally developed by Adorno (Adorno, Frenkel-Brunswik, Levinson, & Sanford, 1950), the construct refers to an individual difference associated with a desire for order, well-defined rules, and an authoritative leadership structure. Individuals who score high on authoritarian measures typically conform to conventional norms and exhibit a desire to punish individuals who deviate from those norms (often with physical punishments). Further, authoritarianism has been shown to relate to prejudicial attitudes manifested in hostility to out-group members (Narby, Cutler, & Moran, 1993), such as "Jews, communists, sexual offenders, members of the women's movement, or any other easily identified group" (Byrne & Kelley, 1981, p. 160). Although authoritarianism is a concept that was first identified in the 1950s to describe characteristics of fascist leaders who emerged during World War II, recent research indicates that it is an attitude that is still relevant to predicting behavior (Narby et al., 1993).

Authoritarianism is typically measured using a scale that asks participants to indicate their level of agreement with a variety of behaviors related to authoritarian attitudes (e.g., "It would be best for everyone if the proper authorities censored magazines and movies to keep trashy material away from the youth," "There is nothing sick or immoral in somebody being a homosexual," "One reason we have so many troublemakers in our society nowadays is that parents and other authorities have forgotten that good old-fashioned physical punishment is still one of the best ways to make people behave properly"; Altemeyer, 1988, pp. 24–25). The original measure of authoritarianism was the California F-Scale (the F standing for fascism), which became quite popular (Christie, 1991) and had high reliability (Narby et al., 1993). Later research showed that the scale had a number of methodological flaws (McBride & Moran, 1967) which were corrected in more recent versions (Christie, 1991).

It is reasonable to assume that authoritarianism would be related to conviction rates in criminal trials because authoritarians have a strong belief in the legitimacy of conventional authority and are driven to punishing deviates from that authority and defendants represent individuals who have rejected the rules of society. Numerous studies have investigated the relationship between authoritarianism and verdicts in trials involving different types of crimes, with the results demonstrating that authoritarians are more conviction prone (e.g., Bray & Noble, 1978; Lamberth, Kreiger, & Shay, 1982; Moran & Comfort, 1982). In addition, authoritarian jurors tend to have better recall of prosecutorial evidence than defense evidence (Garcia & Griffitt, 1978) and are more likely to recommend longer prison sentences for convicted defendants (Bray & Noble, 1978; McGowen & King, 1982).

Not all of the findings on authoritarianism have been completely straightforward, however. For example, Mitchell and Byrne (1973) found that, overall, there was no difference in conviction rates between authoritarian- and egalitarian-oriented jurors. However, participants classified as high authoritarians were more likely to convict defendants whom jurors viewed as different from themselves, and acquit defendants perceived to be similar. Authoritarians are also more punitive toward defendants of low status (Berg & Vidmar, 1975). Other research has shown authoritarians to be less punitive in cases in which the defendant was an authority figure (e.g., a police officer) or when a defendant committed an obedience-oriented crime (e.g., a Marine who followed a superior officer's order or someone who committed murder while disciplining a disobedient son; Garcia & Griffitt, 1978; Hamilton, 1978).

Although authoritarianism is a personality factor that is related to verdicts, on closer inspection the ability to predict verdicts from authoritarianism is actually rather weak. In a meta-analysis of 20 studies that examined the relationship between authoritarianism and perceptions of defendant culpability, Narby et al. (1993) found that the overall correlation between authoritarianism and verdict was $r = .11$, $p < .01$.[1] The effects were stronger among actual or representative jurors than among college students (approximately half the studies used actual jurors or representative participants, as opposed to the use of college students in the remaining studies). Thus, authoritarianism is significantly related to verdicts, but ultimately does not account for a great deal of verdict variance. The effects of authoritarianism also appear to be affected by the context and details of a specific case (Bonazzoli, 1998).

Legal Authoritarianism

Because authoritarianism is a broad personality trait that relates to many aspects of behavior, other researchers created measures of aspects of an authoritarian personality that are more specifically focused on legal issues. These are typically described as *legal authoritarianism measures*.

Legal authoritarianism measures currently focus on attitudes toward civil liberties and the rights of the accused within criminal trials, but theoretically could be applied to other legal issues (e.g., toxic tort litigation in which the defendant is a corporation). Individuals scoring high on legal authoritarian measures express a tendency to convict a defendant rather than upholding safeguards designed to protect the defendant, such as presumption of innocence, burden of proof, reasonable doubt, and due process-oriented restrictions on law enforcement. As Narby et al. (1993) noted,

> Although ignoring civil liberties is illegal and seemingly in contradiction to the law-abiding nature of authoritarian personality, it should be noted that the domain of civil liberties is one in which conventional

---

[1]The letters r and p are commonly used in describing research findings. When research results involving correlations are described, the strength and the direction of a correlation between two variables are identified by the letter r. The r refers to the "Pearson correlation," which can range in value from 0.0 to +/− 1.0. Positive scores indicate a positive correlation, meaning that as one variable increases, a second variable also increases. For example, the amount of money spent by political candidates on campaigns and the number of votes they receive may be positively correlated. Negative scores indicate a negative correlation, meaning that as one variable increases, a second variable decreases. For example, temperature and snowboard sales are negatively correlated, because fewer snowboards are sold in warmer months compared with colder months. When a correlation is close to 0.0 there is almost no relationship between variables. A relationship close to 1.0 indicates a near perfect relationship, so that as one variable increases, a second variable increases–decreases a consistent amount. Correlations close to +/− 1.0 are rare in social science research.

The letter p indicates the "significance level" of a statistical test. For most research, results are considered statistically significant if the significance level is less than .05, meaning that there is less than a 1 in 20 chance that the results are due to chance (e.g., abnormalities in sampling) and not a real effect. This is the general standard used in published social science research. When a statistical test produces a significance level of less than .01, the results are considered highly statistically significant.

norms may conflict with the law. In other words, legal authoritarians may be breaking the law in ignoring civil liberties but may be conforming to the normative viewpoint of their peers. (p. 35)

Thus, even though legal authoritarianism measures attitudes specifically on due process and crime control issues, the measure has been shown to also relate to general authoritarian measures (e.g., Boehm, 1968).

Boehm (1968) first measured legal authoritarianism by developing the Legal Attitudes Questionnaire (LAQ). The LAQ requires participants to rank 10 triads of items. In each case, participants ranked one authoritarian item (e.g., "Police should be allowed to arrest and question suspicious looking persons to determine whether they have been up to something illegal"), one antiauthoritarian item (e.g., "A society with true freedom and equality for all would have very little crime"), and one egalitarian item (e.g., "It is moral and ethical for a lawyer to represent a defendant in a criminal case even when he believes his client is guilty") to indicate their level of agreement. Antiauthoritarian items represented left-wing beliefs that antisocial acts were the result of unfair societal structure and identified individuals who may be disposed to acquitting defendants to demonstrate a rejection of authority. Egalitarian items represented "traditional, liberal, nonextreme positions on legal questions" and were designed to indicate lack of bias (Boehm, 1968, p. 740).

Boehm predicted that conviction proneness should be positively related to authoritarian subscale scores, negatively related to antiauthoritarian subscale scores, and unrelated to egalitarian subscale scores. Support was obtained for these predictions in a mock jury study. However, "her results were only marginally significant, and she did not report a direct comparison between LAQ scores and verdict preferences" (Penrod & Cutler, 1987, p. 298). Jurow (1971) also provided some support for utility of the LAQ scales by examining mock juror verdicts in a robbery case and a murder–rape case. Verdicts in these cases were not predicted by a traditional measure of authoritarianism (using the California F-Scale). Although the LAQ appears to be an improvement over the F-Scale in this case, it is worth noting that only a small proportion of verdict variance was accounted for. This conclusion also holds true for judgments about the severity of a verdict that should be imposed in death penalty trials ($r = .16$; Cowan et al., 1984).

Not all research supports the above findings. Buckhout et al. (1979) and Berg and Vidmar (1975) found that the LAQ was not predictive of mock juror verdicts (although it did predict recall and sentencing trends). The discrepancy regarding the LAQ findings was resolved by Narby et al. (1993) in a meta-analysis of studies performed on the relationship between authoritarianism and verdict decisions. They reported that verdicts were more strongly correlated with legal authoritarianism ($r = .19$, $p < .01$) than with traditional authoritarianism ($r = .11$, $p < .01$).

Cutler et al. (1992) indicated that in their experience (e.g., Moran & Comfort, 1982), participants are confused by the original format of the LAQ, which requires tripartite item rankings to be made. Cutler et al. also noted that there is less confusion and greater internal reliability to the scale when the items are treated as 30 separate items with Likert scales used to measure agreement for each (for a more extensive discussion of empirical limitations of the LAQ, see Kravitz, Cutler, & Brock, 1993). The methodological flaws of the LAQ led a number of researchers to develop revisions of the scale (Cutler et al., 1992; Kravitz et al., 1993; Moran & Comfort, 1982, 1986). For example, Cutler et al. used a revised 30-item measure of legal authoritarianism based on Boehm's (1968) original LAQ and found that legal authoritarians were more likely to convict in an insanity defense case.

Narby et al. (1993) have noted that in general "there is substantial overlap between traditional and legal authoritarianism, but the constructs are not completely redundant" (p. 36). In their meta-analysis of authoritarianism studies, Narby et al. reported that the overall correlation between authoritarianism (collapsing across different measures such as traditional authoritarianism, LAQ, and the Juror Bias Scale, discussed later in this chapter), and verdicts was significant ($r = .16$, $p < .01$). Thus, authoritarians do appear more conviction prone. Given that legal authoritarianism is related to beliefs about defendants' rights, assessing this attitude may be particularly useful to attorneys for identifying and challenging potentially biased jurors during voir dire (Narby et al., 1993). Further, as noted above, Narby et al. found the LAQ predicted verdicts better than traditional authoritarianism measures. However, the overall correlation between authoritarianism and verdict produced by the Narby et al. meta-analysis was .19, which translates to less than 4% of verdict variance being accounted for by this personality factor. As a result, legal authoritarianism does not appear to be an overwhelmingly powerful personality characteristic in predicting verdicts.

Juror Bias Scale

The main personality factors discussed thus far contribute to less than 10% to 15% of the verdict variance in any particular study, and less than 4% when combined across studies. As a result, the Juror Bias Scale (Kassin & Wrightsman, 1983) was developed to be a more sensitive measure of legally relevant attitudes. The scale is based on the assumption that two key factors are related to how jurors formulate ideas regarding guilt. First, jurors assess the likelihood that a defendant committed the crime (known as the Probability of Commission subscale) by indicating agreement with statements such as: "If a suspect runs from the police, then he probably committed the crime." Second, jurors establish some standard of proof that the probability of commission must exceed before voting for conviction (known as the Reasonable Doubt subscale), with items such as "A defendant should be found guilty if 11 out of 12 jurors vote guilty." Kassin and Wrightsman reported correlations between scale ratings and verdicts in a number of mock trials, with an average correlation of .31. Although the Juror Bias Scale is a better predictor of verdicts compared with other personality measures, it still only accounts for less than 15% of verdict variance.

Cutler et al. (1992) found that the Reasonable Doubt subscale was predictive of verdicts in a case where insanity was being used as a defense, but recommended the use of the Legal Authoritarianism Questionnaire (based on Boehm's, 1968, Legal Attitudes Questionnaire over the Juror Bias Scale in insanity defense cases because it emerged as a stronger predictor of verdicts). Further analyses indicated that politically conservative and non-Black people were most likely to endorse legal authoritarian attitudes (as measured by the Reasonable Doubt subscale), as were individuals with negative attitudes toward psychiatrists. In addition, crime victims were marginally significantly more likely to endorse legal authoritarian attitudes.

Cutler et al. (1992) also investigated the relationship of the Reasonable Doubt and Probability of Commission subscales and more traditional measures of legal authoritarianism (based on Boehm's, 1968, questionnaire). The data indicated that reasonable doubt was moderately (but significantly) correlated with legal authoritarianism, but probability of commission was not. On the basis of these findings, Cutler et al. questioned whether the Juror Bias Scale and the Legal Authoritarianism Questionnaire measure the same construct. In addition, although the Reasonable Doubt and Probability of Commission subscales of the Juror Bias Scale are supposed to measure separate concepts, there was high correlation ($r = .60$) between the subscales. As a result, it is not entirely clear what the Juror Bias Scale is measuring (Penrod & Cutler, 1987).

Although the Juror Bias Scale is traditionally composed of the factors of Reasonable Doubt and Probability of Commission, more recent work (Myers & Lecci, 1998) indicates probability of commission is itself composed of two separate factors, confidence in the legal system and cynicism toward some aspect of the criminal justice system. Confidence in the legal system is composed of three items: "If a suspect runs from the police, then he probably committed the crime," "Generally, the police make an arrest only when they are sure about who committed the crime," and "If the grand jury recommends that a person be brought to trial, then he probably committed the crime." Cynicism toward the criminal justice system is also composed of three items: "In most cases where the accused presents a strong defense, it is only because of a good lawyer," "Defense lawyers don't really care about guilt or innocence, they are just in business to make money," and "Many accident claims filed against insurance companies are phony." Myers and Lecci found that three items on the Probability of Commission subscale have little predictive power: "Out of every 100 people brought to trial, at least 75 are guilty of the crime with which they are charged"; "Circumstantial evidence is too weak to use in court"; and "The defendant is often the victim of his own bad reputation." In addition, on the Reasonable Doubt subscale, two items were weak predictors: "The death penalty is cruel and inhuman," and "Too many innocent people are wrongly imprisoned." As a result, it appears that attorneys may not want to waste precious space on jury questionnaires or time during voir dire probing responses to those items. Finally, Myers and Lecci report that their revised structure of the Juror Bias Scale accounted for more verdict variance (3.52%) than the original version (with only 2.63% of the verdict variance accounted for). However, the total variance accounted for is still very low. The validity of Myers and Lecci's research was limited to some extent by their use of college students as participants. However, the basic findings of their research were replicated in a later study (Lecci & Myers, 2002) that used a large sample of 617 jury eligible adults drawn from the community. Thus the Juror Bias Scale does not appear to be much better than other personality measures discussed thus far in terms of predicting verdicts.

Dogmatism

A number of researchers have examined the influence of dogmatism on jury verdicts. *Dogmatism* refers to a more general form of authoritarianism that focuses on how inflexible and closed-minded a person is (Rokeach, 1960; Shaffer & Wheatman, 2000). Dogmatism tends to be "free of the politically rightist ideology that characterizes high authoritarians" (Shaffer & Wheatman, 2000, p. 663). A key component of dogmatism is intolerance of ambiguity.

Research investigating the effects of dogmatism, not surprisingly, has produced findings similar to those regarding authoritarians. Individuals classified as highly dogmatic are more likely to convict defendants and are more punitive in sentencing decisions than individuals who score low on dogmatism measures (Shaffer & Case, 1982; Shaffer, Plummer, & Hammock, 1986; Shaffer & Wheatman, 2000). For example, in a study examining the effects of dogmatism and defendant suffering on sentencing recommendations (Shaffer et al., 1986), nondogmatic jurors sentenced a defendant shot while fleeing a crime scene less harshly than control participants who were told the defendant did not suffer while committing the crime. However, dogmatic jurors acted in a far more punitive fashion by punishing a defendant who had suffered as a result of a gunshot more severely than control participants. Shaffer et al. attributed this finding to dogmatic jurors adopting a just world perspective, believing that the defendant got what he deserved and should receive equally harsh punishment (just world beliefs are discussed in greater extent later in this chapter).

Although the behavior of dogmatic jurors is similar to that of authoritarian jurors, an important distinction between dogmatism and authoritarianism is that dogmatism is focused on a strong dependence upon legitimate authority, whereas authoritarianism tends to be intertwined with prejudicial issues, including limited tolerance and hostility toward out-group members. This distinction has been empirically demonstrated in a number of studies. For example, in the Shaffer et al. (1986) study described earlier, demographic characteristics of the accused were manipulated to create "in-group" and "out-group" conditions. The results showed that these manipulations did not have an effect on either nondogmatic or dogmatic individuals. In a similar manner, Shaffer and Case (1982) presented mock jurors with a robbery and murder trial and varied the characteristics so the defendant was either a heterosexual (in-group member) or homosexual (out-group member). Dogmatic jurors were more conviction prone in general than nondogmatic individuals. However, they were not more punitive to the homosexual defendant (in fact, a leniency bias was demonstrated). Thus, the results of these studies imply that dogmatic individuals were not hyper-punitive toward out-group members specifically.

Although these studies portray dogmatic jurors as punitive regardless of specific case factors, other research indicated that this is not always the case. Kerwin and Shaffer (1991) assigned individuals to six-person juries and classified each jury as either dogmatic or nondogmatic in orientation by having each mock juror complete a dogmatism scale. The juries were then presented with a summary of a murder case in which the defendant was accused of killing his terminally ill mother, who wanted to die. The evidence clearly indicated the defendant was guilty. In addition, participants were given one of two sets of jury instructions. One group received standard jury instructions defining the relevant procedural and substantive law and informing them that it was their duty to follow the law. A second group received nullification instructions (see Lieberman & Sales, 1997, for a more extensive review of nullification instructions) that informed jurors that they had the "final authority to decide whether to apply a given law or the Court's interpretation of it, to the acts of the defendant" (p. 142). The nullification instructions also informed jurors that they represented their community "and it is appropriate to consider the feelings of the community and your own feelings, based on conscience, in reaching [their] decision" (p. 142). If dogmatic people are simply hyper-punitive individuals, they would be expected to be highly conviction prone regardless of the type of jury instructions given. However, the results indicated that this was not the case. Although dogmatic juries given the standard instructions rendered more guilty verdicts than nondogmatic juries, the opposite occurred when nullification instructions were presented. That is, dogmatic jurors given nullification instructions in this euthanasia case rendered fewer guilty verdicts than nondogmatic jurors. Rather than being hyper-punitive, dogmatic jurors rigidly adhered to instructions they were given by a legitimate authority figure (i.e., the judge). When the instructions were written in a standard format that did not allow personal sentiment to be considered, jurors followed the law and convicted the defendant based on the strong evidence against him. However, dogmatic jurors did consider these personal feelings when the nullification instructions allowed them to do so.

Not all research has shown that dogmatism is related to verdict decisions or leads to greater adherence to judicial instructions. Buckhout (as cited in Penrod & Linz, 1986) examined jurors drawn from actual trials and found that there was no difference among individuals who had been on juries that convicted or acquitted defendants, in terms of jurors' scores on the Rokeach Dogmatism Scale (Rokeach, 1960), the Christie and Geis Machiavellianism Scale (Christie & Geis, 1970), or the Marlowe–Crowne Social Desirability Scale (Crowne & Marlowe, 1960). In addition, in experimental studies on instructions to ignore inadmissible evidence (Kerwin & Shaffer, 1994) and on the effects of a defendant invoking the Fifth Amendment (therefore withholding evidence), dogmatic jurors were not more inclined to follow legal instructions (Shaffer & Case, 1982). Shaffer and Wheatman (2000) tentatively attributed these discrepant findings to dogmatism moderating the effectiveness of only "very general *substantive* or *procedural* instructions that defined the relevant points of law or described the jury's responsibilities in applying the law as they deliberate to reach a verdict" as opposed to "*limiting* instructions that pertained to *specific testimony*" (p. 671, italics in original). Thus, it appears more research is needed on the effects of dogmatism before it can be considered a reliable personality characteristic that should be routinely used in jury selection.

Locus of Control

Locus of control (Rotter, 1966) refers to an individual's belief in the source of outcomes in life. That is, are events that occur to a person the result of that person's actions or of outside forces beyond his or her control? According to the locus of control perspective, individuals tend to adopt either an internal or external locus of control. *Internal locus of control* reflects the belief that an individual is responsible for his or her outcomes through his or her skills or efforts. In short, one is in control of one's own destiny. *External locus of control* refers to the tendency to attribute outcomes to factors beyond one's control, such as luck, fate, or the action of others (Phares & Wilson, 1972).

Rotter (1966) developed the Internal–External Locus of Control Scale to measure individual differences on this personality dimension. The scale contains a series of paired statements and respondents are required to select which of the two statements in the pair best reflects their attitudes. For example, respondents must choose between "As far as world affairs are concerned, most of us are the victims of forces we can neither understand, nor control" and "By taking an active part in political and social affairs the people can control world events," or between the statements "Many of the unhappy things in people's lives are partly due to bad luck" and "People's misfortunes result from the mistakes they make."

Because internally oriented people view themselves as responsible for their own outcomes, it is possible they will hold the view that other people are responsible for their outcomes as well. Externally oriented people tend to attribute less responsibility to themselves and may attribute less responsibility for an event to other people (Phares & Wilson, 1972). If this is the case, jurors with an internal locus of control may be more likely to hold defendants personally responsible for charges brought against them than individuals with an external locus of control. A number of studies investigated this possibility, and the findings of those studies present a somewhat mixed and complicated picture.

For example, Sosis (1974) found that individuals classified as *internals* (using Rotter's Internal–External Locus of Control Scale) recommended more severe punishment for a defendant in a drunk driving case than did *externals* or a group of *moderates* whose scores on the scale fell in the middle of the range. In addition, internals viewed the defendant as more responsible for his actions than externals did. However, there was no relationship between locus of control scores and perceptions of guilt. The lack of significant effects on verdict decisions may have been the result of the details of the case being largely prosecution oriented, leading most participants to render a guilty verdict. Hence, the situational factors associated with the case may have overpowered individual differences. Sosis also examined the impact of several demographic factors, including sex, religion, and ethnicity and found that these variables had no effect on participant responses in the case. Thus, in the context of the materials used by Sosis, personality factors were a more useful predictor than demographic characteristics.

Phares and Wilson (1972) also found that individuals classified as internals attributed more responsibility to defendants in automobile accidents than those classified as externals. However, there was a complex interaction between locus of control classification, ambiguity of the defendant's actions (whether or not it was clear the defendant was at fault), and severity of the injuries sustained by the victim. When injuries to the victim were severe and the defendant's actions were ambiguous, internals attributed more responsibility to the defendant than externals. This indicates that the locus of control personality dimension becomes more influential when the situation is more important (i.e., because of injury severity)— that is, jurors are more likely to need additional information because of the situational ambiguity.

However, internals did not respond differently than externals when the defendant was clearly at fault. In addition, when injuries were not severe there was no difference between internals and externals in ambiguous conditions, but internals attributed greater responsibility than externals when the defendant's behavior was not ambiguous. Phares and Wilson (1972) attributed the lack of locus of control effects in the less-severe, ambiguous conditions to participants' unwillingness to attribute much responsibility under these circumstances.

Kauffman and Ryckman (1979) also reported a complex picture for locus of control effects. They found that mock jurors classified as internals found a defendant who committed a severe crime more criminally responsible than those classified as externals when the defendant was attitudinally similar to them. However, externals attributed greater responsibility to a defendant who was dissimilar to them when a severe crime was committed. There was no simple main effect of locus of control found in their study. Not surprising, not all empirical investigations found the internal–external locus of control distinction a useful predictor of juror decisions (Osborne, Rappaport, & Meyer, 1986). For example, Lussier, Perlman, and Breen (1977) found that recommendations for punishment of drug offenders were not predicted by locus of control.

Although the studies discussed in this section present somewhat conflicting findings, perhaps the most important implication is that the relationship between locus of control and juror behavior is not straightforward and may be heavily dependent on specific case factors. For example, type of case (criminal vs. civil) may be important. For the most part, locus of control studies have focused on criminal defendants in cases in which responsibility attributions are made by considering only the defendant's actions. However, during a civil trial, when a victim's contribution is often considered by jurors, it is possible that individuals high in locus of control could attribute greater responsibility to a victim and be more lenient to a defendant. In addition, it should be noted that studies on conformity show internals are more resistant to conformity pressures than externals. As a result, the locus of control personality dimension may be related to the dynamics of deliberations and may indirectly be of some use to attorneys (Osborne et al., 1986).

Just World Beliefs

Just world beliefs (Lerner, 1980; Montada & Lerner, 1998) refers to the attitude that people get what they deserve in life. This concept is based on principles of equity. Individuals who believe in a just world tend to believe that good things will happen to good people and bad things will happen to bad individuals (or that if something bad happens to someone, he or she probably did something that instigated it). For example, if a person who believes in a just world hears a report on the news about a carjacking, although he may feel some sympathy for the victim, he or she may also believe that the victim did something that encouraged the crime to occur (e.g., the victim should not have put expensive rims on his or her car, driven his or her car through a bad part of town at night, or should have been more cautious and alert when stopped in traffic).

Believing in a just world is not a rare phenomenon. A survey conducted in England found that 33% of respondents agreed that women who were victims of rape are usually responsible for the attack (Wagstaff, 1982). By making such attributions, perceivers can believe that if they alter their behavior they can avoid succumbing to the same fate. As a result, just world beliefs create a buffer against the anxiety related to perceptions that the world is a random place where negative events can befall us or our loved ones at any time, or that actions in the world are outside of our control.

Belief in a just world is typically measured using a self-report scale (see Furnham, 1998, for an extensive review of belief in just world measures). For example, the frequently used Rubin and Peplau's (1975) Just World Scale requires respondents to indicate their level of agreement with items that reflect a just world (e.g., "By and large people deserve what they get") and items that reflect a random world where outcomes are not predictable (e.g., "Careful drivers are just as likely to get hurt in traffic accidents as careless ones"). Using this measure, belief in a just world has been shown to correlate with a wide variety of factors, including locus of control beliefs, authoritarianism, religiousness, admiration of political leaders, and negative perceptions of underprivileged classes (Furnham, 1998).

From a legal perspective, one might expect individuals who believe in a just world to be more punitive toward lawbreakers, because such individuals may be motivated to facilitate a negative outcome toward defendants who are charged with reprehensible behaviors. Some research has supported this possibility. For example, in homicide cases both mock jurors and real jurors classified as high in just world beliefs had less favorable impressions of a defendant and recommended more severe sentences than individuals who scored low on a just world belief measure (Gerbasi & Zuckerman, 1975, as cited in Gerbasi, Zuckerman, & Reis, 1977; Rubin & Peplau, 1975). It is interesting to note that Moran and Comfort (1982) found that gender was a moderator of the effects of just world beliefs. There was a stronger relationship between just world beliefs and guilty verdicts for women serving as mock jurors than for men, with women's just world belief scores predicting about 6% of verdict variance. Unfortunately, the authors offer no explanation for this difference.

Although the research mentioned above indicates that belief in a just world is associated with greater punitive reactions to offenders, it is important to remember that just world beliefs allow for protection against anxiety of negative outcomes by holding victims responsible for their misfortune. As a result, although just world-oriented jurors may have a desire to punish a defendant for his or her wrongdoing, jurors may also consider the actions of the victim to see if the victim deserved his or her fate. This assessment of victim behavior or characteristics could lead jurors to show greater leniency to defendants if jurors feel the victim did something that contributed to the harmful act. For example, the tendency to hold victims responsible may be highly relevant in sexual assault cases. Janoff-Bullman, Timko, and Carli (1985) reported that observers described a woman who acted in a friendly manner toward a man as behaving appropriately. However, when another group of observers was told that the woman had been raped by the man, she was judged to have had acted inappropriately, thus instigating the rape, even though her behaviors were identical to those observed by the first group.

Several other researchers examined the effects of belief in a just world in rape cases. For example, Zuckerman and Gerbasi (1973, as cited in Gerbasi et al., 1977) found that individuals who scored high on just world belief measures held a rape victim more responsible for the attack than did those with low scores. In addition, more respectable victims were held less responsible than individuals of questionable moral character (but see Jones & Aronson, 1973). Montada (1998) reported that scores on a General Belief in Just World Scale were correlated with a Blaming the Victim for Self-Infliction Scale that measures tendencies to blame rape victims, excuse the perpetrators, and minimize the impact of the rape experience on the victim. Visher (1987) found that a tendency to blame victims was significantly negatively correlated with verdict preferences; that is, greater victim blame was associated with fewer convictions. However, Visher found that blaming the victim attitudes did not independently affect verdict decisions when other relevant factors had been taken into account; these factors included jurors' attitudes toward crime and beliefs in a need for more severe sentences and tougher laws.

Several other interesting effects regarding just world beliefs have been found in legally oriented studies. Moran and Comfort (1982) reported a relationship between just world beliefs and verdict flexibility in women. That is, women who scored high on a just world belief scale were less likely to change their verdict after engaging in deliberations than individuals who were not inclined to endorse just world beliefs. In addition, just world scores are correlated with confidence in the court system; those who believe the world is a just place where people get what they deserve express more confidence in the courts (Hans & Lofquist, 1994).

Much of the application of the belief in a just world to legal decision making has involved criminal cases. However, just world cognitions appear to extend to civil trials as well. The relationship between belief in a just world and civil litigation is inherently complex (Bonazzoli, 1998), particularly in trials in which jurors may consider the contributory negligence of a plaintiff, because jurors are instructed to consider assigning blame to both defendant and plaintiff. Although there have not been many studies that have examined this relationship, Hans and Lofquist (1994) reported that individuals who believe in a just world are not supportive of tort reform. Related civil decision making research has shown that positive attitudes toward tort reform are associated with lower damage awards (Goodman et al.,

1990; Moran et al., 1994). Thus, it appears that jurors who believe in a just world may be inclined to award greater damage awards.

As was the case with the other personality and attitudinal measures discussed in this chapter, the relationship between belief in a just world and juror behavior is a complex one. The findings have been mixed, relatively weak, and highly dependent on other case relevant factors, such as victim characteristics. One reason for the obfuscated findings may be that the factors mentioned thus far represent broad personality characteristics and attitudes that are applicable to a wide variety of social behavior or legal cases. Attempting to predict behavior in a specific type of case using broad concepts such as authoritarianism, locus of control, and belief in a just world may be impossible. Instead, successful prediction may require more precise instruments. As a result, recent research on the influence of personality and attitudes on juror decision making has focused on specific characteristics, which we discuss in the rest of this section.

Attitudes Toward Tort Reform and Legal Claims

The measurement of attitudes toward tort reform and legal claims illustrates recent attempts to identify more specific legally oriented attitudes that may be predictive of behavior. For example, concerns about frivolous litigation have led states to explore and implement tort reform measures. As tort reform is designed to reduce frivolous litigation, individuals who believe frivolous litigation is a problem and are concerned about exorbitant damages may have negative attitudes toward plaintiffs and a general inclination toward defendants in civil trials.

Several research studies have supported the hypothesized relationship between tort reform support and civil trial damage awards (Goodman et al., 1990; Moran et al., 1994, Study 4). For example, Goodman et al. found that although demographic variables were not predictive of the magnitude of damage awards, specific attitudes about tort reform were. Individuals who felt that a litigation crisis existed were more likely to award lower damages.[2]

Similar results have been obtained using the Litigation Crisis Attitudes Scale (LCAS) developed by Hans and Lofquist (1992, 1994). The LCAS is a seven-item scale that measures attitudes toward excessive litigation (e.g., "there are too many frivolous lawsuits today") and criticism of civil juries

---

[2]However, as the attitudinal measures were administered after participants rendered damages, it is possible that their damage decisions influenced their attitudinal responses.
In a similar study, Diamond et al. (1998) found that jurors who held favorable attitudes toward plaintiffs in general—were inclined to think it is legitimate to sue and thought it was difficult to win a lawsuit—were more likely to find a defendant liable in a product liability case. Diamond et al. also found that mock jurors who held favorable attitudes toward business on items measuring overall attitude toward business, the extent to which regulation and lawsuits interfere with business, and the need for regulation to ensure public safety were less likely to find the defendant liable. A composite model accounting for nine related attitudinal characteristics accounted for 11.5% of liability verdict variance, which was twice the amount of variance accounted for by demographic characteristics.

(e.g., "the money awards that juries are awarding in civil cases are too large"). The LCAS was administered to jurors who had served on civil cases and LCAS responses were related to verdict awards: the greater the jurors' collective belief that a litigation explosion existed, the lower the jury's award (Hans & Lofquist, 1992).

Hans and Lofquist (1994) also found that LCAS scores were positively correlated with a seven-item measure of claims consciousness that assessed respondents' inclination to contemplate and pursue legal claims, indicating that individuals who support tort reform are also most likely to pursue litigation themselves (see also Vidmar & Schuller, 1987). That is, those who are inclined to pursue their own claims tend to view others as having "illegitimate claims" (Hans & Lofquist, 1994, p. 189) and those who are unlikely to claim for themselves are more inclined to view others as having "legitimate claims." This finding is counterintuitive and is indicative of the need to pursue extensive voir dire questioning. If a juror simply says he or she has pursued litigation in the past, the individual may be viewed as a good plaintiff's juror; however, this conclusion may be premature.

Attitudes toward tort reform have been shown to relate to a number of other individual difference measures. For example, beliefs regarding political efficacy were negatively correlated with LCAS scores, in that people who favor tort reform tend to feel less confident about the political system and their own political clout. Although Hans and Lofquist (1994) did not find a relationship between LCAS and measures of authoritarianism or locus of control, they did find a negative correlation between LCAS and Belief in Just World Scale responses. This relationship indicates that jurors who believe people get what they deserve in life are less likely to believe a litigation crisis exists.

Although one would expect attitudes toward tort reform to be relevant to civil trial decision making, there is evidence that this attitudinal dimension also has some predictive ability in criminal trials. Moran et al. (1994) examined the relationship between attitudes toward tort reform and verdict inclinations in several studies, using a representative sample of jurors contacted. Respondents' attitudes toward tort reform were associated with greater perceptions of defendant culpability in three cases: a controlled substance conspiracy case (Study 1), a criminal RICO case (Study 2), and a medical insurance fraud case (Study 3).

One limitation of Moran et al.'s (1994) research is that survey participants were presented with a brief overview of the key evidence of the case, rather than with more extensive trial materials (including a substantial cross-examination). As a result, although it is clear that biased participants can be identified and that case relevant attitudes can be useful predictors, it is not entirely apparent that such factors can predict a jury's final verdict. However, although a brief case summary was used, research has shown that the format of presenting stimulus materials to participants has a minimal influence on their final verdict (Bornstein, 1999).

In conclusion, the studies regarding attitudes toward legal claims and tort reform present far more consistent findings than those of the more global personality and attitudinal measures discussed previously in this chapter. This may be the result of an increased level of specificity regarding the attitudes that are measured and the type of trial they are applied to (although there also is evidence of predictive ability in less relevant criminal trials).

Attitudes Toward the Death Penalty

The landmark U.S. Supreme Court decision in *Witherspoon v. Illinois* (1968) established a standard for excusing individuals from the penalty phase of a trial in a capital case. According to the Court in *Witherspoon*, a juror can be constitutionally excused when he or she would never vote for the death penalty or when his or her opposition to the death penalty prevents him or her from being impartial in the penalty phase. These individuals were labeled *Witherspoon-excludables* and the resulting jury was labeled *death-qualified*. The U.S. Supreme Court in *Wainwright v. Witt* (1985) clarified the death qualification standard by stating that jurors can be constitutionally excused if their opposition to the death penalty would prevent or substantially impair the performance of their duties during the sentencing phase of the trial.

In 1986, the U.S. Supreme Court in *Lockhart v. McCree* (1986) addressed the question of whether the death qualification process would affect jurors during the guilt phase (as opposed to the penalty phase) of the trial. The Court held that death qualification did not violate a defendant's constitutional right (under the Sixth and Fourteenth Amendments) to have his or her guilt or innocence determined by an impartial jury selected from a representative cross section of the community. McCree argued that the death qualification process resulted in a jury comprised of persons who were proconviction because prospective jurors who were against the death penalty were excluded. A considerable number of jurors end up being excused under these standards, with estimates ranging from about 9% under *Witherspoon* and up to 29% to 40% under *Witt* (Fitzgerald & Ellsworth, 1984; Neises & Dillehay, 1987; Thompson, 1989).

The critical issue that emerges is whether juror attitudes toward the death penalty are related to juror behavior. In general, research has shown that death penalty attitudes are related to verdict decisions, leading death-qualified juries to be more conviction prone. For example, using a mock trial design, Cowan et al. (1984) demonstrated that juries made up of individuals qualified to serve using the *Witherspoon* standard were more likely to convict a defendant. Seventy-eight percent of death-qualified jurors were inclined to convict the defendant, whereas only 53% of excludable jurors were conviction prone. Thus, Thompson, Cowan, Ellsworth, and Harrington (1984) speculated that death-qualified jurors may have a lower conviction threshold.

These findings replicated earlier research on death penalty qualification and attitudes (e.g., Jurow, 1971; Zeisel, 1968, who conducted a survey with jurors and measured actual juror verdicts). In a similar study, Ellsworth, Bukaty, Cowan, and Thompson (1984) found that attitudes toward the death penalty were correlated with the insanity defense. Those who supported capital punishment were more likely to convict in insanity cases.

It appears that attitudes toward the death penalty also influence how trial evidence is interpreted. Thompson et al. (1984) found that more than one third of the variance in jurors' evaluation of witness testimony in a death penalty case was accounted for by attitudes toward the death penalty. Similarly, positive attitudes toward the use of the death penalty have been shown to be associated with positive attitudes toward police and prosecutors and less favorable attitudes toward defense attorneys and due process factors in death penalty cases (Bronson, 1970; Fitzgerald & Ellsworth, 1984; Thompson et al., 1984; Vidmar & Ellsworth, 1974).

Evidentiary factors, however, may overpower juror attitudes toward the death penalty. Moran and Comfort (1986) examined the relationship between attitudes toward capital punishment and verdicts, as well as a variety of other demographic and personality differences, in two studies involving impaneled jurors. In the first study, jurors in favor of capital punishment were only marginally more likely to favor conviction, and the effect was primarily driven by the behavior of female participants. This gender effect was not replicated in the second study. However, jurors in the second study who strongly favored capital punishment were more likely to favor convicting defendants in capital cases, with the correlation between death penalty attitudes and convictions being stronger with weak evidence ($r = .44$, $p < .01$) than with strong evidence ($r = .02$, ns). This issue is discussed to a greater extent in chapter 8.

From a jury selection standpoint, perhaps the most important results of the studies were the data showing a relationship between death penalty attitudes and demographic and personality factors. Moran and Comfort (1986) found that individuals who were White, male, married, of upper income levels, and with authoritarian and conservative personalities were most likely to favor the death penalty (see also Fitzgerald & Ellsworth, 1984; Haney, Hurtado, & Vega, 1994). Other studies have also shown that positive death penalty attitudes are related to antilibertarian attitudes (Bronson, 1970; Buckhout, Baker, Perlman, & Spiegel, 1977). This relationship between death penalty attitudes and other juror characteristics is important because jurors may not be honest during voir dire. For example, if an attorney did not observe consistency between juror responses to death penalty related questions and the demographic and personality factors mentioned above, he or she might consider questioning the juror more extensively and possibly using a peremptory challenge to exclude the juror.

Although the studies reviewed in this section generally indicate a relationship between death penalty attitudes and verdicts and this finding has been observed in a multitude of studies conducted by independent researchers, the relationship is best characterized as weak or moderate. Thus, although excluding jurors using the *Witherspoon–Witt* standard is likely to produce a jury that is more homogeneous and conviction prone, substantial variability still exists in juror decisions. As a result, something other than individual differences appears to be driving verdict decisions. Indeed, the lack of strong predictive power for an attitudinal measure has been a consistent theme throughout this chapter. Before addressing this issue we discuss a number of additional personality and attitudinal factors that have produced similar results.

Attitudes Toward Psychiatrists

Moran et al. (1994) found that the verdict inclinations of community members in an insanity case were predicted in part by attitudes toward psychiatrists. Unfortunately, respondents in this study were not given the opportunity to render a verdict following the presentation of trial evidence, so it is difficult to know if these attitudes can account for verdict variance. However, the findings of this study are strengthened by consistency of the results with previous research (Cutler et al., 1992).

Cutler et al. (1992) conducted a series of studies examining the effects of legal authoritarianism, attitudes toward psychiatrists, and attitudes toward the insanity defense on verdict decisions in insanity defense cases. They initially noted that jurors tend to hold negative attitudes toward the insanity defense, driven in part by high profile "not guilty by reason of insanity" verdicts, such as the infamous acquittal of John Hinckley for his attempted assassination of President Ronald Reagan. Such negative attitudes may influence verdict decisions. To investigate this issue, Cutler et al. conducted a telephone survey of community residents in which respondents were given a case scenario describing an insanity trial. Respondents were asked to provide a verdict and to answer a series of questions regarding their attitudes and demographic characteristics. Among the questions were Kassin and Wrightsman's (1983) Juror Bias Scale (described earlier), as well as a question regarding attitudes toward insanity as a defense ("Every sane individual is responsible for his every action," Cutler et al., 1992, p. 169) and an item regarding attitudes toward psychiatrists as expert witnesses ("I don't put much faith in the testimony of psychiatrists," Cutler et al., 1992, p. 169). The results indicated that females, Hispanics, legal authoritarians (individuals scoring high on the Reasonable Doubt subscale of the Juror Bias Scale), politically conservative individuals, and those who had negative attitudes toward psychiatrists were more likely to convict. Combined, these variables accounted for 22% of verdict variance. Further, several variables predicted possessing negative attitudes toward psychiatrists; these variables included being older, less educated, employed full time, and non-Hispanic status. Politically conservative individuals and non-Blacks were more likely to endorse legal authoritarian attitudes. Thus, a number of demographic variables predicted legal authoritarianism and attitudes toward psychiatrists, attitudes that were in turn predictive of verdict decisions.

In two additional studies Cutler et al. (1992) expanded the number of questions assessing attitudes toward psychiatrists, the insanity defense, and legal authoritarianism. The results indicated that all three factors produce significant and moderately strong correlations with verdict. For example, attitude toward psychiatrists and verdict correlated at $r = .28$, and the correlation between attitude toward the insanity defense and verdict was $r = .33$. Further, Cutler et al. found that an alternative measure of legal authoritarianism (Boehm's [1968] Legal Authoritarianism Scale) predicted reactions to psychiatrists and the insanity defense, as well as reactions to aspects of the case (e.g., "Did the defendant appreciate the nature and quality or wrongfulness of his act?") somewhat better than the Juror Bias Scale. Thus, when case specific attitudes, such as with the insanity defense, are assessed, and demographic factors are examined in the context of those case-specific factors, attitudes appear to be more relevant to verdicts.

Additional Attitudinal Factors

Several other studies drew similar conclusions about the predictive value of case-relevant attitudes. For example, Schuller (as cited in Vidmar & Schuller, 1989) assessed agreement with myths about battered women (e.g., battered women can always leave home) and found that participants who endorsed more myths about battered women were more likely to convict when exposed to a mock trial in which a battered woman was accused of killing her husband.

Field (1978a) examined the relationship between attitudes toward rape and judgments in rape cases (see also Penrod, 1979, as cited in Fulero & Penrod, 1990). In Field's study, 896 participants made verdict and sentencing decisions in response to a trial summary of a rape case. Demographic characteristics of age, education, sex, marital status, occupational prestige, previous jury service experience, and personal experience with a rape victim were obtained from participants. In addition, participants completed an eight-factor Attitudes Toward Rape Questionnaire (Field, 1978b). In general, attitudes about rape were better predictors of sentencing decisions than were demographic characteristics (which were weak predictors). Unfortunately, Field measured the effect of background and attitudinal factors on sentencing rather than on verdict decisions, so it is unclear what juror behaviors would be when making the actual judgments required of them in the courtroom. However, other studies have also shown that attitudes regarding empathy toward rape victims predicted verdicts in simulated rape trials, with mock jurors who reported greater empathy more likely to believe the victim and hold the defendant responsible (Deitz, Blackwell, Daley, & Bentley, 1982; Deitz, Littman, & Bentley, 1984; Weir & Wrightsman, 1990).

Moran et al. (1990) found that the best predictors of verdicts in a case where a lawyer was accused of a number of drug crimes were attitudes toward lawyers and drugs. In addition, attitudes toward drugs predicted verdicts in a major drug trafficking case. It is unfortunate that in this study respondents did not render verdicts after exposure to trial evidence, so it is difficult to assess how powerful this effect is.

LIMITATIONS OF USING PERSONALITY AND ATTITUDINAL CHARACTERISTICS AS PREDICTORS

In this chapter, we have seen that attitudinal and personality factors tend to be more powerful predictors of verdicts than demographic characteristics, and this has been found in both civil and criminal cases (Goodman et al., 1990; Moran et al., 1990; Narby et al., 1993; Wiener & Stolle, 1997). However, the total amount of verdict variance accounted for by personality and attitudinal characteristics still tends to be low and is affected by a number of factors, including case type and evidence strength.

Case Type

The predictive power of attitudinal measures varies greatly from case to case (Penrod, 1990; Wiener & Stolle, 1997). For example, Penrod (1990) examined the verdict preferences of 367 participants who were in the process of serving jury duty in a Massachusetts Superior Court. Participants were exposed to evidence in three criminal (murder, rape, and robbery) cases and one civil case. Penrod obtained information regarding 12 attitudinal and 15 demographic factors. The predictive ability of the variables was relatively case specific, and none of the variables emerged as useful predictors in more than two of the four cases. Further, the variables had little predictive ability when examined independently (accounting for less than 2% of verdict variance in most cases). The average variance explained by the combination of variables was 11% across the four cases examined.

Thus, variables that predict verdicts in one case may not predict verdicts in other cases. Individual characteristics tend to interact with situational factors about the trial in complex ways, making basic generalizations highly unreliable (Hans & Vidmar, 1982). It is probably unrealistic to expect "that the age of a juror will relate to the verdict in the same way in a drug trial involving a youthful defendant and in a trial involving a corporate executive accused of price fixing" (Hans & Vidmar, 1982, p. 57). In addition, gender of a juror may be far more relevant in a rape case than in a murder case. Penrod and Cutler (1987) argued that the influence of attitudinal factors may even vary from locality to locality.

Although it may be impossible to draw generalizations about personality factors that allow one to predict verdicts in all cases, it may be possible to predict verdicts in specific cases. As a result, it is critical to identify the effects of case specific attitudes on specific case factors in the particular jurisdiction where a trial will be held, to maximize predictive ability. It is impossible to achieve such specificity from general principles contained in trial tactics manuals or other jury selection texts written by "jury experts." As a result, Vidmar (1999) argued the need to "[a]pply logic and common sense when a jury consultant proposes simplistic theories of personality to predict a jurors' [sic] behavior: e.g., handwriting analysis; the colors of clothes the juror wears predict personality traits and ultimately behavior" (p. 274).

It is fortunate that a high level of specificity regarding attitudes, case factors, and geographic locality can be achieved by consultants who use standard scientific jury selection techniques. However, it is important to remember that although increased specificity may increase predictive ability somewhat, it will not provide a magic formula through which the behavior of all jurors can almost certainly be predicted. In certain cases (e.g., child molestation), for example, personal beliefs may have a stronger effect than in more mundane trials (e.g., robbery). In ambiguous trials with less powerful evidence, "juror attitudes are likely to have a greater impact on verdict than in cases in which the evidence points definitively in one direction or another" (Narby et al., 1993, p. 40). Thus, a huge amount of verdict variance is likely to be left unaccounted for by personality and attitudinal factors, with the result that there is no guarantee that it will be possible to correctly predict the ultimate behavior of jurors (Kovera, Dickinson, & Cutler, 2003). For example, Narby and Cutler (1994) found that attitudes toward eyewitnesses did not predict verdicts in cases in which eyewitness testimony was present. Even when demographic and attitudinal variables are combined, predictive power is still low, ranging from about 5% to 14% (e.g., 8%, Hepburn, 1980; 13%, Saks, 1976; 4.9% to 14.1%, Penrod, 1990).

Evidence Strength and Presentation

Perhaps not surprising, a general conclusion in the literature is that strong evidence may overpower individual differences (e.g., Hepburn, 1980; Narby et al., 1993; Saks, 1976; Visher, 1987). For example, Saks (1976) reported the results of mock jury research indicating the "amount of evidence was more than three times as powerful" as juror attitudes, and that "strength of evidence was more than seven times as powerful" (p. 18; this important finding is discussed in greater detail in chap. 8, this volume). In addition, it is also likely that attorney litigation tactics and strategy may also explain a significant portion of the verdict variance. However, the importance of strength of evidence or attorney advocacy does not mean that using personality characteristics to predict verdict decisions is a fruitless venture.

Can Minimal Information Still Be Useful?

Penrod and Cutler (1987) argued that even if minimal verdict variance can be accounted for by background or personality factors, such information may give attorneys an important advantage.

> If half the [jury] pool [members] were favorable and half unfavorable, the attorney's guesswork would correctly classify half the jurors [at] chance level of performance. However, if we consider a situation in which a jury survey detected a reliable relationship in which 5 percent of the variance in verdict preferences was accounted for by attitudinal and personality measures, successful use of that information would increase the attorney's performance significantly [and] 61 percent of jurors could be correctly classified. With 15 percent of the variance accounted for, 69 percent of the jurors could be correctly classified. Thus weak relationships can produce dramatic changes in jury selection performance. (p. 302)

Further, even though demographic and attitudinal variables may have a minimal amount of influence on verdict decisions, Hepburn (1980) found that such factors may have an important indirect effect on verdict by serving to influence perceptions of the strength of the prosecution's and defense's evidence. In turn, strength of evidence variables were shown to be important mediating variables that directly linked to verdict decisions.

Thus, it may be premature to dismiss juror characteristics as unimportant factors in verdict decision making. Rather, it may be more useful to explore the subtle ways background characteristics influence verdict decisions, particularly on a case-by-case basis. Ideally, case-specific evidentiary factors should be included in both a pretrial survey and in a mock jury group research. Evidence can then be treated as an intervening variable, allowing for clearer relationships between background factors and verdicts to be identified. After pretrial community surveys have revealed which evidentiary factors appear to be critically important, consultants can use mock juries to refine the presentation of key factors and arguments (we discuss the mock jury technique in chap. 9).

CONCLUSION

In this chapter, we discuss the major personality factors that have been empirically examined over the years. To be sure, this list is not exhaustive, as many other personality factors have also been examined. For example, socialization, autonomy, and empathy (Mills & Bohannon, 1980b), social desirability (Moran & Comfort, 1982), cognitive complexity (Graziano et al., 1990), and even newspaper preference (Hastie et al., 1983) have been empirically investigated. Extensively covering every personality and attitudinal factor that has ever been included in jury decision-making studies would go beyond the scope of this chapter, and would probably be a book in itself. Yet, as the main factors have been addressed in this chapter, a number of conclusions can be fairly drawn. Most notable, it is possible to identify a variety of personality and attitudinal characteristics that have some relationships to juror verdict inclinations, and these characteristics tend to be more powerful predictors than demographic characteristics (e.g., Moran et al., 1994). However, personality and attitudinal factors still tend to be weak predictors overall and predict minimal amounts of verdict variance (Saks, 1976). Whether the weak effects obtained for the factors discussed in this chapter can meaningfully influence a trial outcome is more extensively discussed in chapter 8.

However, we first need to address several other aspects of the scientific jury selection process: in-court questioning of prospective jurors (chap. 6), and in-court observation of nonverbal behaviors of prospective jurors during questioning (chap. 7). Both topics are relevant to determining if prospective jurors are attempting to be deceptive or are withholding information when answering judges' or attorneys' questions during voir dire.

6

IN-COURT QUESTIONING
OF PROSPECTIVE JURORS

After the community survey results are analyzed and predictors of juror behavior are known, the scientific jury consultant can make recommendations to an attorney about the types of jurors that are likely to be most favorable or antagonistic to their side. Effectively applying these recommendations requires that the attorney gather detailed information from the prospective jurors. Prospective jurors are usually first questioned about basic demographic information, including name, residence, marital status, education level, age, and occupation. In addition, prospective jurors are questioned about whether they previously served on a jury; the type of case and the verdict in that case; their experiences relevant to the case under consideration (e.g., in a criminal case, whether they were ever arrested for a crime or were the victim of a crime); and whether they personally know any of the parties involved in the present case (e.g., attorneys, defendant, or witnesses). These types of general questions are typically asked, regardless of whether the judge or attorneys do the questioning. Although these questions may produce somewhat informative responses, they may not be able to detect hidden biases on the part of many jurors. As a consequence, there is a need to gather more in-depth information.

Unfortunately, there are a number of procedural and situational constraints on voir dire that may restrict the amount of useful information gathered during this process. First, in federal courts and numerous state courts the trial judge, rather than the attorneys, questions prospective jurors, and the judge may be unwilling to ask specific questions of interest to an attorney. In addition, juror candor may be affected by the status of the individual asking questions. Second, even if attorneys are allowed to question prospective jurors, the trial judge may place restrictions on the questioning process, such as on the scope of allowable questioning, because the trial judge feels certain issues are legally irrelevant. The judge may also limit the time attorneys can spend questioning jurors. In a similar way, an attorney may be reluctant to inconvenience jurors by conducting lengthy voir dire questioning, particularly after the judge has spent considerable time doing so. As a result, an attorney may not ask questions about issues that might illuminate the juror's attitudinal dispositions. Third, the attorney may ask questions in a manner that encourages responses that are devoid of sufficient detail to identify relevant biases. As a result, the attorney may not be able to make a persuasive argument for a causal challenge or exercise an intelligent peremptory challenge. Fourth, prospective jurors are often questioned in front of a group of other jurors. The social demands of this setting may lead jurors to give socially desirable responses. In addition, the authoritarian setting of the courtroom may increase conformity pressure on jurors (Hafemeister, Sales, & Suggs, 1984). This chapter focuses on these issues and discusses how jury selection consultants and existing social science research findings can improve the process of questioning jurors.

WHO SHOULD DO THE QUESTIONING?

In federal courts, the judge usually conducts voir dire (although federal judges have the discretion to allow lawyers to conduct voir dire). Approximately 75% of federal district judges conduct voir dire examinations themselves and do not permit the attorneys to ask questions directly; however, most allow attorneys to provide questions that the judge then asks (Bermant, 1977, 1985). The process in state courts varies from jurisdiction to jurisdiction, with some states' systems following the procedures of federal courts by restricting questions to the judge's interrogatories, whereas other states allow attorneys to question jurors as well. Only seven states restrict voir dire to questioning conducted exclusively by judges. In four states, only attorneys conduct questioning. In the remaining 39 states, the District of Columbia, and Puerto Rico, both attorneys and judges are permitted to question jurors (Bureau of Justice Statistics, 1998). However, in jurisdictions in which both attorneys and judges are permitted to ask voir dire questions, judicial discretion may limit how often attorneys actually question prospective jurors directly. In determining whether it is better to have the attorneys or judge do the questioning, it is important to consider which approach will produce the most informative responses from jurors, which will be most efficient, and how each approach will affect perceptions of fairness in the process.

Informativeness of Juror Responses

Suggs and Sales (1981) noted that "voir dire may be ideally characterized as a self-disclosure interview because it purports to obtain background and attitudinal information which might affect a juror's decision in a case" (p. 247). As a result, it is important to take steps that facilitate self-disclosure. Jurors may be more likely to substitute honest and candid answers with socially desirable responses when questioned by the judge, because the judge is perceived as an authority figure. Jurors are usually more concerned with pleasing the judge than with pleasing an attorney, who is closer to the jurors in terms of status level (Jones, 1987; Mogill & Nixon, 1986; Padawer-Singer, Singer, & Singer, 1974). Opponents of attorney-conducted voir dire, however, maintain that jurors may be more honest when questioned by the judge because of the degree of respect they have for the judge (Jones, 1987).

The judge certainly has the highest status of any person in the courtroom. Physically, the judge is separated from the other trial participants, put on a raised platform above all others, and is the central figure in the courtroom. In addition, attorneys speak to the judge respectfully, addressing him or her as "your honor." In general, research indicates that individuals should be more willing to disclose information to those who are more similar to them (Suggs & Sales, 1981). As a result, the high status of the judge is likely to increase the perceived social distance between jurors and the judge, and this increased social distance should reduce self-disclosure. It would appear, therefore, that attorneys would be more effective at extracting useful information from prospective jurors.

This proposition is supported by direct empirical research. Jones (1987) compared the effects of judge- versus lawyer-conducted voir dire in a fairly realistic mock jury study using jury-eligible participants and trained actors with legal backgrounds (e.g., a law professor at a major southern university) playing the roles of judge and attorney. Jones found that participants were more consistent in their attitude reports when attorneys conducted voir dire. In fact, participants changed their answers (between initial private disclosure on a questionnaire and public disclosure in the courtroom) almost twice as often when questioned by a judge. Further, Jones found that participants were more consistent in their self-reported attitudes when attorneys used a more relaxed and personable demeanor, as opposed to behaving in a more formal manner. It is interesting to note that judicial demeanor (personal vs. formal) did not affect participant responses, and in both cases participants were less consistent under judicial questioning than when attorneys questioned them. Thus, attorneys may be better than judges at extracting honest responses from jurors, particularly if they interact with jurors in a personable manner.

Finally, proponents of attorney-conducted voir dire have argued that it is essential that the person who questions prospective jurors have an extensive knowledge of the case (Mogill & Nixon, 1986). Before evidence has been presented in court, the attorneys' awareness of the legal issues relevant to the case and of the parties participating in the case will be far greater than the judge's knowledge.

Time Constraints

Empirical evidence (described in chap. 2) suggests that attorneys are typically not much better than chance at selecting favorable jurors. Thus, time (and expenses) could be saved if attorneys are prevented from asking questions that have minimal predictive value (Hastie, 1991, p. 726). Opponents have noted that voir dire takes longer when attorneys conduct it, with estimates ranging from 10% longer to as much as one third the total trial time ("Judge Conducted Voir Dire," 1970; Levit, Nelson, Ball, & Chernick, 1971). The reasoning here is that judges may be less likely to ask extensive and probing questions of jurors, either because of demands to move the trial along as quickly as possible or because of partiality to one of the sides (Van Dyke, 1976). Although it is important that trials are conducted in a speedy manner, speed should not come at the expense of failure to exclude prospective jurors who hold strong pretrial biases that could have been identified through more thorough questioning.

Other scholars, however, have found that attorney-conducted voir dire does not take substantially longer than judge-conducted voir dire (Corboy, 1980; Mogill & Nixon, 1986). In support of this latter position, a study of felony voir dire by Johnson and Haney (1994) indicated that even when attorneys are allowed to question jurors during voir dire, it is court personnel who do most of the talking, with judges accounting for 24% of verbal interactions during voir dire, and defense attorneys and prosecutors accounting for 21% and 16% of the statements, respectively. Jurors accounted for 39% of voir dire statements. It appears that although judge-conducted voir dire may save a small amount of time, the total time saved over the course of a trial may be negligible.

Perceptions of Fairness

Opponents of attorney-conducted voir dire have argued that public perceptions of the justice system may be lowered when attorneys conduct voir dire, because of attorneys' ability to identify and eliminate potential jurors who are partial to one of the parties in a case, thus creating a stacked jury (Hastie, 1991). However, it is the duty of attorneys to use their skills to eliminate jurors biased against their client.

Further, proponents of attorney-conducted voir dire have argued that the practice of preventing attorneys from asking questions may produce a perception on the part of a convicted defendant that the trial was not fair because of a perception that judicially directed voir dire will produce more juries with a proprosecution bias. Having a judge conduct voir dire removes an element of the fundamentally adversarial process of the trial and brings elements of an inquisitional system of justice into U.S. courtrooms. If voir dire is looked at through the procedural justice lens (Lind & Tyler, 1988; Thibault & Walker, 1975), there may be some merit to the argument that judicially conducted voir dire will lead to lower trial satisfaction on the part of defendants. In a series of studies, Thibault and Walker compared the outcomes of adversarial and inquisitional justice procedures and found that both in the United States and cross-culturally, participants prefer adversarial procedures. They also found that the adversarial system leads to greater effort on the part of attorneys, a reduction in the impact of preexisting biases in jurors, a more balanced presentation of facts, and greater satisfaction on the part of defendants when the final verdict was unfavorable to their side.

Attorneys' behaviors during voir dire may also lead to changes in perceptions of fairness if attorneys try to take advantage of the voir dire process by ingratiating themselves with jurors (Hastie, 1991; Johnson & Haney, 1994). In addition, as attorneys try to present some of the issues in their case during voir dire, they may attempt to get pretrial verdict commitments of jurors. In a study of four felony voir dire cases, Johnson and Haney found that prosecutors, defense attorneys, and judges frequently attempted to get public commitments of one form or another from jurors. Over the four trials, 236 attempts were made to elicit public commitments. Prosecutors made almost half of these attempts (46%), whereas defense attorneys accounted for about one third (34%), and judges, 20%. Although judges have the power to curtail attorney abuse of voir dire, there is no research to suggest that they exercise their powers in this way. In addition, there is no research assessing how variations in attorney voir dire strategies affect perceptions of justice.

Conclusions Regarding Judge- Versus Attorney-Conducted Voir Dire

Opponents of attorney-conducted voir dire (e.g., Bermant, 1985; Hastie, 1991) present a variety of reasons for limiting attorney participation in the process of questioning jurors, including saving time, increasing fairness and juror honesty, and preventing perceptions of unfairness during voir dire. However, many of the objections have not been supported by empirical research. The goal of voir dire is to select fair and impartial jurors (*People v. Love*, 1991) and to allow trial counsel to intelligently exercise their peremptory challenges (*Bal Theatre Corporation v. Paramount Film Distributing Corporation*, 1962; Bermant, 1985). As it appears that jurors may be more willing to disclose information to attorneys, we recommend that attorneys be allowed to question jurors whenever possible.

In some cases, pretrial community surveys may indicate strong bias toward parties involved in a trial among the population of the jurisdiction where a trial will be held. If the case is held in a court in which attorneys do not routinely question jurors but judges have the flexibility to allow attorney-conducted voir dire, the presentation of the results of pretrial community surveys may convince the judge to allow attorneys to question prospective jurors. In addition, such information may be useful in making an argument to allow for expanded voir dire questioning.

EXPANDED VOIR DIRE

The scope of voir dire questioning needs to be broad enough to allow attorneys to make intelligent use of the allowed challenges. However, federal courts typically limit questions to demographic factors, including: age, marital status, occupation, spouse's occupation, children's ages and occupations, residence, whether jurors have close personal contacts with individuals who work in the legal system (e.g., police officers or lawyers), membership in social organizations, prior experiences involving the legal system, and any case-related experiences (Moran, Cutler, & Loftus, 1990). Voir dire for civil cases is also conducted on a limited scale in both federal and state courts, with questioning frequently conducted by the court. Civil lawyers often have to base their challenges on limited demographic information (Goodman, Loftus, & Greene, 1990).

An alternative approach to this restricted voir dire is to expand questioning beyond basic demographic characteristics to ascertain information regarding "jurors' personality, attitudes, habits, authoritarian tendencies, case-relevant opinions and experiences, attitudes toward crime, and political views" (Moran et al., 1990, p. 334). As expanded voir dire allows for more information to be gathered, it is likely to be more useful for attorneys in terms of making intelligent challenges and accurate decisions.

Moran et al. (1990) compared the predictive value of restricted and expanded voir dire across two controlled substance trials. The results indicated that expanded voir dire provided information that was able to explain more of the variance in mock juror verdicts. In the first trial, the overall increase in explanatory power rose from explaining 1% of verdict variance in restricted voir dire to 5% in expanded voir dire, which is certainly still low. However, analysis of data in a second trial was far more impressive. In that case, explanatory power rose from 8% (restricted voir dire) to 31% (expanded). Moran et al. speculate that the difference in variance accounted for between these studies may have been due to methodological limitations in the first study. For example, there was minimal variability in verdict decisions in the first study, with 84% of the sample being conviction prone. As a result, there was little variance for predictor variables to account for. Moran et al. claim "the data suggests that extended voir dire may increase accuracy in predicting individual verdicts from 50% [chance level of selecting a favorable or unfavorable juror] to 78%" (p. 331). Although such success may not occur in all cases, it does appear that expanding voir dire provides useful information to guide the intelligent use of challenges. In particular, individual differences may exert a larger influence in cases in which the evidence is equivocal.

In a similar study, Nietzel and Dillehay (1982; see also Nietzel, Dillehay, & Himelein, 1987) examined the effect of different voir dire procedures in actual death penalty trials in Kentucky and compared restricted and expanded voir dire procedures. They report that attorneys were able to exclude more jurors through a challenge for cause when attorneys were allowed to interview prospective jurors in an expanded voir dire format, particularly when jurors were questioned individually rather than en masse (discussed in greater detail in the "Sequestering Jurors During Voir Dire" section later in this chapter). As challenge for cause dismissals result from uncovering juror bias, the implication of these findings is that an extended attorney-conducted voir dire may produce a more impartial jury.

Treger (1992), however, argued that expanded voir dire is a waste of the court's time and resources because even if additional case-relevant attitudinal information is gained, that information does not address how jurors will ultimately interact during deliberations. That is, other factors may affect the dynamics of group interaction during jury deliberation. Two jurors may hold attitudinal characteristics that are associated with a proplaintiff position. However, they may also possess other characteristics irrelevant to voir dire questioning (e.g., sexual preferences—one may be openly gay, the other a homophobe). These characteristics may cause conflict in the deliberation room, causing one juror to be inclined to disagree with the other. In this case there may be competing attitudes and motivations for jurors ("I want to make the right decision" vs. "I don't want to agree with a person who is a member of a group I don't like"). According to Treger, expanded voir dire questioning would do nothing to identify these factors and prevent this dynamic from occurring.

Although this is a valid point and echoes issues brought up in previous chapters about the unintended consequences of selecting jurors on the basis of demographic or personality and attitudinal characteristics, it appears to be a secondary issue. The primary concern for attorneys in voir dire should be to eliminate biased jurors. As empirical evidence suggests, expanded voir dire questioning leads to greater detection of juror biases (Moran et al., 1990; Nietzel & Dillehay, 1982; Nietzel et al., 1987), and therefore is preferable to restricted voir dire.

Cutler, Moran, and Narby (1992) noted that "[i]n 1989 Alabama Senator Howell Heflin introduced legislation to require judges to allow attorneys at least 30 minutes to address and question the prospective jurors during the voir dire" (p. 181). Although this proposed bill did not become law, many judges have the flexibility to allow for expanded voir dire. As previously noted, presenting pretrial community survey data demonstrating bias against parties involved in the case may make a compelling argument for expanding voir dire. If a judge insists on using a restricted voir dire, community survey data would provide attorneys information regarding the demographic characteristics of community members who are likely to hold strong biases.

ANALYTIC JUROR RATER

Abbott (1987, 1999a) argued that because judges frequently conduct voir dire questioning and jurors may not be honest in their responses, alternative approaches to identifying relevant juror biases are necessary. Traditional scientific jury selection approaches involving pretrial community surveys provide a potential solution. However, hiring a consultant to conduct such research is often costly and beyond the means of individuals and small corporate clients. As a result, Abbott proposed the use of an Analytic Juror Rater (AJR) method that uses the responses of individuals in the United States who have participated in the well-known General Social Survey (GSS). The GSS is conducted each year by the National Opinion Research Center and is designed to measure a wide variety of attitudes among the population of the United States.

According to Abbott (1987), there are a number of scales in the GSS that are useful for predicting juror verdicts: Authoritarianism, Economic Orthodoxy (conservatism), Cosmopolitan and Traditional Lifestyles, and Racial Tolerance. Later, Abbott (1999a) revised the Analytic Juror Rater method by adding GSS measures of *anomia* and *wordpower*. Abbott (1987) defined *authoritarian values* (described in detail in chap. 5) as "the predisposition to use coercion and to impose retribution" (p. 25), and maintained that authoritarian jurors are responsive to the prosecution rather than the defense in criminal cases. *Economic orthodoxy* is a measure of "the individual's tendency to assess evidence based on traditional values of the American economic system" (p. 30), and consists of items such as individuals' attitudes toward confidence in institutions (such as major companies and financial institutions) and spending on welfare programs. Abbott (1987) argued that "[j]urors rating high on the economic orthodoxy scale are more likely to favor corporations in litigation between individuals and corporations" (p. 30). The Cosmopolitan and Traditional Lifestyle Values Scale includes items measuring attitudes toward legalizing marijuana, premarital sexual relations, abortion, pornography, and legalized suicide. According to Abbott (1987), this scale is most appropriate in victimless crimes, with individuals scoring high on the measure being more likely to acquit in such crimes. The Racial Tolerance Values Scale measures "the extent to which [W]hites will accept [B]lacks as full members of a [W]hite dominated society" (pp. 40–41). The scale is intended to be used when either the client or attorney is Black. Presumably, a White juror who was rated as having high racial tolerance would not rely on race of the defendant or attorney in his or her decision making. The scale measures bias in terms of interactions between Blacks and Whites, and is not applicable to other minority groups. *Anomia* refers to an individual's sense of isolation because he or she is not integrated into society. Abbott (1999a) made the assumption that anomic jurors will "empathize with a person who has been wronged" (pp. 15–26). The scale is best applied to civil cases, with persons scoring high on an anomia scale predicted to be more plaintiff-oriented. Finally, *wordpower* refers to a juror's vocabulary level. The GSS has a 10-word measure of verbal skills. Strong vocabulary skills are desirable in cases of complex litigation.

Abbott (1987) suggested that an attorney choose the particular scale that is most applicable to the specific case factors. He then provided a means for classifying jurors along these scales, based on key demographic factors (e.g., age, sex, race, occupation, marital status and spouse's occupation, religion). The classification scheme is based on correlations between these demographic factors and responses to the scales, using GSS data. Using this approach, an attorney will have an idea of the predisposition of particular jury members and the jury pool as a whole. The attorney can then attempt to intelligently exercise his or her peremptory challenges to increase the probability of obtaining a favorable jury.

Abbott's (1987, 1999a) Analytic Juror Rater method provides an intriguing approach to scientific jury selection. Unfortunately, a number of limitations and questions about the approach exist. First, the GSS reports national data, and the population of any given particular jurisdiction may hold attitudes discrepant from the general trends. Second, in many situations the scales may not be applicable. For example, the Economic Orthodoxy Scale is applicable to litigation between individuals and corporations. However, it is "unclear how the scale should be used in civil suits in which both plaintiff and defendant are corporations or both are individuals" (Abbott, 1987, p. 35). In addition, the racial tolerance scale measures only attitudes of Whites toward Blacks, not the interaction between members of other races or ethnic groups, who may frequently be trial participants. Third, in many cases multiple scales may be applicable, such as when White jurors are presented with a case about a Black defendant accused of a victimless crime, in which case both racial tolerance and cosmopolitan lifestyle scales could be applied. In a similar way, a Black plaintiff might sue a corporation, making both the racial tolerance and economic orthodoxy scales relevant. It becomes much more difficult to use the AJR in these situations, requiring attorneys to use such solutions as weighting the scales and relying on advanced social science methodological and statistical techniques. As a result, it is more appropriate for consultants who have social science backgrounds to use the scales than attorneys who do not have training in this area. In short, Abbott's approach of simplifying the selection process for attorneys so they do not need a selection consultant may actually complicate matters to the point that a consultant is needed to help the attorney avoid critical errors that might adversely affect the jury composition. Finally, and most important, Abbott did not report any direct measures of the success of this approach. Rather, he supported the use of his technique by applying his classification approach to the composition of previously constructed juries, such as the Harrisburg Seven jury (described in chap. 1). Without a true validation, it is impossible to know how much verdict variance can be accounted for by the AJR.

STRUCK VERSUS SEQUENTIAL APPROACHES TO CHALLENGING JURORS

The effectiveness of voir dire may be limited by the method used to challenge jurors. There are two approaches that are typically used—a struck method and a sequential method. When the struck method is used, the trial judge rules on all challenges for cause before any peremptory challenges are exercised. This method results in a pool of jurors equal to the number of jurors that will sit on the final trial jury, the number of alternate jurors that will be used, and the total number of peremptory challenges allotted to both parties. With this method, attorneys can rank order the jurors after challenges for cause have been made and eliminate those jurors they find most objectionable. However, such is not the case when a sequential method is used. With a sequential method, jurors are interviewed one at a time and causal and peremptory challenges are exercised immediately after each interview. As a result, when an attorney eliminates a juror, they do so without knowing whether the remaining jurors will be less desirable (Hafemeister et al., 1984).

Jury selection consultants can provide information to aid peremptory challenges under both voir dire methods. Their consultation can be used to overcome the limitation with the sequential method. As the sequential method requires attorneys to challenge any particular juror before they know the responses of prospective jurors who will be interviewed subsequently, any information attorneys have about the dispositions of the remaining jurors will assist in their decision making. If a consultant conducts a pretrial community survey with a sample that is representative of the pool of citizens from which the venire will ultimately be drawn, data can be gathered about the general tendencies of the community (e.g., information regarding the percentage of individuals favorably and unfavorably predisposed to an attorney's case and the characteristics of each type of individual). This pretrial research might indicate that Christian men who work in blue-collar jobs and hold conservative attitudes express unfavorable attitudes toward the defense's case. In addition, the research might show that 26% of the people living in the community where the trial will be held possess this combination of demographic characteristics. Armed with this information, a defense attorney can act like a person who is counting cards at a blackjack table in Las Vegas, aware of the number of high cards that have been played. If one knows the composition of cards that were originally in a deck and the characteristics of the cards that have already been played, one is able to make an educated guess as to whether the next card will be high or low. The attorney will know the characteristics of the jurors who have previously been interviewed and will have a good sense of the number of unfavorable jurors who are likely to remain in the venire. If the attorney is interviewing a juror who appears to be modestly unfavorable to their case, and the attorney has come across few unfavorable individuals thus far during voir dire, he or she may want to save peremptory challenges.

Of course, this practice assumes that a representative sample of people has been drawn from the community and that the sample has not been biased by the exclusion of people ineligible to serve. For example, if individuals in white-collar positions are more likely to be excused from jury service because of the demands of their occupations, the percentage of blue-collar workers will increase. An attorney must take this possibility into account when applying pretrial research data. Thus, the consultant must be careful to identify not only whether respondents are eligible for jury service, but also other characteristics that might lead them to be excused from jury service.

Finally, it is important to know whether given characteristics in a jury pool are normally distributed, or distributed in a skewed or bi-modal manner (Abbott, 1987). For example, a characteristic like authoritarianism may be normally distributed in the jury pool, with most members possessing moderate attitudes and only a few individuals with extremely high or low scores on the measure. However, it may be distributed in a negatively skewed pattern, with most individuals classified as high in authoritarianism and only a few with moderate or low levels (a positively skewed distribution is the opposite, with most scores on the low end of a measure and only a few in the moderate or high range). A bimodal distribution occurs when most individuals tend to fall at the high or low ends of a scale, with only a few expressing moderate values. If an attorney uses a peremptory challenge to exclude a prospective juror, it is extremely important to know if there is a high probability that the next juror drawn will be favorable or unfavorable. For example, an attorney may use a peremptory challenge to excuse a juror who is classified as a moderate in terms of authoritarianism and is hoping that the replacement juror will be less authoritarian. However, if the jury is drawn from a population that is negatively skewed and most individuals have strong authoritarian attitudes, with only a few at moderate or low levels, the attorney may be doing him- or herself a great disservice. It is far more likely in this case that the replacement juror will strongly endorse authoritarian values than if the population were normally distributed. Jury selection consultants may be useful at providing information regarding the distribution pattern of attitudes in the relevant population.

QUESTION STYLE

Mogill and Nixon (1986) argued that when attorneys question prospective jurors during voir dire, they should attempt to

> (1) obtain as much explicit and inferred information as possible about prospective jurors; (2) based on the information received, assess each individual's likely ability to be impartial in this particular case; and (3) based on the information received about an individual juror and others in the panel, assess the likely impact on the group dynamic if this individual is included or excluded from the jury. (p. 54)

Unfortunately, these goals may be limited by the question style used by attorneys and judges.

Prospective jurors are often asked questions that can be answered with a simple "yes" or "no" response, such as "Have you or any members of your family or close friends ever been the victim of this type of crime?" or "Can you set aside any personal beliefs or feelings and any knowledge you have obtained outside the court and decide this case solely on the evidence you hear from the witness stand?" (Wrightsman, Greene, Nietzel, & Fortune, 2002, p. 392). In fact, Balch, Griffiths, Hall, and Winfree (1976) found that the majority of statements (63%) made during voir dire by jurors consisted of either "yes" or "no" responses. Such questions are similar to the type of closed-ended questions attorneys direct toward witnesses in the courtroom.[1] Although these types of interrogatories are useful at controlling the responses of people on the witness stand, they are not optimal for revealing useful information about jurors' attitudes, beliefs, and relevant influential life experiences (Wrightsman et al., 2002).

Attorneys may be able to draw out more honest and useful information from venire members by using open-ended questions. This assumption has been supported by empirical research. For example, Middendorf and Luginbuhl

---

[1] In addition, jurors are not always required to respond verbally but allowed to respond by simply raising their hands, which further restricts the amount of information generated (Cutler et al., 1992; Jones, 1987). If a juror does not raise his or her hand to show an affirmative response to the question, the judge is unlikely to follow up with further questions on that point to the juror. In addition, if jurors answer the majority of questions by a show of hands, it may be impossible to determine the charisma level of particular jurors. As a result, this potentially important interpersonal quality that may play a role in a juror's leadership qualities and persuasiveness during deliberation discussions (Moscovici, 1985) may not be revealed in any way during voir dire.

(1995) found that participants were more likely to admit they were unable to abide by legal due process guarantees when asked open-ended questions that did not direct their responses, such as,

> Another legal principle is that the State has the entire burden of proof. The burden rests with the State and never shifts to the defendant. How do you feel about the State having to prove the defendant guilty, and the defendant not having to prove his innocence? (p. 138)

Participants were less likely to admit inability to adhere to due process guarantees when questions were framed in a manner in which a single word answer would suffice, such as,

> Another legal principle is that the State has the entire burden of proof. The burden rests with the State and never shifts to the defendant. Could you accept the principle that the State has the entire burden of proof and that the defendant is never required to prove anything to you? (p. 137)

In addition, participants tended to view the voir dire process more positively and were more comfortable when nondirective (open-ended) questions were asked.

It should be noted that a nondirective voir dire is distinct from an extended voir dire. The goal of a nondirective voir dire is not necessarily to ask more questions, but to get jurors to provide more detailed responses to each question. The responses can, in turn, be probed to uncover biases that may have been impossible to reveal if directive questions had been asked. Thus, nondirective questioning may be useful to reveal likely attitude trends identified in pretrial community surveys. Further, if time constraints prohibit an attorney from using nondirective questioning of all jurors, it may be possible to target nondirective questions to jurors whose demographic backgrounds reveal a potential for bias, on the basis of a pretrial community survey.

EFFECTS OF EVALUATION ANXIETY AND DEMAND CHARACTERISTICS

Jurors may also reveal more information during voir dire when attempts are made to reduce the influence of the social psychological factors of *evaluation anxiety* and *demand characteristics* (Marshall & Smith, 1986). Evaluation anxiety refers to a situation in which a person is concerned whether he or she will be evaluated positively by an observer. In a courtroom setting, jurors may be concerned with how they are perceived by attorneys or judges, which may cause jurors to selectively reveal information so they are perceived in a positive, rather than negative, light.

The concept of demand characteristics comes out of methodological concerns in psychology experiments. Demand characteristics refer to aspects of an experimental procedure that convey the experimenter's hypothesis to a participant (Orne, 1962, 1969). In turn, rather than behaving naturally, the participant may behave in ways that confirm the experimenter's hypothesis. Demand characteristics may also be conveyed to experimental participants through subtle verbal and nonverbal behavior on the part of the experimenter, which is known as *experimenter bias* (Rosenthal, 1969) or *expectancy effects* (Marshall & Smith, 1986). In the context of a courtroom, the judge or attorney may inadvertently convey to participants the type of answers they would like to receive to their questions (Suggs & Sales, 1981). As a consequence, participants may provide responses that correspond with those expectations, rather than revealing their true attitudes and behavior.

Marshall and Smith (1986) conducted a study to determine the influence of evaluation anxiety, demand characteristics, and expectancy effects on juror responses during voir dire. A survey was mailed to 422 individuals who had recently served on a jury. The results indicated that former jurors who had higher levels of evaluation anxiety during voir dire reported that they were less likely to answer questions honestly than jurors with lower levels of anxiety. Expectancy effects (i.e., how difficult respondents felt it was to guess what the judge and attorneys wanted to hear as answers to voir dire questions) had a small and marginally significant effect on honesty as well. However, other demand characteristics, such as the formality of the courtroom setting, the oath to tell the truth, and the seriousness of the situation, had no effect on juror honesty. Unfortunately, the analyses were based entirely on juror self-report. As a consequence, it is possible that jurors were not aware of all the factors that influenced their behavior (or may simply have been dishonest about their dishonesty).

SEQUESTERING JURORS DURING VOIR DIRE

Jurors may not only be anxious about how they appear to attorneys and judges but also may be concerned with their self-presentation in terms of the impression other jurors have of them. Jurors are usually required to respond to voir dire questions in the presence of fellow prospective jurors, regardless of whether the questions are directed at the entire group or at specific jurors. This questioning style may affect the honesty and depth of juror responses, making it more difficult to accurately assess a juror's true attitudes and experiences. This may be particularly true when jurors are required to provide personal, sensitive information.

Rose (2001) conducted a study on juror reactions to voir dire questioning and found that slightly over half the respondents felt uncomfortable with some questions or felt that the questions were "too private" (p. 13). The questions that made jurors uncomfortable involved experiences they or their family members had with crime and the courts, in terms of victimization or being charged with crimes; questions regarding personal characteristics about themselves or their families (e.g., questions about children, marital status, or residency); and questions associated with their activities, organizational memberships, or interests (e.g., hobbies, religious affiliation, gun ownership). Not surprisingly, jurors also found objectionable questions about drug or alcohol problems, or experiences of being raped.

In addition, some of the earliest findings in social psychological research demonstrated that when individuals are forced to make public responses they will conform to responses provided by other individuals in a group, even if those responses go against their true beliefs (Asch, 1955, 1956). Conformity rates increase as group size increases and when a person is responding to high-status individuals. Middendorf and Luginbuhl (1995) also noted that jurors may learn what attorneys and judges want them to say (or what to say to be dismissed or accepted on a jury) by observing other jurors during voir dire. If jurors adjust their responses after making such observations, it may interfere with an attorney's ability to eliminate jurors who are most unfavorably predisposed to his or her case. Ideally, jurors would be questioned in private to avoid the influences of social observation and social pressure.

Occasionally, if jurors must discuss prejudicial or sensitive information they may be sequestered during voir dire, when each juror is questioned privately. Several studies examined the effects of sequestration and found this approach is superior at detecting juror biases (Nietzel & Dillehay, 1982; Nietzel et al., 1987). Nietzel and Dillehay (1982) examined the voir dire procedures of 13 capital murder trials in Kentucky and found that there were more sustained defense challenges for cause when jurors were questioned using individual sequestration. Sustained defense challenges were used as the primary dependent variable of interest because such a challenge is issued when an attorney believes a defendant is biased, and the judge concurs with this conclusion. Although the sample used by Nietzel and Dillehay was small (13 cases) their findings were supported in a replication study (Nietzel et al., 1987) that examined 18 capital cases in Kentucky, South Carolina, and California. This second study also showed individual sequestration to be associated with more sustained defense challenges (22%) than group questioning (10%).

It is worth noting that of the eight juries in the Nietzel and Dillehay (1982) study that underwent individual sequestration sentencing, only one returned a death penalty sentence (this trend emerged, but to a nonsignificant degree, in Nietzel et al., 1987). Thus, there is evidence that the greater number of sustained defense challenges that emerged from the practice of sequestration were successful at eliminating jurors biased toward the prosecution.

Nietzel et al. (1987) found that the influence of pretrial publicity produced the most frequent category of sustained defense challenges (43.4%); followed by automatic belief in imposing the death penalty (25.8%); refusing to accept certain legal principles, such as burden of proof and defendant's right to silence (13.5%); close affiliation with the victim (10.3%); and other reasons (6.6%). The type of voir dire conducted, however, had no effect on health and hardship excuses. This is most likely because the setting voir dire is conducted in does not affect jurors' comfort expressing information related to these excuses.

In addition, Christie (1974, reported in Ginger, 1977), one of the consultants who worked with Schulman in many of the early cases where scientific jury selection was used, examined the type of voir dire used in trials where consultants were involved (Harrisburg Seven, Gainesville Eight, Mitchell–Stans, Wounded Knee, Camden 28, etc.). Christie found that exclusive judicial questioning of jurors as a group (lawyers were not permitted to ask questions) led to the lowest level of sustained defense challenges (3%); however, judge and attorney questioning of individual jurors, with attorneys having "[a] wide latitude in questioning" (p. 324), led to the highest rate (25%). Given Broeder's (1965) report that many jurors conceal information during voir dire, these results are not surprising (see also Seltzer, Venuti, & Lopes, 1991).

As noted previously, en masse questioning of jurors is used far more often than individual sequestration. However, jury selection consultants may be able to provide attorneys with useful data to strengthen an argument for the sequestration approach during voir dire. In high-profile cases, community surveys may reveal substantial biases in the population from which the venire is drawn. The presentation of such evidence, combined with presentation of such empirical work as that showing the superiority of individual sequestration at eliminating biased jurors, may help convince the judge to allow the use of this approach in a trial. Even if the media have not covered the case extensively, pretrial community survey research may uncover important biases related to verdict inclination that can be presented to a judge in an attempt to obtain individual sequestration, or at least more extensive questioning, during voir dire.

PRETRIAL JUROR QUESTIONNAIRES

If individual sequestration is not allowed, attorneys may be able to make a successful argument for the use of extensive pretrial juror questionnaires (Moran et al., 1990). Pretrial questionnaires serve as a supplement to direct oral questioning of jurors during voir dire. Although courts may be inclined to use limited questionnaires to assess basic background characteristics (e.g., demographic information), more expanded questionnaires can delve into topics jurors may not feel comfortable revealing in a public setting. As a consequence, juror questionnaires are particularly useful in cases dealing with sensitive issues (e.g., homosexuality, AIDS, attitudes toward race); in cases in which there has been extensive pretrial news coverage; and in cases in which jurors are likely to hold strong opinions because the case involves a heinous crime or some highly charged issue (Wiley, 1997).

Some jurisdictions automatically use questionnaires in all cases, whereas others allow them on a case-by-case basis, most often in criminal cases with serious charges (such as murder or sexual assault) or complex civil cases (Wiley, 1997). For example, Hannaford-Agor, Hans, Mott, and Munsterman (2002) found that case-specific juror questionnaires were used in about one third of trials in Los Angles and the Bronx, but in only 19% of trials in Washington, DC, and in no trials in the Phoenix area (Maricopa County).

Advantages of Pretrial Juror Questionnaires

Pretrial questionnaires have become popular in recent years because they offer several advantages over oral questioning of jurors. First, questionnaires allow jurors to answer questions privately. As a general rule in conducting research, self-administered questionnaires lead to greater response honesty than face-to-face interviews (Babbie, 1998). As a result, jurors may be more likely to report experiences related to victimization, substance abuse, criminal activity, or other topics that are awkward to speak about in a public setting with pretrial questionnaires. Second, questionnaires provide jurors with more time to think about their responses and to reflect on relevant beliefs and experiences, which may improve the quality of information reported (Hans & Jehle, 2003). Third, questionnaires expedite the selection process, by allowing attorneys to quickly review basic information about jurors (Wiley, 1997). Fourth, pretrial questionnaires may help attorneys identify areas in which they should question particular jurors in greater detail. Finally, pretrial questionnaires may be useful in federal courts (or certain state courts) where attorneys are not allowed to question jurors orally during voir dire. In these cases, the questionnaires will provide more information to the attorneys, with the result that they may more effectively exercise challenges during voir dire.

Disadvantages of Using Pretrial Juror Questionnaires

Despite the benefits of pretrial juror questionnaires, there are a number of disadvantages to using them. First, because both parties in the case will have access to the responses, there is a chance that the opposing side will see strengths that may not have been as apparent if questionnaires were not used. For example, the questionnaire may reveal that the jury pool is strongly predisposed toward the opposing side. In that case, the opposing side may easily identify a few key jurors to eliminate with peremptory challenges. As a consequence, an attorney should exercise caution when determining the cases in which he or she wishes to request pretrial juror questionnaires. Second, a questionnaire response does not allow for an observation of the intensity with which a juror delivers a response (DecisionQuest, 1997). As a result, the attorney should question jurors about highly relevant attitudes or experiences orally, even if a written questionnaire is used.

Administering Pretrial Juror Questionnaires

Usually, a questionnaire that is 4 to 12 pages long will suffice when the trial is not complicated or has not received considerable publicity (Wiley, 1997). However, pretrial questionnaires can be much more extensive when pretrial publicity is present. For example, in the O.J. Simpson criminal trial, prospective jurors were given a 75-page questionnaire with over 300 questions (Wiley, 1997). Not all high-profile trials are accompanied by such lengthy questionnaires. For example, in the Oklahoma City Bombing trial of Timothy McVeigh, prospective jurors received only a four-page questionnaire (Hans & Jehle, 2003).

Juror questionnaires may be filled out when jurors arrive at the courthouse or at home. When questionnaires are to be completed at home, they are usually mailed to prospective jurors. However, in some jurisdictions jurors are able to download questionnaires from the courthouse Web sites (e.g., New Hampshire Courts, see http://www.courts.state.nh.us/jury/juror_questionnaire.htm; U.S. District Court for South Carolina, see http://www.scd.uscourts.gov/DOCS/JURYQUES.PDF). When Internet questionnaires are used, they are typically general questionnaires given to all jurors across different cases. As a result, the questionnaires are quite limited and do not allow case-specific information to be asked.

Although completing juror questionnaires at home may save time (which may be important if a lengthy questionnaire is used) and provide additional privacy, there is a possibility that a juror may receive suggestions from other people regarding how to respond. As a result, it may be better to have prospective jurors complete questionnaires at the courthouse; this appears to be the common approach (Hans & Jehle, 2003).

Content of Pretrial Juror Questionnaires

Pretrial questionnaires usually include a number of questions about the background of the jurors and their family members (e.g., education level, marital status, income, and ages and sexes of children), as well as additional questions about their activities (e.g., newspaper and television viewing preference) and relevant relationships, experiences, and attitudes toward law enforcement. Questionnaires may also contain case-specific information.

If the judge allows additional case-specific questions to be asked, the trial consultant can work with attorneys to develop optimal questions that tap into important case-related issues, are easy to read, and are methodologically sound. Various items relating to personality characteristics (e.g., authoritarianism, just world beliefs, attitudes toward tort reform, etc.) may also be included. When these items are included, the attorney and consultant are usually forced to pick one or two questions that tap into these characteristics, rather than being able to include the entire scales. Thus, it is important for a jury selection consultant to know which items on a scale have the greatest predictive power.

The questionnaire should consist of a combination of closed- and open-ended questions. For example, a person may be asked a closed-ended question regarding his or her general feelings about police officers and provided with response options of positive, negative, and mixed. The question may be followed up with an open-ended "Please explain your answer" statement. In a discrimination case, jurors may be asked if they or anyone close to them has ever been discriminated against, with yes or no response options and a space that allows them to explain their response if they answer in the affirmative. In addition to being asked if they are in favor of or against capital punishment, jurors in a capital murder case may be asked a number of questions requiring them to articulate the strongest arguments in favor or in opposition to the death penalty. It is important to include open-ended questions such as these to give prospective jurors an opportunity to fully articulate relevant attitudes and experiences. In general, the principles of survey construction discussed in chapter 3 apply to the development of pretrial questionnaires. For an example of a pretrial jury questionnaire, see Wiley (1997).

The Utility of Pretrial Juror Questionnaires

Jury selection consultants can develop pretrial juror questionnaires for attorneys. In addition, they can summarize the information in a statistical manner, which may give the attorney greater insight into the predisposition of the jury pool than could be achieved through relying solely on an oral questioning approach. As previously mentioned, research on survey methodology has indicated that self-administered questionnaires usually lead to greater respondent honesty than when questions are asked face-to-face (Babbie, 1998). Unfortunately, there is no published, peer-reviewed research evaluating the utility of pretrial questionnaires.

ADDITIONAL EFFECTS OF VOIR DIRE

Although the primary purpose of voir dire is to identify characteristics that may prevent jurors from being impartial in their decision making, voir dire also affords an opportunity to educate jurors about the key facts of the case and relevant legal issues (Loh, 1984). There is empirical evidence that voir dire provides some educational benefits. For example, Middendorf and Luginbuhl (1995) found that mock jurors who heard other jurors undergo voir dire tended to be more familiar with and accepting of due process guarantees than participants who only heard the judge explain the law to them.

However, there may be negative consequences of voir dire. Haney (1984) found that jurors who were exposed to questions that are typically asked to qualify jurors for a death penalty case were more likely to convict and sentence a defendant to death than were jurors who had not been questioned about their attitudes toward the death penalty. Further, a study by Freedman, Martin, and Mota (1998) found that questioning jurors about their exposure to pretrial publicity increased (rather than decreased) the damaging effects of hearing pretrial crime details. In that study, negative pretrial publicity did not affect mock juror verdicts unless participants were initially asked to express their pretrial opinions on the guilt of the defendant. Freedman et al. speculated that the effects of questioning may be due to participants becoming more committed to their positions after rendering initial pretrial opinions of guilt.

In addition, Dexter, Cutler, and Moran (1992) found that mock jurors were more punitive toward defendants after exposure to pretrial publicity, despite an extended voir dire with questions focused on educating jurors, making them accountable, and directly asking them about the influence of the publicity. Finally, a meta-analysis of studies on the effects of pretrial publicity found a greater pretrial publicity effect in studies in which participants expressed pretrial judgments (Steblay, Besirevic, Fulero, & Jimenez-Lorente, 1999). Thus, even if voir dire serves to educate jurors, it may also make their biases more salient and difficult to overcome. Selection consultants, through the use of mock juries, may help an attorney determine the effects specific voir dire questions may have on jurors (see chap. 9).

CONCLUSION

Voir dire represents a gate-keeping process in which prospective jurors are interviewed in an attempt to discover any attitudes, characteristics, or experiences that would interfere with their ability to impartially consider the evidence presented to them. Unfortunately, a number of aspects of the typical procedure for questioning jurors may cause jurors to be less likely to disclose important relevant information. For example, jurors may be less likely to provide honest or extensive responses when questioned by the judge in a group setting, especially when questions are heavily restricted by the judge and respondents are encouraged to respond in a simple "yes–no" manner. If jurors are worried about how they are perceived by the judge, attorneys, or fellow jurors, they are also less likely to be candid.

Taking steps to reduce the impact of these factors by allowing attorneys to question jurors in an expanded manner, using open-ended questions, allowing jurors to respond in a private setting, and allowing in-court surveys should provide useful information for making successful challenges for cause and intelligent peremptory challenges. Although judges may be reluctant to allow these modifications to typical voir dire procedures, providing community survey data reflecting a strong pretrial community bias may help convince judges to deviate from their traditional practices. Further, consultants may be useful at revealing the unintended consequences of voir dire questioning.

Although this chapter focuses on steps that can be taken to improve the questioning process so jurors can provide more useful responses, verbal responses may not be the only way jurors reveal important information about themselves. The manner in which jurors react when responding to voir dire questions may provide insight as to whether jurors are favorably or unfavorably predisposed to parties in a case. In the next chapter, we address the issue of using jurors' nonverbal behavior to reveal underlying biases.

7

IN-COURT OBSERVATIONS
OF NONVERBAL BEHAVIOR

Effective scientific jury selection requires that attorneys are able to intelligently use the challenges available in voir dire. This requires that they understand prospective jurors' attitudes toward the opposing parties, the counsel representing those parties, and the factual and legal issues that are relevant to the case. However, as discussed in chapter 6, a number of obstacles may prevent attorneys from extracting sufficient detail from jurors. These obstacles include having judges (rather than attorneys) question jurors, restricting the scope of questions attorneys are permitted to ask, and imposing time limits on attorney questioning. In addition, self-presentation concerns may prevent jurors from honestly expressing privately held attitudes that may be relevant, particularly when jurors are questioned in the presence of other jurors. As a result, attorneys often must exercise their challenges even though they have not been able to gather sufficient information about the attitudes of jurors. To reduce the resulting level of ambiguity, some social scientists and legal writers have advocated the observation and use of jurors' nonverbal behaviors to detect underlying biases (e.g., Suggs & Sales, 1978b). This technique is an additional service that jury selection consultants may provide (e.g., Dimitrius & Mazzarella, 1999; Frederick, 1984; McConahay, Mullin, & Frederick, 1977; Starr & McCormick, 2000).

The study of nonverbal behavior has become increasingly popular as a tool in jury selection (Mauet, 1992). Some attorneys have argued that in-court observation and interpretation of nonverbal behavior may give "a more accurate picture of jurors' attitudes than the verbal responses" (Mauet, 1992, p. 27) and may be the most important part of voir dire related social science techniques (e.g., Blue, 2001). Although such claims have not been empirically verified to date, top jury selection consultants place considerable faith in the utility of nonverbal behavior. For example, perhaps the best known selection consultant today, Jo-Ellan Dimitrius, has published a popular book on interpreting the nonverbal signals produced by others, which was inspired by her courtroom experience (Dimitrius & Mazzarella, 1999).

Nonverbal behaviors can be classified in terms of paralinguistic cues and kinesic cues. *Paralinguistic cues* refer to aspects of how a message is delivered, including the speaker's pitch and tone of voice, pauses and latencies, speech disturbances (disruptions to normal speech delivery) and speed of communication. Thus, paralinguistic cues focus on how a message is said, rather than the content of the message. *Kinesic cues* refer to body language, including factors such as facial expressions, eye contact, hand movements, body movements, and body orientation.

Typically, attorneys are trained on how to effectively extract verbal statements from witnesses and jurors but are not trained to focus their attention on jurors' nonverbal behaviors. If attorneys try to analyze nonverbal behavior, they may do so in a way that is not particularly systematic and effective, given the other tasks they must manage during voir dire (attending and recalling verbal statements from a large number of people). Jury selection consultants may provide useful support to attorneys in this regard because they may have greater training in the examination of nonverbal behaviors and can focus their attention specifically on jurors' kinesic and paralinguistic behaviors while others (the attorney or a second consultant) focus their attention on the content of a message. In this chapter, we review research related to nonverbal behavior and discuss the possible effectiveness of this technique.

THE LOGIC UNDERLYING OBSERVING NONVERBAL BEHAVIOR

The goal of observing nonverbal behavior during voir dire is to determine prospective jurors' general attitudes toward parties and issues involved in a case and to try to identify deceptive responses. To accomplish this, Suggs and Sales (1978b) suggested observing cues that may reveal heightened anxiety. There are a number of reasons why it may be useful to identify the anxiety level of jurors. First, a prospective juror may experience greater levels of anxiety when questioned by an attorney he or she dislikes, or when questioned by an attorney who represents a party toward whom the juror has a negative bias. Second, anxiety should be increased when a juror must respond to questions regarding "sensitive issues [about] which he has strong feelings (e.g., racial prejudice, death penalty, 'law and order')" (Suggs & Sales, 1978b, p. 632). Third, greater anxiety should be experienced when jurors provide deceptive responses.

The observation of nonverbal behaviors is based on determining *situational anxiety*, which refers to "anxiety [that] is generated by the particular situation at hand rather than being a stable personality trait of the individual" (Suggs & Sales, 1978b, p. 632). Thus, it is helpful to establish a baseline for the individual's typical nonverbal behaviors while responding to questions that are not likely to produce anxiety before observing behavior displayed during responses to critical questions. Later in this chapter we present a procedure for making such observations. However, we first address different communicative behaviors that may be useful to observe.

Paralinguistic Cues

Suggs and Sales (1978b) identified four aspects of the speaking process that may reveal situational anxiety: pauses and latencies, speed of speech and breath rate, speech disturbances, and the length of speaking time.

Pauses and Latencies

Pauses refer to extended periods of silence within a given sentence or phrase. *Latencies* refer to the length of time between a question being posed to a respondent and the beginning of the respondent's answers. Some research has shown that pauses and longer latency periods are associated with greater levels of anxiety, particularly when a speaker is being deceptive (deTurck & Miller, 1985; Knapp, Hart, & Dennis, 1974; Vrij, 2000; Zuckerman & Driver, 1985).

Speed of Speech and Breath Rate

There is some evidence that individuals speak at a faster rate when they are responding to questions that produce anxiety and when being dishonest (Suggs & Sales, 1978b; Vrij, Edward, & Bull, 2001). However, the relationship between speech and anxiety may be curvilinear. Conditions of minimal discomfort (which may occur when a speaker is being honest) and extreme discomfort (which might arise if a speaker is being dishonest about an important issue) are associated with a faster speaking rate. Moderate discomfort (which might occur if a speaker was being deceptive about an issue of minimal importance to them) has been associated with a slower speaking rate (Miller & Burgoon, 1982; see also Vrij, 2000). Although speaking in an accelerated rate may seem contradictory to the pause and latency indicators discussed previously, these are not necessarily exclusive behaviors. A respondent could have a prolonged latency before engaging in accelerated speech. In both the case of faster speech or greater delay, the key issue is whether the respondent deviates from their normal pattern of speaking when responding to questions that could be anxiety producing. Anxiety may also be associated with more labored breathing (Cutrow, Parks, Lucas, & Thomas, 1972; Knapp et al., 1974).

Amount of Speech

Several researchers reported that individuals engage in speech for a longer duration of time when they are speaking to someone who arouses positive emotions (Suggs & Sales, 1978b) and decrease their talking time when being deceptive (deTurck & Miller, 1985). As a result, the total verbal output of prospective jurors in response to attorneys for both sides of a case could be measured and used as an indicator of favorable disposition. However, this measure would be confounded by the fact that the respondent would almost certainly be answering different questions for each party, so a better indicator might be a measure of the average time of response to each question posed by both sides.

Speech Disturbances

Finally, general speech disturbances may be indicators of anxiety. Speech disturbances refer to a wide range of behaviors that are associated with disruptions to the speaking process. For example, stuttering, inappropriate laughter, voice changes, unfinished sentences, repeating words or statements, and interrupting sentence flow by introducing new thoughts have been shown to be related to situational anxiety (Dibner, 1956; Suggs & Sales, 1978b; Vrij, 2000). In addition, when individuals are anxious their speech pattern may change entirely. That is, a person might change from responding in an informal manner to a more rigid and formal style when questioned about issues they feel hesitant to answer publicly (Suggs & Sales, 1978b). Changes in voice pitch have been shown to be associated with deception, with higher voice pitch occurring in deceptive interviews (Ekman, Friesen, & Scherer, 1976).

It has also been reported that respondents saying "I don't know" as a general statement of resignation or disgust, rather than in direct response to a question, may be an additional indicator of anxiety (Dibner, 1956). However, attorneys should be careful about overestimating the use of the phrase "don't know" as an indicator of deceptive speech. Porter and Yuille (1996) conducted an experiment in which participants were put into situations in which they were interrogated about behavior they had performed (taking either a folder or $100 from a room). Participants were instructed to either admit to behavior of which they were accused, provide a legitimate alibi, or deceive the interrogator. The results indicated that participants who were telling the truth, as compared with those trying to be deceptive, were more likely to report a lack of memory for the details of the incident, even though they actually were able to provide more details in their accounts and were more coherent (the accounts made more sense) when describing their behavior.

Kinesic Cues

In addition to paralinguistic cues, respondents may exhibit a wide range of kinesic cues when experiencing situational anxiety. These behaviors can include eye contact, facial cues, body movements, and hand movements.

Eye Contact

A number of investigators have found that eye contact is decreased (fewer mutual glances and briefer duration of glances) when an individual is anxious or providing deceptive responses (Ekman & Friesen, 1974; Knapp et al., 1974; Miller & Burgoon, 1982). Suggs and Sales (1978b) noted that eye contact may not only reveal anxiety but also may be a good indicator of the nature of the relationship between two people. Increased eye contact may indicate a positive feeling toward an individual. In addition, Efran (1968) found that individuals maintain greater eye contact when interacting with people with whom they have a high expectation of approval. Suggs and Sales (1978b) suggested that Efran's work may have important implications for the voir dire process. If it is assumed that the typical prospective juror begins the voir dire process without knowing either of the parties involved in the case, the juror should have neither positive nor negative feelings toward the trial participants. Therefore, if there is a difference in the amount of eye contact directed toward attorneys for the different parties, then the party that receives greater eye contact from the prospective juror may be the one from whom the juror expects approval and has positive feelings toward.

Facial Cues

Lay people are natural observers of facial cues. People constantly look at the facial expressions of others to gauge their emotional state. In fact, cross-cultural research has shown that there are universally common attributions in the expression of happiness, sadness, surprise, anger, disgust, and fear (Ekman 1973). As a consequence, facial cues may be useful indicators of juror attitudes (Ekman, O'Sullivan, Friesen, & Scherer, 1991). There is evidence that facial cues may be more effective in communicating attitudes than either verbal or paralinguistic cues (Mehrabian, 1971; Mehrabian & Ferris, 1967; Zaidel & Mehrabian, 1969).

Ekman and Friesen (1969) argued that individuals may be quite aware that faces are a good indicator of emotions. As a result, people may try to control their facial expressions to hide true emotions and may present false emotions through contrived facial cues. Although some individuals may be able to control their facial cues, they may have more difficulty controlling body postures and movements, which may also reveal cues to the current emotional state. It may then be possible to detect deception by focusing on body cues. Ekman and Friesen termed this phenomenon the *leakage hypothesis* (the idea that individuals may be able to control their faces, but that deceptive cues will leak out of the body).

The leakage hypothesis has been tested by presenting observers with videotapes of targets who present either truthful or deceptive accounts, and who have been videotaped from either above or below the neck. Ekman and Friesen (1974) found that observers could detect deception in the body better than in the face, but only when they had first seen targets present truthful statements before the deceptive statements. Therefore, it may be critical to closely observe prospective jurors as they answer mundane questions (e.g., questions about their occupation) before answering questions when they may be more likely to be deceptive. Later research by Hocking, Bauchner, Kaminski, and Miller (1979) showed that individuals were better able to detect deception about emotionally oriented information by observing body cues, but better able to detect deception about factual information by observing facial cues. This may be due to individuals being more accustomed to using their face to express emotions and thus better able to control facial cues for emotion.

Ekman et al. (1991) suggested that the body leakage may only occur when the motivation to deceive is at a moderate level. When motivation to lie is very high, people may exert greater monitoring and control over their entire body to prevent having the deception detected. The key issue for attorneys and consultants ultimately appears to be attending to the consistency between facial and body cues. If body cues appear to contradict the cues revealed by the face, the attorneys should be suspicious of the information provided by the prospective juror.

Body Cues

Attorneys have long been advised to examine the body language of jurors. For example, Katz (1968–1969) suggested that attorneys focus on jurors' body cues, rather than on facial or eye cues, because body movements are harder to conceal. A variety of body postures and movements have been identified as relevant to revealing deceptive cues. For example, individuals who have positive attitudes and who are being honest toward a target tend to have a slight forward body lean and squarely face the person, as opposed to leaning back or turning away (Ekman et al., 1976; Knapp et al., 1974). Suggs and Sales (1978b) maintain that it

> could be safely assumed that if a prospective juror was trying to be deceptive, he would be emotionally aroused and this emotional arousal would

become manifest either in an observable increase in body movements or in a tense, still body posture. (p. 637)

In addition, body positions that indicate a relaxed state, such as arm position asymmetry (with one hand in the lap and the other arm placed on the back of a chair) or leg position asymmetry, hand relaxation or a sideways lean, have been shown to be associated with positive affect (Mehrabian, 1969). Of course, the formality of the courtroom setting may inhibit prospective jurors from exhibiting these "relaxed" behaviors.

Hand Movements

A prospective juror's hand movements may also reveal deception during voir dire. A variety of behaviors, such as finger-tapping, scratching, wringing the hands, or hand shrugs (indicating uncertainty or vagueness), have been associated with increased body tension and anxiety (Freedman & Hoffman, 1967; Ekman & Friesen, 1972; Knapp et al., 1974). However, other researchers found that individuals who are being deceptive make fewer hand and finger movements (Vrij, 2000). This discrepancy in findings may be the result of liars' attempts to control obvious signs of deception. When a person's anxiety does not stem from attempts to conceal deception, but stems from other factors (such as negative emotional arousal toward the interviewer), he or she may not feel a need to control hand movements. Hand movements may increase or decrease as a function of whether anxiety or deception is present, so rather than looking for one of these behaviors specifically, the attorneys should take note in cases in which the prospective juror alters his or her frequency of hand movements.

MAKING SYSTEMATIC OBSERVATIONS OF PARALINGUISTIC AND KINESIC CUES DURING VOIR DIRE

Nonverbal behavior in the form of paralinguistic and kinesic cues can be observed during voir dire to provide a measure of prospective jurors' situational anxiety. However, interpretation of nonverbal behavior may be difficult because situational anxiety may be caused by any one of a number of factors. First, a juror may attempt to make deceptive statements during voir dire, and this deception may produce anxiety. Second, even if the juror is telling the truth, anxiety may be produced by the strong emotional feelings he or she has about the particular issues being discussed at any given moment. Third, a juror may be anxious because he or she has negative feelings toward the person who is questioning him or her. Finally, a juror may be anxious simply as a result of being forced to give public responses in the courtroom. For nonverbal cues to provide a somewhat useful indicator of juror acceptability, it is important to determine the cause of juror anxiety. Suggs and Sales (1978b) provided a technique for doing so.

TABLE 7.1
Nonverbal Rating Grid

Behavior	Judge questioning	Prosecutor/Plaintiff attorney questioning	Defense attorney questioning
Eye contact	+	+	+
Facial cues	0	+	–
Body orientation	+	+	0
Body movements	0	0	–
Body posture	0	+	–
Hand movements	+	+	+
Speech disturbances	0	0	0
Pauses and latencies	0	0	0

Note. From "Using Communication Cues to Evaluate Prospective Jurors During the Voir Dire," by D. Suggs and B. D. Sales, 1978, *Arizona Law Review, 20,* p. 639. Copyright 1978 by the University of Arizona. Adapted with permission.

Timing of the Observations

Suggs and Sales (1978b) suggested attorneys begin observing prospective jurors during initial questioning, when interrogatories are not likely to produce anxiety. Prospective jurors are almost always initially questioned by the judge and attorneys (depending on jurisdiction) about background information, such as marital status, occupation, and residence. As these questions will probably not produce strong emotional reactions or a need for deceptive responses, the behavior of jurors can be observed to produce a baseline for responses. Later, when the judge or attorneys for either side question the jurors about more critical or sensitive information, jurors' nonverbal behavior can be compared with this initial baseline.

Using a Ratings Grid

Suggs and Sales (1978b) reported that in their experience they found it most convenient to rate a variety of specific juror behaviors on a three-point rating system: negative, neutral, and positive. They suggest using a grid for easy coding (see Table 7.1).

A grid such as this should be used for each juror, and, as noted previously, observations should be made twice. First, when the judge or attorneys ask initial background questions, and again when the prospective juror is asked about case relevant attitudes or experiences. As observations will be subjective, two (or more) observers should be used to independently rate each juror, and the reliability of the observations should be checked.

As different individuals may express affect and anxiety in different ways, it may be most useful to compute an overall score for each juror in response to each interviewer. Overall scores may be more useful than analyzing specific behaviors, because they allow for a general picture of the person's behavior. Dimitrius maintains, on the basis of her experience as a consultant, that "it is important not to focus on any single trait or characteristic: taken alone, almost any trait will be misleading" (Dimitrius & Mazzarella, 1999, pp. xiii–xiv). In a similar way, Vrij et al. (2001) have noted "there is no infallible cue such as a Pinocchio's nose" (p. 899), meaning there is not one specific behavior all individuals who are attempting to be deceptive show in all cases (DePaulo, Stone, & Lassiter, 1985; Vrij, 2000; Vrij et al., 2001). Ekman et al. (1991) found that observers who viewed a combination of behaviors (different types of smiles and voice pitch combined) had higher deception detection accuracy rates than when these different behaviors were observed independently. Observing a combination of behaviors produced an 86% deception detection accuracy rate, which is far superior to the typical 50% to 60% accuracy rate found in most studies (Bond, Kahler, & Paolicelli, 1985; Ekman et al., 1991).

An overall score for each juror can be computed by converting ratings to scores of –1 (negative cues revealed), 0 (neutral cues), or +1 (positive scores), and adding scores for all behaviors. Thus, in response to judicial questioning, a respondent could receive a score ranging from –8 (negative behavior exhibited for all 8 behaviors) to +8 (positive behavior exhibited for all 8 behaviors). A score would be computed in response to judicial questioning, plaintiff–prosecutor questioning, and defense attorney questioning, thus producing three separate scores. As ratings should be made twice (once during initial baseline questioning, and once during critical questioning for each juror), there will ultimately be a total of six scores that can be compared.

Interpreting Grid Ratings

Juror responses can be compared both across interviewers and within a given interview. That is, juror responses to baseline questions can be compared between plaintiff–prosecutor questions and defense attorney questions, or between each party and the judge. If there are initial differences in baseline questions to each party, the observed behavior may reflect preexisting biases toward different sides in the case.

Comparisons can be made within each interview as well. If there is a shift from relatively neutral behaviors to extreme positive or negative behaviors during questioning about trial relevant attitudes–experiences, this may reflect a juror's becoming positively or negatively aroused by the content of the questioning. Attorneys should pay particular attention to such shifts, particularly when prospective jurors are expressing socially appropriate responses but producing a variety of behaviors that indicate anxiety or negative attitudes (stiffened body posture, less eye contact, increased pauses and latencies, etc.).

Challenges to Using the Ratings Grid

Although the general approach to making observations of nonverbal behaviors is relatively straightforward and does not require the sophisticated statistical analyses or difficult sampling procedures associated with other scientific jury selection techniques, it is not necessarily an easy process. It is almost impossible for an attorney to make such observations in any systematic way by him- or herself. The attorney will be too busy generating questions and attending to prospective jurors' verbal responses and will not be able to carefully observe, interpret, and record a wide variety of nonverbal behaviors from the prospective juror being questioned or other empanelled prospective jurors (discussed later in this chapter). It is critical that the lead attorney use several other observers to make the observations.

It is also critical that the observers are seated where they can clearly see the behaviors of the jurors in a head-on position. When the venire is questioned, the prospective jurors may initially be seated in the spectator section of the courtroom during voir dire questioning because they are being questioned as a group. Unless observers are seated at the attorney's tables, immediately next to, or behind her or him, it may be impossible to observe many of the nonverbal behaviors of jurors, such as facial expressions and eye contact. If the observers are jury selection consultants instead of attorneys, the attorneys may want to introduce the consultants to the venire members. Suggs and Sales (1978b) maintained that this should always be done, because in their experience serving as jury selection consultants jurors did not express objection to the use of social scientists when interviewed after the trial.

Observations will have to be made at a very rapid pace during voir dire, particularly because jurors are often not questioned in the order of their juror numbers. Thus, steps should be taken to streamline the observation process. As a result, as many grids as possible should be placed on each sheet of paper (preferably 12–14; Suggs & Sales, 1978b). This will minimize the amount of paper shuffling (and reduce the noise from paper shuffling, which may annoy prospective jurors or the judge).

When a prospective juror makes a statement that may indicate an underlying bias, an attorney (or judge) may be inclined to probe the issue further with the juror. However, Buller, Comstock, Aune, and Strzyzewski (1989) found that when individuals are probed after making a deceptive statement they are less likely to exhibit nonverbal cues of deception. This may occur because individuals exert greater control over their behaviors when they believe an interviewer is suspicious of them (see also Buller, Strzyzewski, & Comstock, 1991; Burgoon, Buller, Dillman, & Walther, 1995). Thus, nonverbal cues may not be good predictors of deception when motivation to deceive is high.

Because nonverbal behavior requires the subjective interpretation of juror behavior, it is possible that behaviors may be incorrectly classified. For example, Bond et al. (1992) found that observers tended to incorrectly judge whether people were lying when the targets they observed exhibited weird nonverbal behaviors, such as excessive staring, head tilting, and arm raising. They interpreted this as the result of a tendency in individuals to believe that lie detection is an obvious process, causing perceivers to ignore more subtle nonverbal behaviors that may actually be better indicators of deceit. As a result, untrained observers in laboratory studies typically perform at about a chance level when attempting to detect deception (Bond et al., 1985; DePaulo et al., 1985; Ekman et al., 1991; Zuckerman, DePaulo, & Rosenthal, 1981).

If jury selection consultants advertise nonverbal behavior analysis as part of the services they can provide, one would expect that their professional experience would be associated with higher accuracy rates. Training has been shown to improve deception detection (Landry & Brigham, 1992). In addition, Secret Service agents have been shown to perform at a greater than chance level at detecting deception (Ekman & O'Sullivan, 1991), so it is possible that other professionals, such as trained jury selection consultants, might also do better than chance. However, social science research has found that professionals who must regularly try to detect deception, such as law enforcement officers, custom agents, and federal polygraphers, have usually demonstrated similar levels of accuracy rates to that of lay people (DePaulo & Pfeifer, 1986; Ekman & O'Sullivan, 1991; Koehnken, 1987; Kraut & Poe, 1980). Thus, attorneys should determine the basis for, and what level of, expertise jury selection consultants have with evaluating nonverbal behaviors.

If a judge does the voir dire questioning entirely by him- or herself, the amount of information will be greatly limited and comparisons between parties cannot be made. As minimal verbal information may be obtained in such a restricted voir dire, the additional nonverbal observations made about each juror may provide a useful secondary source of information. Thus, we believe that there is evidence to suggest that anxiety-based observations of nonverbal behavior may be a useful component of scientific jury selection. However, more research is clearly needed to validate this approach. In one of the few existing relevant studies, Frederick (1984; see also McConahay et al., 1977) reported the use of nonverbal observations as a jury selection aid in a criminal trial. The results indicated that there was a correlation between ratings of authoritarianism (as noted in chap. 5, a trait generally associated with conviction proneness), and nonverbal behaviors that indicated negative attitudes toward the defense. However, Frederick was not able to provide any validation data for nonverbal communication measures.

Finally, in early work on the use of nonverbal observations, Sales and Suggs (1978b) divided the prospective jurors so that they were observing different people, not just the person being asked a direct question by the judge or attorneys. The logic of their approach was that jurors would reveal nonverbal information that would indicate how they would answer a question if it was posed to them rather than to the juror actually questioned. For example, in one of the Wounded Knee cases, one juror started breathing deeply while another juror was questioned about potential biases he held toward Native Americans. As it turned out, the deep breathing occurred because the observed juror held deep biases against the defendants and was thus excused from the jury. Mogill and Nixon (1986) also suggested observing for "mimicking of body posture among panel members, as this may indicate initial formation of subgroups" (p. 55). Unfortunately, there is almost no research to suggest how accurate these nonverbal cues are for revealing attitudes of nonquestioned jurors.

IMPORTANCE OF EMPIRICALLY SUPPORTED, THEORETICALLY BASED OBSERVATIONS

The techniques described in this chapter have been based on studies that often involved participants who engaged in basic research on nonverbal behavior and deception rather than on jury decision making. However, there is no reason to think the basic findings cannot carry over to voir dire observations. The basic principle of observing behaviors that may reveal situational anxiety provides a legitimate basis for making decisions.

We encourage attorneys to be skeptical of claims regarding the utility of nonverbal behavior when the techniques used do not have empirical or solid theoretical grounding. For example, Vaughan (as cited in Belli, 1982) noted that specific facial features can be used as indicators of a person's character. Belli makes note of Vaughan's assertions that individuals with a concave or turned-up nose are good helpers, but do not handle money well as they are not primarily motivated by financial concerns. However, if an individual has a hook nose it is an indication that he or she is an excellent business person who understands the value of a dollar. Similar personality inferences are made in Belli's book regarding the shape of other features, such as eyes, eyebrows, lips, and nostrils. These attributions appear to be based on gross generalizations and stereotypes, with no empirical basis. As a result, there is no reason to believe these indicators will have any utility in the courtroom.

The absence of an empirical or theoretical approach has led to conflicting recommendations in trial manuals regarding some types of nonverbal behavior (Kovera et al., 2003). For example, Wishman (1986) suggested attorneys avoid a juror whose face he or she doesn't like, because "chances are he doesn't like yours either" (pp. 72–73). This amusing suggestion is in accordance with guidance from Clarence Darrow (1936), who advised selecting jurors who often smile, particularly when they are smiling at the attorney. However, others (Harrington & Dempsey, 1969; Wagner, 1989) cautioned against smiling jurors, because the jurors may be trying to ingratiate themselves with attorneys so they can get on the jury. Such individuals may have hidden agendas and may produce unexpected and undesirable verdicts. These conflicting recommendations may be the result of lack of awareness of different types of smiles. Smiles can be classified as Duchenne, or D-smiles, or masking smiles. D-smiles occur when a person is truly experiencing enjoyment, whereas masking smiles occur when smiles are accompanied by indicators or subtle indicators of negative emotion (Ekman et al., 1991).

In addition to conflicting information, a variety of techniques of dubious reliability and validity have also been suggested over the years. For example, factors such as clothing style, handwriting style, and basic body shape have all been mentioned as characteristics worthy of observation during voir dire.

Clothing

Starr and McCormick (2000) argued that consultants should carefully examine the way potential jurors are dressed to discern cues as to their personality and ideology. Mauet (1992) maintained that a prospective juror's attire may provide information regarding a variety of issues, such as whether the juror is a person who is "meticulous and analytically oriented," "what he would like to be, but isn't," and whether his clothes are worn to compensate for "a perceived inadequacy" (p. 27). We know of no existing published research that has demonstrated clothing to be a useful predictor of juror behavior. However, it is possible for clothing to provide a crude indicator of wealth or of tendencies to adopt or reject conventional norms, which may have implications for behavior during deliberations (discussed in the juror deliberation roles section later in this chapter). Such inferences may only be possible with a few members of the jury, so this approach can be considered supplementary at best.

Graphology

Graphology refers to the study of handwriting to identify psychological traits as well as developmental and situational factors. The analysis of handwriting is based on the assumption that writing is a self-generated and expressive activity (Allport & Vernon, 1933; Farrell & Bunch, 1999; Nevo, 1989) that can be analyzed in a manner similar to other projective tests, such as the Rorschach Inkblot Test (Farrell & Bunch, 1999). Handwriting is a potentially useful characteristic because it is easily recorded on paper and remains relatively constant throughout a person's adult life. A variety of handwriting factors can be examined, including the size and width of letters, and amount of pressure used to write them, details about the letters such as where loops are placed and how *i*'s are dotted and *t*'s are crossed (Furnham, Chamorro-Premuzic, & Callahan, 2003). If jurors are given a pretrial survey with open-ended questions on it, then a sufficient sample of handwriting should exist for analysis. Although there is some anecdotal evidence of graphology being a useful contributor to attorney success (Farrell & Bunch, 1999; Reagh, 1992) there have not been any published studies regarding graphology and jury selection.

However, a number of general graphology studies have been published in academic journals over the years. Although some studies reported that graphology can be useful for screening employees (e.g., Nevo, 1988; Taylor & Sackheim, 1988), other research indicated that graphology does not have sufficient criterion-related validity (predictive ability) and may be harmful for use in personnel selection (Simner & Goffin, 2003). Ben-Shakhar, Bar-Hillel, Bilu, Ben-Abba, and Flug (1986) speculated that graphology may simply appear to be useful in some cases because of the *Barnum effect*. The Barnum effect, named after P.T. Barnum, refers to the tendency of individuals to believe that vague or general characterizations about themselves (such as horoscopes) are highly accurate (Glick, Gottesman, & Jolton, 1989).

In general, the typical conclusion of published research is that graphology is not a useful predictor of personality or behavior (e.g., Bar-Hillel & Ben-Shakhar, 2000; Ben-Shakhar et al., 1986; Furnham et al., 2003). For example, studies have shown that graphologists did not perform significantly better than chance at judging the profession of 40 successful professionals (Ben-Shakhar et al., 1986), a finding substantiated in a later meta-analysis of graphological studies (Neter & Ben-Shakhar, 1989). Other research has shown that handwriting analyses are not reliable predictors of scores on the Eysenck Personality Questionnaire (Furnham & Gunter, 1987).

Individuals who believe in the utility of graphology might respond to the lack of social science research supporting the predictive ability of graphology by saying that graphology requires skilled subjective interpretation of handwriting, and the graphologists used in research studies were simply not talented enough to accurately classify individuals on the basis of their writing style. It is certainly possible that a trial consulting firm could use a talented graphologist. However, we believe the best advice is for attorneys to avoid accepting handwriting-based prospective juror profiles until convincing empirical research can be conducted that demonstrates strong support for graphology and provides clear protocols (associated with sufficient predictive ability) for collecting, measuring, and classifying handwriting data (Bar-Hillel & Ben-Shakhar, 2000; Farrell & Bunch, 1999). Even if graphology can be shown to be a reliable predictor of personality factors, personality characteristics have been shown to be weak predictors of juror verdict decisions (as previously discussed in this volume); therefore, there is no theoretical reason to expect robust effects.

Body Types

Several legal authors, applying the work of Sheldon (1949), have proposed using a person's body type to predict verdicts (Bailey & Rothblatt, 1971, 1985; Lane, 1984). Sheldon distinguished among different personalities by creating three classifications for individuals: endomorphs, mesomorphs, and ectomorphs. The *endomorph* is a round, heavyset person whose body is soft. This type of individual is even-tempered and tends to be outgoing and jolly. The *mesomorph* is a physically fit, athletic person whose body is hard and muscular. Mesomorphs enjoy risk-taking behaviors and can be aggressive and challenging in nature. Finally, *ectomorphs* are thin and often weak. They tend to enjoy mental activity and engage in activities by themselves. As a result, they are introverted people. The belief that has been articulated by some in the legal community is that endomorphs, with their easygoing nature, are better jurors for the defense in criminal cases than ectomorphs and mesomorphs (Bailey & Rothblatt, 1971, 1985; Lane, 1984). However, if a mesomorph can be convinced to adopt an attorney's viewpoint, he or she is typically an ideal juror because the mesomorph's aggressive and dominating nature can cause him or her to be a leader in the deliberation room. As we discuss in the next section, the issue of identifying characteristics of leaders may be important for use in juror selection.

Unfortunately, the basic assumptions about body types have not been empirically tested within the context of jury decisions. In addition, as the assumptions are based on gross generalizations about individuals, they are likely to be inaccurate.

USING NONVERBAL BEHAVIOR TO IDENTIFY JUROR DELIBERATION ROLES

Up to this point, we have discussed the issue of nonverbal behavior in terms of identifying jurors who may be deceptive or who may have a preexisting bias against one of the parties involved in the case, as indicated by negative affect exhibited to that party. However, observations of nonverbal behavior may serve other useful purposes. Most notably, paralinguistic and kinesic cues may provide indications of the type of role individuals may adopt in deliberation interactions. That is, nonverbal behavior may be useful at indicating which jurors are likely to emerge as leaders. Leadership is one of a number of roles that jurors may adopt in their deliberation interactions (Blue, 2001; National Jury Project, 2004). The National Jury Project has identified five roles of jurors during deliberations: leaders, followers, fillers, negotiators, and holdouts.

Leaders are individuals who are influential during deliberations and drive other jurors to reach the goal of a unanimous verdict by supporting their interpretation of the case facts. This type of leadership role is sometimes referred to as a task-oriented leadership role (Bales, 1958; Kassin & Wrightsman, 1988). Leaders tend to walk with an air of confidence, holding their head up as they walk, and sitting upright in the courtroom. Leaders may be well-dressed or dressed conservatively with conservative haircuts and hairstyles (Dimitrius & Mazzarella, 1999).

Blue (2001) suggests that attorneys watch each juror as they enter the courtroom and observe their stride, posture, and the degree of confidence with which they appear to carry themselves, as such factors may be indicative of leadership qualities. However, this advice may prove to be impossible to follow for voir dire purposes, because it may be extremely difficult to observe the behavior of a large group that enters the room at the same time, or even the behavior of 12 jurors as they walk to the jury box as a group. However, the technique of making systematic observations using the grid method described in this chapter may allow for useful information to be collected during the questioning of jurors. In that case, it would be useful to create a separate grid for leadership characteristic observations to be made. Ideally, additional observers who were focused solely on the characteristics of leadership would be used.

Negotiators are individuals who serve to increase group cohesiveness. Negotiators tend to adopt a socioemotional leadership role. Socioemotional leaders tend to provide emotional support to other members of the group, which serves to increase the morale and cohesiveness of the group. In that process, socioemotional leaders may reduce tension created by task-oriented leaders (Bales, 1958; Kassin & Wrightsman, 1988) and are important for a group to achieve a conflict resolution stage. Without such individuals, a jury may end up split between two positions, ultimately ending in a deadlock. Negotiators may be difficult to detect in terms of body language, but the fact that they must get some members of their group to accommodate others implies a certain degree of confidence and self-assurance. It may be best to combine their verbal responses with their body language.

Followers tend to be passive and do not actively participate in deliberations. These individuals are easily persuaded by leaders. Followers tend to speak only after they are spoken to and provide nonverbal cues that indicate a lack of assertiveness (e.g., having a walk or posture that indicates a lack of confidence).

Fillers tend to take an almost silent role in deliberations. They do not want to serve on juries and will typically vote with the majority opinion. According to Hastie, Penrod, and Pennington (1983), this type of person may be fairly common on juries. Hastie et al. conducted a study in which over 800 people were assigned to juries that deliberated after the jurors had watched a videotaped reenactment of a homicide trial. The deliberations were recorded and content analyzed to determine the level of participation of each juror within the group. The results indicated that in most juries, as many as three jurors were almost silent during the deliberations. Typically, deliberations were dominated by only a few jurors (leaders), with others speaking much less frequently (followers). Fillers give off nonverbal cues that indicate they are disinterested in the voir dire process. Dimitrius and Mazzarella (1999) noted that indicators of boredom in a juror's behavior may include letting eyes wander; gazing into the distance; yawning or sighing heavily; playing with objects such as pens, eyeglasses, or fingers; leaning forward and backward in the chair; crossing and uncrossing legs and arms; or moving the head from side to side, or stretching.

Holdouts are individuals who are resistant to group pressure. They will firmly defend their position and are comfortable going against social norms. As rebels are comfortable going against majority influence, their appearance may reflect unique choices. That is, holdouts may not be concerned with dressing in the latest fashions or having conventional hairstyles. However, it is important to remember that norms exist even in deviant subgroups, and a unique appearance may reflect adoption of the conventional appearance of one's subgroup.

CONCLUSION

Nonverbal cues potentially provide additional information for attorneys to use in trying to determine whether jurors' responses are honest and whether jurors possess attitudes that may negatively influence their decision making. There has been considerable research over the years on nonverbal behavior. The research has shown that individuals do display certain nonverbal behaviors when experiencing a variety of emotions, when under anxiety, and when attempting to deceive others. Unfortunately, most of the research involved observers watching videotapes of individuals making statements and then attempting to determine if the person is lying or not. The observers are not required to watch the interaction between an interviewer and a group of people. Making individual observations of a large group of people during a fast-paced voir dire, when attorneys or the judge may constantly jump from one prospective juror to another during the questioning is likely to be far more difficult than what has been done in the laboratory studies conducted to date.

In addition, relevant nonverbal behavior studies typically focus on the detection of deception. Although attorneys are certainly interested in detecting juror deception, they may also be interested in a variety of behaviors unrelated to deception, such as determining whether a juror has preexisting negative attitudes toward a party in the case or identifying the qualities of individuals that may affect the participation role (i.e., leaders, followers, negotiators, etc.) that jurors adopt in the deliberation process. To date there have been almost no published studies done on these issues with a specific focus on jury decision making.

The research that has been conducted outside the context of jury decision-making studies does not suggest particularly encouraging results for attorneys who rely on nonverbal cues without the aid of a jury selection consultant who is expert in evaluating nonverbal behaviors. Most studies find that untrained observers rarely do much better than chance at detecting deception. In the courtroom, it may be even more difficult to detect deception because jurors are more motivated than targets of observation in experimental studies to mask their deception. Prospective jurors may be so concerned with how they are being evaluated by the judge and attorneys that they attempt to guard all their nonverbal behaviors or express consistently neutral behaviors during voir dire questioning. In addition, the level of stress generated by the voir dire experience may be so high that it masks naturally expressed anxiety, making the observed nonverbal behaviors impossible to interpret.

It is possible that jurors may be so concerned about the content of their verbal responses that they will neglect to exert control over their nonverbal behaviors. In addition, nonverbal behavior information may be useful for identifying jury leaders. If an attorney is told by a jury selection consultant that a particular individual is exhibiting behaviors indicative of leadership, and that juror provides verbal responses indicating they are somewhat predisposed to the other side in the case, an attorney might want to use a peremptory challenge to exclude the juror. It is ultimately necessary to conduct more research in this area to get a better indication of whether nonverbal behaviors can be effectively used, and, if so, how to use them most effectively.

8

OVERALL EFFECTIVENESS OF SCIENTIFIC JURY SELECTION

Is scientific jury selection effective? Ultimately, this is the fundamental, relevant question for attorneys and their clients. That is, are attorneys more likely to win cases if they call on jury selection consultants, as opposed to relying on their own hunches? There have been no precise estimates of the effectiveness of the scientific jury selection approach. Unfortunately, selection consultants typically do not publicly report success rates, and the social science literature has relatively few published estimates.[1]

---

[1]Several researchers have noted that the marketplace should be used as a barometer of the effectiveness of jury selection consulting. That is, it can be assumed that scientific jury selection is useful because trial consulting as an industry has grown dramatically in the past 3 decades. As top attorneys routinely employ trial consultants in major litigation and have even gone as far as hiring in-house consultants for their firms, the technique must be reasonably useful (Shartel, 1994; Stolle, Robbennolt, & Wiener, 1996). Although there is some logic to this position, it is important to keep in mind that practices in the marketplace have shifted over the years. In the early years of trial consulting there was a major focus on jury selection, but over time that focus has shifted to an emphasis on assistance related to trial presentation ("Development in the Law," 1997; Strier & Shestowsky, 1999). As a consequence, because trial consultants spend much of their time engaged in other activities (e.g., witness preparation, case theme identification, development of demonstrative aids, etc.), the existence of a booming marketplace by itself is not enough to defend the use of scientific jury selection. More important, the marketplace supports many goods and services that have little value. Thus, reliance on the purchase of these services should not be used to supplant scientific proof of the validity of scientific jury selection.

However, the success rates that have been reported are encouraging for the practice of using social science techniques. Nietzel, Dillehay, and Himelein (1987) reported that in an examination of 18 capital cases in Kentucky, South Carolina, and California, death sentences were returned in 33.3% of the cases on which they served as trial consultants versus 64.7% of the cases they did not work on. Other research reported accuracy rates as high as 70% (Kairys, Schulman, & Harring, 1975; Silver, 1978). The estimates are based on posttrial interviews with selected jurors and those who were challenged and excused from jury service. However, these reports "fail to provide either the size of the data base or, more important, the precise meaning of 70 percent accuracy" (Penrod & Cutler, 1987, p. 297). For example, did the consultants win 7 out of 10 or 700 out of 1,000 cases? Other methodological concerns are also prominent. For example, what is the definition of jury selection success? In a criminal case, is a conviction on a lesser charge enough to be considered a success? Does a hung jury count as a success? Where exactly is the line of effectiveness drawn and why?

In this chapter, we first present a brief discussion of the problems with assessing the effectiveness of scientific jury selection and discuss skepticism that exists in the academic community regarding the utility of this service. Next, we consider a theoretical reason why scientific jury selection may be superior to attorney selection strategies and follow with a critical review of the research assessing the effectiveness of scientific jury selection. We then consider why selection techniques may not work better and how this may be remediated and explore whether minimally improved predictive ability is useful.

PROBLEMS IN ASSESSING SCIENTIFIC JURY SELECTION

In general, the effectiveness of scientific jury selection is a difficult issue to assess. Although there may be a high winning percentage for legal teams that use consulting services, the inherent cost of these services usually limits their use to cases in which clients can afford not only the consultants but also perhaps the best legal representation. As a result, it becomes difficult to tell if success in a given case is due to a jury selection consultant's services, other trial consulting services (e.g., the development and use of computer graphics to aid the attorney's adversarial presentation), or the skills of top-level attorneys and the general resources at their disposal. High-end attorneys usually have large staffs and the financial resources to pay for everything from high-priced expert witnesses to compelling graphic and computer animated displays to use as courtroom exhibits. In addition, attorneys may simply work harder in cases in which jury selection consultants are used, because such cases are in some ways more important than cases in which consultants are not used.

Although consultants and their clients may be confident in the effec-tiveness of scientific jury selection, there is far less confidence in the aca-demic community (Moran, Cutler, & De Lisa, 1994). Academic researchers have argued that demographic and attitudinal variables are poor predictors of verdicts (Berman & Sales, 1977; Diamond, 1990; Hastie, 1991; MacCoun, 1989, 1993), thereby casting doubt on the effectiveness of scientific jury se-lection. For example, Vidmar (1999) maintained that "[t]here is little or no evidence that in-court selection of jurors by jury consultants has any validity or reliability, particularly if the criterion is marginal accuracy over an experi-enced trial lawyer" (p. 268). Further, MacCoun (1989) argued that

> a large body of empirical research calls into question the premise that jurors' votes during deliberation can be reliably predicted from juror char-acteristics that are observable before the trial. In general, jurors' demo-graphic attributes, personality traits, and general attitudes are associated weakly and unreliably with jurors' verdicts. (p. 1048)

This can cast doubt on "the efficacy of both traditional and scientific jury selection strategies" (MacCoun, 1993, p. 151).

However, MacCoun (1993) also cited data that, to some degree, sup-ports the importance of background factors. He noted that plaintiffs' victory rates vary among jurisdictions, with some locations, such as Bronx County, New York, being particularly plaintiff prone (citing research by Daniels, 1991). Daniels found that from 1981 to 1985 there was a plaintiff success rate in medical malpractice cases of 58% in the Bronx, compared with an average rate of 32.4% across a national sample of 46 cities. Daniels argued that this trend may be a function of socioeconomic conditions (e.g., wealth, area popu-lation growth, and an "urban" dimension consisting of such factors as a population's age, racial composition, and population density) or of environ-mental factors (availability of health care in the area, and legal reforms such as arbitration provisions and limits on noneconomic damages). A model con-taining these factors accounted for about one third of the variance in ver-dicts, with wealth found to be the most important predictor. It is possible that more variance could have been accounted for if relevant attitudinal factors had been measured, but this was not done. Thus, Daniels provided an indication that background factors have some predictive power.

Further, Moran et al. (1994) noted that there has been a shift from the view held during the 1970s that attitudes are unrelated to behavior, and that much of the research that indicates a weak relationship between predictor variables has used jury simulation studies rather than examining the behav-ior of real jurors and real verdicts. In addition, Moran et al. argued that scien-tific jury selection does improve the predictability of verdicts, particularly when the evidence in a case is equivocal (see the "Evidence Strength" sec-tion later in this chapter) and when case specific attitudes are assessed.

A THEORETICAL REASON WHY SCIENTIFIC JURY SELECTION MAY BE SUPERIOR TO ATTORNEY SELECTION STRATEGIES

There may be a solid theoretical reason to expect superior results from scientific jury selection methods, compared with attorneys relying on their gut-level hunches. An attorney choosing to rely on his or her own experience when challenging jurors in voir dire, as opposed to using a scientific jury selection approach, is quite similar to the distinction between clinical and actuarial based assessments (Grove & Meehl, 1996; Saks, 1976). For example, expert witnesses may be called on to inform a court of their prediction regarding the likelihood that a defendant charged with murder or a sexual offense will continue to pose a threat to the community. The expert may testify after interviewing the defendant that in her or his opinion based on experience, the defendant may or may not be a high risk to reoffend. Such a prediction based on personal experience is known as *clinical decision making*. Alternatively, the expert may use an assessment tool that measures the presence of a variety of risk factors and has been validated on individuals who have committed similar crimes. This approach is referred to as *actuarial decision making*. It has long been demonstrated that judgments based on a clinician's experiences are, in many cases, less accurate at predicting future behavior than those based on statistically oriented judgments using validated assessment tools (Krauss, Lieberman, & Olson, 2004; Krauss & Sales, 2001; Meehl, 1954; Saks, 1976). When individuals rely on personal experience they tend to make a number of errors in judgment, such as ignoring base rate information, or being overly influenced by heuristics (Kahneman & Tversky, 1982; Tversky & Kahneman, 1974), such as the representativeness heuristic (i.e., overestimating the likelihood of something because it matches a particular mental prototype, such as believing that a person who has a short haircut is conservative and therefore conviction prone). As statistically based assessment tools and judgments have been shown to be equal or superior to reliance on personal experience, one would expect scientific jury selection to be a superior approach.

RESEARCH ASSESSING THE EFFECTIVENESS OF SCIENTIFIC JURY SELECTION

What does the empirical research assessing the effectiveness of scientific jury selection indicate? The initial published research on the effectiveness of scientific jury selection was limited because the work was more qualitative in nature and reported the results of particular trials in which scientific jury selection was used. For example, to assess the effectiveness of the scientific jury selection procedure that Schulman and his colleagues developed (Schulman, Shaver, Coleman, Emrich, & Christie, 1973), they compared the verdicts of the actual jurors who decided the case with the verdict prefer-ences of potential jurors who were excused during voir dire and jury eligible community members who did not go through jury selection. Such compari-sons are not terribly meaningful, because the groups differ not only in the fact that they either were or were not selected with use of scientific jury selection but also that only the actual jurors were exposed to trial evidence and the lawyers' arguments.

However, other studies have attempted to more directly examine the effectiveness of scientific jury selection. Zeisel and Diamond (1976) provided a detailed report of the Mitchell–Stans conspiracy trial, in which scientific jury selection was used. John Mitchell, then United States Attorney General under President Nixon, and Maurice Stans, Secretary of Commerce in the first Nixon cabinet and finance chairman for the Committee for the Reelec-tion of President Nixon, were charged with conspiring to impede a Securities and Exchange Commission investigation of a financier, Robert Vesco, in return for a $200,000 contribution to President Nixon's reelection campaign. In that trial, the defense team used a scientific community survey to deter-mine profiles of ideal and undesirable jurors. The defendants were acquitted, which implies that the use of social science data in jury selection was success-ful, particularly because when the jury began deliberations they were initially split, with eight jurors voting for conviction and only four voting for acquittal. The fact that the defense ultimately prevailed despite this initial split is rather remarkable. Previous research demonstrated that in an overwhelming percent-age of cases, if there is an initial minority and majority verdict split, the posi-tion held by the majority is almost always the final verdict. In less than 5% of cases is the minority able to sway the majority members to their verdict opin-ion (Kalven & Zeisel, 1966; Zeisel & Diamond, 1976).

Despite the optimistic findings of the case studies regarding the success of scientific jury selection, it is impossible to definitively determine the ef-fectiveness of this approach because no true comparison can be made be-tween scientific and traditional approaches to jury selection. A true experi-mental comparison would require that two actual juries decide a case, one picked by intuition and the other by scientific jury selection. Both would be exposed to the same evidence, and both would render binding verdicts with a defendant's fate at stake. However, a trial cannot be conducted a second time with both juries rendering a binding decision.

Horowitz (1980) attempted to overcome the practical limitations of measuring the success of scientific jury selection by using a simulated test. Law students were assigned to a scientific jury selection condition and trained in the fundamentals of this approach. They were then given a variety of statistically oriented information based on pretrial surveys conducted on the population from which a venire for the study was drawn and from the venire itself. The law student participants were also given profiles of jurors, ranging from "most friendly" to "least friendly" jurors. In the other group, law students were trained in the conventional method; that is, they were trained to select jurors by observing actual local attorneys conducting voir dire using nonscientific methods. Overall, the results indicated that the social scientific method was not superior to the conventional method. Rather, the strength of each method largely depended on the type of case. The social scientific method was more accurate at predicting juror verdicts in cases in which there was a strong relationship among the personality, demographic, and attitudinal variables used in this approach. In cases in which the relationship among these factors was weak, the conventional approach worked better.

Of course, as with all experimental studies, there are validity concerns associated with this comparison of jury selection techniques; most notable, the experience of the "lawyers" in this study. These law students had neither the courtroom experience of actual attorneys nor the methodological and statistical background of social scientists and competent jury selection consultants. However, even with this caveat in mind, Horowitz's (1980) conclusion that the effectiveness of scientific jury selection is dependent on the type of case seems reasonable. In certain cases (e.g., sales of illegal drugs), personal attitudes and experiences may exert a stronger effect on verdict decisions. This possibility is in accordance with research on jury nullification that indicates in certain types of trials (e.g., euthanasia, gambling, avoiding the military draft), jurors rely on their own beliefs rather than the written letter of the law when making verdict decisions (Lieberman & Sales, 1997).

Horowitz (1980) also noted that although the social science method was not a more effective approach across all cases in his study, the power of this method is in its potential ability to predict verdict predispositions on the basis of minimal juror information. As the scope of voir dire questioning is expanded and more information about the jurors is made available to attorneys, the differences in effectiveness between these approaches should be minimized. Thus, in cases of limited voir dire, especially those in which the judge does the questioning and attorneys are not able to ask questions they feel are important, scientific jury selection should provide a more reliable basis for making peremptory challenge decisions.

Frederick (1984) reported the results of several rating systems used by jury selection consultants in a criminal and civil trial. In the first trial, scientific jury selection techniques were used by the defense. The consultants conducted a community survey of 952 residents from the community where the trial was to be held. A factor analysis of the survey results led to the identification of 14 key items. These items were made into a scale that prospective jurors were questioned on in court. In addition, the consultants made in-court ratings of authoritarianism and nonverbal behavior of jurors. An analysis of the characteristics of the initial jury pool indicated that the group was generally unfavorable for the defense as it was relatively authoritarian (a trait that was viewed to be unfavorable for the defense), expressed negative attitudes on the survey, and exhibited generally unfavorable nonverbal behavior to the defense. A comparison of excluded jurors with those retained as actual jurors and alternates indicated that the jurors who were not excluded were more favorably predisposed to the defense than those who were excluded.

An examination of the correlations among the juror rating measures used by the consultants in the case provides some degree of validation for the techniques. Authoritarianism was significantly correlated with in-court survey ratings, as low authoritarians expressed more favorable survey responses for the defense. In addition, there was a significant correlation between authoritarianism and nonverbal behavior, with those rated less authoritarian likely to exhibit more favorable nonverbal behavior for the defendant. The relationship between in-court survey responses and nonverbal behavior was not significant. A posttrial interview (see chap. 9) of the actual jurors and alternates indicated that in-court survey responses and ratings of authoritarianism also predicted responses to the original questionnaire given to community members, providing some additional validation of these techniques.

The jury's verdict in the trial was unanimous for acquittal on the first ballot, and the lack of variation among juror verdict preferences makes it impossible to directly assess the relationship between juror ratings and behavior. However, this limitation was overcome to some extent in an additional case reported by Frederick (1984) in which scientific jury selection techniques were used. In the second study, a community survey and mock jury trial (see chap. 9) were held in preparation for a civil case. A factor analysis of the community survey led to the identification of several critical items regarding attitudes toward the case that were developed into a scale used to identify the verdict preferences of mock jurors. The results indicated that it was possible to identify mock jurors as either proplaintiff or prodefense on the basis of responses to survey items and that these classifications correctly predicted the verdict preferences in a majority of jurors. Eighty-six percent of mock jurors classified as prodefense found for the defendant, and 71% of those classified as proplaintiff rendered verdicts for the plaintiff. Unfortunately, the case settled the day before trial was set to begin, so Frederick was not able to provide any validating data from jurors exposed to actual trial evidence.

Although the results of the studies reported by Frederick (1984) provide support for scientific jury selection techniques, the studies are limited to some extent by the small samples used in each case. For example, in the first study only 13 jurors completed posttrial interviews. In addition, in the second study nonverbal behaviors were not measured, and the data was based on mock juror responses rather than on responses by actual jurors who were likely to be exposed to complex civil litigation.

Finally, Tindale and Nagao (1986) evaluated the potential utility of scientific jury selection using computer modeling. Attempting to mathematically explore the influence of scientific jury selection on obtaining changes in venue and selecting jurors, they created data using different potential assumptions (e.g., the likelihood of picking an unbiased juror being 20% or 30%, etc.) to estimate success. Their model showed that the successful use of scientific jury selection for obtaining a change of venue would have a strong effect on trial outcomes. Further, they also reported that when they assumed that scientific jury selection was only moderately successful at identifying biased jurors (i.e., assuming a hypothesized increase in the likelihood of selecting a juror from an unbiased population increased from 20%–50%), an increase in approximately 11% of not guilty verdicts occurred.

It is difficult to make much of these results because the findings are based on multiple assumptions about the circumstances in which scientific jury selection would be used. For example, assumptions were made regarding the distribution of verdict predisposition or that scientific jury selection would only be used by the defense. Thus, Tindale and Nagao (1986) cautioned that the results only indicate that there is potential for scientific jury selection to be useful and that "no conclusions should be drawn from these results as to whether [scientific jury selection] should or should not be used" (p. 423).

Thus, on the basis of the few existing studies that directly assess the utility of scientific jury selection, it appears that this approach may be useful. However, more simulated studies assessing its effectiveness are clearly needed.

Perhaps the pragmatic difficulty of conducting direct research on scientific jury selection has led most researchers to research the effects of specific variables likely to be used in scientific jury selection. As the research discussed in chapters 4 and 5 about the influence of demographic and personality factors indicated, these variables contribute a minimal amount of variance (usually less than 10%–15%). However, the predictive value of these characteristics increases when more case specific case relevant attitudes are measured. For example, Moran et al. (1994) argued that scientific jury selection is superior to clinical judgments during voir dire. As support for this assertion, they presented the results of four studies that measured the specific legally oriented personality characteristic of attitudes toward tort reform and found a significant relationship between this personality characteristic and perceptions of defendant culpability in criminal cases and support for defendants in a civil case. However, a number of methodological limitations are associated with this study and need to be considered before accepting its conclusions. Most notable, in all four studies participants were given brief summaries of cases (i.e., typically six or seven statements, and in one case just a two-sentence scenario) and asked to indicate their verdict preference in those cases before indicating their attitude toward tort reform. The results are certainly a good indication that jurors may hold personality characteristics related to pretrial biases. However, it cannot be determined if these biases would have affected the outcome of actual cases. Participants did not undergo voir dire, were not presented with an actual trial, and were not given an opportunity to deliberate.

Similar limitations exist with many other studies reported in this book. These studies often use artificial scenarios, rely on small sample size or low response rates, or ignore other legal realities such as allowing deliberation or using representative jurors (Diamond, 1997; Penrod & Linz, 1986). Hans and Vidmar (1982) argued that one limitation of many jury simulation studies is that the studies have not included judicial admonishments to jurors to set aside biases they may hold and render a verdict based only on the evidence that has been presented to them. Such instructions are always given in real trials. However, research in the area of pretrial publicity and inadmissible evidence in general indicates such admonitions are largely ineffective (Lieberman & Arndt, 2000). Thus, we would expect that if demographic, personality, attitudinal, or experiential factors produce pretrial biases, these biases would remain despite any judicial admonitions.

WHY SCIENTIFIC JURY SELECTION TECHNIQUES MAY NOT WORK BETTER

On the basis of research previously cited in this book, it appears that attitudes and background factors are not strong predictors of verdicts, often accounting for less than 15% of verdict variance. Thus, a scientific jury selection approach based on these factors may have some, but not overwhelming, utility. The question we may then pose is, why don't these techniques offer greater predictive accuracy? There are a number of reasons why predictive accuracy may be low, including: sampling limitations, a generally weak relationship between attitudes and behavior, insufficient information obtained during voir dire to make useful predictions, evidence strength, general validity and reliability problems with scientific jury selection, and uncertainty about how to systematically combine the sources of information gathered during scientific jury selection to reach a selection decision.

Sampling Issues

Scientific jury selection is largely based on the application of community surveys. These surveys must initially be administered in an appropriate manner for the results to have useful predictive ability. However, a number of problems arise when applying findings obtained through survey research. First, there may be a substantial difference between the characteristics of the population of interest (individuals in the local community who are registered voters or on other lists from which the venire is drawn) and the population of venire people, which the results are applied to. Although the venire should initially match the characteristics of the population, individuals who argue that serving on a jury would create an undue hardship on their jobs or home life are often excused from jury service. In addition, many jurisdictions still exclude members of certain occupations almost automatically, including judicial officers, public officials, police officers, and physically disabled individuals (Bureau of Justice Statistics, 1998). Thus, the remaining population may be substantially different from the initial population that was summoned to the courthouse. Care must be taken to limit such differences during the construction of the sample and in generalizing the findings (Berman & Sales, 1977). In addition, the sample must be of adequate size to allow for greater precision in the prediction of true population responses (Arnold & Gold, 1978–1979).

Relationship Between Attitudes and Behavior

If an individual possesses background characteristics that are related to case-relevant attitudes favorable to the defense in a criminal trial and that individual is not excluded during voir dire, will that translate to a vote for acquittal from that juror? The attitude–behavior connection has long been a major focus of study in the social sciences, particularly in social psychology. Initially, it was generally believed that only a modest relationship between the two existed, and researchers concluded that in most cases, expressed attitudes account for about 10% of the variation in behavior (e.g., Calder & Ross, 1973; McGuire, 1985; Wicker, 1969).

However, a more recent meta-analysis of 88 attitude–behavior studies indicated that attitudes are a substantial predictor of future behavior (Kraus, 1995). Over half the studies analyzed by Kraus had attitude–behavior correlations above .30, with 25% above .50. A number of factors affect the strength of the relationship between attitudes and behavior, including: the level of attitude specificity assessed; the stability, certainty, affective–cognitive consistency, direct experience, and accessibility of the attitude; personality characteristics of the target; and situational demands impinging on the target.

Level of Specificity

General attitudes have been shown to be poor predictors of *specific* behaviors (Ajzen & Fishbein, 1977; Fishbein & Ajzen, 1975). For example, asking participants about their attitude toward scientific research does little to predict whether they will participate in a particular psychology experiment (Wicker & Pomazal, 1971). However, the attitude–behavior correlation can be greatly magnified by increasing the level of specificity of the assessed attitude. Davidson and Jaccard (1979) demonstrated the importance of specificity in a study in which they attempted to predict self-reported use of birth control pills by women, 2 years after assessing attitudes on the subject. Women were asked their attitude toward birth control in one of four ways: their attitude toward *birth control*; their attitude toward *birth control pills*; their attitude toward *using* birth control pills; or their attitude toward *using* birth control pills in the *next 2 years*. As the question measuring the attitude became more specific, the attitude–behavior correlation became stronger (*r*s = .08, .32, .52, .57, respectively).

Thus, questions should be as specific as the behavior one is trying to predict. For example, an attorney interested in whether a particular juror would be willing to render a death sentence in a trial held in a state where electrocution was the means of execution should assess an attitude as precise as that behavior. Although an individual may have a positive attitude toward the use of the death penalty in general, he or she may be unwilling to impose the death penalty in a particular case. That may be especially true if the method of execution is one the juror has reservations about, such as the electric chair. The questions "What is your attitude toward the death penalty?" or "Are you willing to impose the death penalty?" will likely not predict behavior as accurately as more specific inquiries. Actual behavior might be better predicted if respondents in either a community survey or during voir dire were asked, "Would you be willing to sentence the defendant to die by electrocution?" The correlation between attitudes and behaviors tends to be quite high (typically above .50) when they are measured at corresponding levels of specificity (Kraus, 1995).

Thus, attitudes toward specific case factors can predict verdict inclination (see chap. 5). For example, verdicts in a criminal case involving a lawyer charged with drug-related crimes were best predicted by attitudes toward attorneys and drugs (Moran, Cutler, & Loftus, 1990, Study 1). In addition, in a case involving drug trafficking, attitudes toward drugs were a key verdict predictor (Moran et al., 1990, Study 2). In both the lawyer and drug trafficking trials, case-specific attitudes were superior to demographic factors at predicting verdict inclination. In a similar way, attitudes toward psychiatrists and the insanity defense were predictive of mock juror verdicts in insanity cases (Cutler, Moran, & Narby, 1992). Mock jurors who agreed with myths about battered women were more likely to convict a defendant with a history of being battered who eventually killed her husband (Vidmar & Schuller, 1989). Within the domain of civil trials, it has been shown that attitudes toward tort reform are strong predictors of verdict (Caiola & Berman as cited in Cutler et al., 1992; Goodman, Loftus, & Greene, 1990; Moran et al., 1994). Further, in a meta-analysis, Narby, Cutler, and Moran (1993) demonstrated that within the domain of authoritarianism, a more specific measure of legal authoritarianism was more strongly related to verdicts (*r* = .19) than was traditional authoritarianism (*r* = .11).

Moran et al. (1994) argued that "studies cited as evidence against [scientific jury selection] did not employ case-specific attitudes" (p. 313). However, not all case-specific attitudes appear to be good predictors of behavior. For example, Narby and Cutler (1994) found that attitudes toward eyewitnesses were not good predictors of verdict preferences. Eyewitness confidence, however, was a significant predictor. Further, factors such as the stability and certainty of the attitudes, and the history of how attitudes develop (i.e., whether it is a result of direct experience), will affect the predictive utility of attitudes. In addition, limitations placed on voir dire may prevent attorneys from asking questions in sufficient depth to be able to identify case-specific attitudes.

Stability and Certainty

Attitudes that are stable over time predict behavior better than attitudes that are less stable (Davidson & Jaccard, 1979; Schwartz, 1978). Thus, it may be useful to ascertain how long individuals have held their attitudes (e.g., has a relevant case attitude changed as the result of information heard recently in the news or has it existed for a long time?). In addition, the level of certainty of an attitude has been shown to moderate the predictive power of that attitude. In two studies reviewed in Kraus's (1995) meta-analysis (Sample & Warland, 1973; Warland & Sample, 1973), expressed attitudes toward voting in a student election were significant predictors of actual voting behavior only when respondents also reported that they were certain about their attitudes.

Direct Experience

Several studies have shown that attitudes that are produced by direct experience are stronger than other types of attitudes (Fazio & Zanna, 1981; Regan & Fazio, 1977). Direct experience may produce more influential attitudes because the experience creates a clearly defined attitude that individuals are more certain of. In an alternate way, direct experience may make attitudes more accessible from memory (Fazio, 1986). In addition, an attitude based on repeated experiences will be a better predictor of behavior than attitudes based on minimal experience (Fazio & Zanna, 1981). Thus, attorneys should be cautious about putting much faith in attitudes based on limited experience when making voir dire judgments.

Accessibility

Accessibility refers to how likely it is that an attitude will come to mind after an individual encounters the target of that attitude. This issue has been measured by using the time it takes to respond to a question regarding that attitude. The faster the reaction time of expressing an attitude following an inquiry, the stronger the relationship between the attitude and the expressed behavior (Kraus, 1995). Reaction time for key attitudinal questions could be measured relatively easily in both telephone surveys or during voir dire. Starr and McCormick (2000) have suggested that one way to increase attitude accessibility is for the attorneys during voir dire to repeatedly make references to jurors' attitudes that are favorable to the attorney's side, in an effort to make those attitudes more salient and accessible to jurors.

Self-Awareness

Self-awareness (Duval & Wicklund, 1972) refers to a state of heightened self-consciousness during which attention is focused on oneself. When self-awareness is increased, individuals are more influenced by their own dispositions and attitudes, and behavior becomes more consistent with these values. For example, people are more likely to steal (Beaman, Klentz, Diener, & Svanum, 1979) and cheat (Vallacher & Solodky, 1979) when self-awareness is low. Self-awareness can be enhanced through a variety of methods, such as having people perform an act in front of an audience, video camera, or mirror (Carver & Scheier, 1978, 1981; Duval, Duval, & Mulilis, 1992; Duval & Wicklund, 1972; Hass & Eisenstadt, 1990; Wicklund, 1975; Wicklund & Frey, 1980). Although this may seem of little relevance to the courtroom because it is unlikely that a deliberation room will be encased in mirrors or that an attorney will hold up a looking glass during closing arguments, jurors may be required to sit on cases in which cameras are allowed in the courtroom. Courts typically take steps to prevent the identity of jurors from being revealed in these cases, but the presence of a camera (whether or not it is pointed at a juror) may still be sufficient to heighten self-awareness (Orive, 1984). Even without cameras present, attorneys might try to capitalize on the effects of increased self-awareness by crafting the language of closing statements to remind jurors not to forget who they are (e.g., remind them to consider their own attitudes and values). This may be especially important to counter the possible effects of deindividuation in the deliberation room.

Deindividuation occurs when a person experiences a loss of self-awareness. It is produced in group situations that foster anonymity and draw attention away from the individual. Deindividuated people are less likely to act in ways commensurate with their values, less restrained, less sensitive to long-term consequences, and more responsive to situational demands (Diener, 1980). Deindividuation is typically produced when people are in a highly stimulating environment (e.g., being at a rock concert or sporting event), are physically anonymous (e.g., by wearing masks or uniforms), or have consumed alcohol. However, certain characteristics of courtroom procedures may enhance a juror's sense of deindividuation and reduce self-awareness, such as when the anonymity of a juror is emphasized. Jurors who are told their identities will remain anonymous have been shown to be more conviction prone than nonanonymous jurors (Hazlewood & Brigham, 1998).

Self-Monitoring and Need for Structure

Numerous studies have investigated the personality trait of self-monitoring (Snyder, 1987). *Self-monitoring* refers to the tendency of individuals to adjust their behavior to the reactions of others and the demands of the social situation. High self-monitors are quite concerned with managing their self-presentation and act like social chameleons. As a consequence, the behavior of high self-monitors is driven far more by the expectations of others than by their internal attitudes. Low self-monitors behave in ways more consistent with their attitudes.

The construct of self-monitoring can be measured with a self-monitoring scale (Snyder & Gangestad, 1986). Agreement with items such as "In a different situation and with different people, I often act like a very different person" indicates high self-monitoring, whereas low self-monitoring is exhibited by agreement with items such as "I can only argue for ideas that I already believe." Kraus (1995) reported that the average attitude–behavior correlation for low self-monitors was .50; for high self-monitors, it was .25.

Self-monitoring effects have been examined in several mock jury studies conducted by Jamieson and Zanna (1989). It is interesting to note that the correlation between attitudes and behavior among low self-monitors was enhanced when mock jurors were under time pressure. For example, in one study individuals classified as either low or high self-monitors rendered verdicts in a premeditated murder case, in which the evidence was largely circumstantial. Participants also indicated their attitudes toward capital punishment. Half the participants were asked to read over the case materials and render verdicts quickly, and half of the participants were not placed under any time pressure. Attitudes toward capital punishment were much better predictors of verdicts ($r = .69$) for low self-monitors under time pressure than for any other group of participants ($rs < .14$). Jamieson and Zanna attribute this finding to individuals relying on attitudes more when a "need for structure" had been aroused.

A need for structure (Kruglanski & Freund, 1983) represents a desire for clear and unambiguous information to guide behavior. A heightened need for structure motivates a person to halt or "freeze" the process of acquiring knowledge and to rely on existing information (often in the form of preexisting beliefs such as stereotypes). Although time pressure has been repeatedly shown to increase need for structure, it may be difficult, if not impossible, for an attorney to manipulate this factor in a courtroom. However, an individual's need for structure is likely to also be aroused when he or she is faced with a variety of cognitive demands (Gilbert & Hixon, 1991). For example, when subjects are faced with what they perceive to be complex judgments, they are more likely to use stereotypes to simplify the task, resulting in differential judgments based on stereotypes. However, when subjects perform what they think will be a simple task, stereotypes are not used (Bodenhausen & Lichtenstein, 1987). The implication of this finding is that when participants face a long or difficult trial, they may be more likely to rely on preexisting attitudes to guide their behaviors.

Affective–Cognitive Consistency

Attitudes are better predictors of behavior when there is greater affective–cognitive consistency of the behavior. Attitudes are often described as having three components: thoughts, feelings, and behavior (Myers, 1999). For example, negative attitudes toward a minority group could be expressed by pejorative beliefs about the group, such as "prisons are filled with people of that minority group"; feelings, such as "I don't like members of that group"; and behaviors, such as "I won't sell my house to members of that group." Of course, from a jury selection consultant's point of view the goal is to predict the behavioral component of attitudes from the affective (feelings) or cognitive (thoughts) dimensions. When there is consistency between these latter two dimensions, it is considered a good indicator of a stronger attitude (Miller & Tessler, 1989; Rosenberg, 1960). As a consequence, in conducting any type of survey or voir dire questioning, a jury selection consultant or attorney should ask about multiple dimensions of attitudes. For example, an attorney concerned about potential jurors' negative attitudes toward Muslims should be skeptical of an individual who indicated that he or she liked Muslims or has friends who are Muslim but held stereotypic beliefs, such as that Islam is a violent religion or Muslims value life less than other people.

Conclusion Regarding the Relationship of Attitudes and Behavior

A variety of social psychological factors influence the strength of the relationship between attitudes and behavior. If scientific jury selection is used to identify demographic characteristics that are associated with personality factors and case relevant attitudes, it is important that lawyers attempt to maximize the influence of attitudes on behavior by using some of the techniques described in this section. Consultants who have a strong social psychology background may be able to assist attorneys by helping them tailor their presentation to capitalize on these strategies.

Jurors Not Responding Honestly or at All

As noted in chapter 6, in most cases jurors are questioned in a group setting, rather than privately. As a result, jurors may feel pressure to provide socially desirable responses, distorting their true attitudes about certain issues (Diamond, 1990). The demographic profiles of desirable and undesirable jurors, based on pretrial research provided by jury selection consultants, can provide attorneys with needed information on the types of jurors that should be questioned in greater detail, particularly when those jurors provide socially desirable answers. Hence, the ability to uncover deception during voir dire may be a valuable component of scientific jury selection.

An alternative problem to jurors misrepresenting their attitudes and experiences during voir dire questioning is jurors simply failing to respond to questions during voir dire. That is, if voir dire is conducted by questioning prospective jurors in groups and jurors respond by raising their hands, jurors may simply remain silent during questioning. Attorneys and judges may be inclined to follow up with individual questioning of jurors who have responded affirmatively to questions, but it is difficult to know what to make of jurors who have not responded to any of the questions. Mize (2003), a judge on the District of Columbia Superior Court, recommended questioning silent jurors outside the presence of the other jurors, so that all jurors are ultimately questioned individually. Although this process takes more time, Mize maintained that it is more effective at discovering biases. In private questioning, 28% of silent jurors in criminal and civil cases revealed information that they were unwilling to admit to in open court; this led to a number of jurors being struck by challenges for cause. Thus, there may be a serious need to question silent jurors. However, if a judge is unwilling to spend the time further interviewing unresponsive jurors, consultants may be useful at identifying potential biases in jurors. As previously mentioned, pretrial surveys may be useful at developing profiles of jurors likely to hold case relevant biases. In addition, as discussed in chapter 7, there is potential that the body language of jurors may reveal hidden biases.

Evidence Strength

As already noted, the general conclusion of the research is that juror characteristics exert less effect on jury verdicts than the strength of the evidence. Support for this conclusion has been obtained in a number of studies that specifically examined evidentiary factors. For example, Hepburn (1980) examined the influence of demographic, attitudinal, and case-specific evidentiary factors on juror decisions, using a sample of 305 individuals selected from a list of jury eligible registered voters in St. Louis, Missouri. Home interviews were conducted with these respondents in which characteristics and experiences of the respondents were obtained. The respondents were also given a case summary regarding an actual murder trial. Hepburn found that demographic and attitudinal factors had almost no predictive ability for jury verdicts. However, perceptions of the strength of the prosecution's evidence and the defense's evidence were strongly correlated with verdicts (rs = .45 and –.66, respectively). In addition, Saks (1976) reported the results of previous research by Saks, Werner, and Ostrom (no citation given) in which the strength of evidence was shown to be seven times more powerful than juror attitudes at predicting verdicts.

Kaplan and Miller (1978) conducted a mock jury experiment in which participants were classified on a trait basis as being either harsh or lenient toward the punishment of criminals. In addition, Kaplan and Miller manipulated the reliability of evidence presented to jurors. The results of their study indicated that individuals who advocated harsh treatment for offenders were more conviction prone when evidence against a defendant was described as unreliable or when no information was given about the reliability of evidence. However, when evidence was described as reliable, there was no significant difference between the verdicts of jurors classified as harsh or lenient, providing further support for the conclusion that evidence strength is far more important than individual differences among jurors.

Evidence strength effects are not limited to simulated studies. Visher (1987) interviewed 331 jurors who had served on 38 sexual assault trials regarding their background characteristics (sex, race, age, education, and occupation); attitudes toward being "tough on crime" and "blaming the victim"; attitudes toward the defendant (e.g., appearance, education, prior record) and victim characteristics (e.g., use of alcohol or drugs before incident, sexual activity outside marriage); and evidence and case characteristics (e.g., use of a weapon, physical evidence, use of force, eyewitness testimony). Visher found that strength of evidence (particularly use of a weapon, physical evidence, and evidence of force) was a much stronger predictor of verdict variance (accounting for 34% of the variance) than victim and defendant characteristics (8% variance accounted for) and juror characteristics (2%). None of the juror demographic factors analyzed by Visher had a significant effect on verdict decisions. The "tough-on-crime" attitude measure was predictive of verdicts, but as noted previously, this factor barely increased the verdict variance accounted for.

Fulero and Penrod (1990) argued that the relative influence of the factors investigated in Visher's (1987) study may have been influenced by the way the data was analyzed (in a multiple regression). It is possible that preexisting differences in the jurors' backgrounds affected their perceptions of evidence, and that juror characteristics would exert a stronger influence on verdict if analyzed in the first step of a regression rather than the last. However, as mentioned previously, other research has supported Visher's findings. It should also be noted that the type of case used in Visher's research (sexual assault) allowed for a particularly stringent test of the strength of evidentiary and juror characteristic factors, because such cases are more likely to be emotionally charged when extra-legal factors may play a larger role (Visher, 1987).

Thus, it appears that scientific jury selection does not work in all cases (Diamond, 1990; Moran et al., 1994), including cases in which the weight of the evidence is so strong (or weak) that a particular verdict is almost certain:

> In some cases, a jury consultant may even be less accurate than the trial attorney operating without consultant advice. Statistical prediction is usually, but not always, more accurate than clinical prediction. . . . The trial attorney knows the evidence in the case, both on the client's and on the opposition's side, better than does the consultant. In addition, the attorney operating in a familiar court may be able to use the incidental information that emerges during voir dire (e.g., the strike at a local business where a prospective juror is employed). The attorney can eliminate some hostile jurors without expert advice. . . . Accordingly, the attorney should accept advice from a survey formula for jury selection only when provided with hard evidence that the advice offers the genuine prospect of improved prediction. (Diamond, 1990, p. 181)

General Validity and Reliability Problems

One problem with scientific jury selection is that research is often carried out in the absence of theory. Significant predictors may be identified, but in the absence of theoretical reasons why they should affect verdict, it is difficult to understand why some factors are likely to influence decision making. Despite this, valid surveys of the community and statistical analyses of the results will reveal effects that do not occur by chance. Traditionally, significance levels are set at the .05 level, meaning that there is only 1 chance in 20 that these findings would occur if the relationship between the variables (e.g., between religion and verdict) was not true. The stronger the effect, the more likely it is to surpass the significance level. Weak effects, which may be due to oddities of sampling (i.e., several atypical respondents in the sample) are identified and removed from the model that predicts verdicts. Significance levels work well in scientific research because they assure that the vast majority of relationships identified will be true. But this is most true when theory-guided research is conducted and a limited number of theoretically determined variables are examined.

An alternative research approach is to conduct exploratory research, in which many variables are examined to determine which relationships emerge. Scientific jury selection tends to adopt this latter approach, in which the consultant may examine the influence of a wide variety of variables. It is unfortunate that with the more variables that are examined, the greater the likelihood of factors emerging by chance. At the .05 level, chance would cause 1 variable in 20 to emerge as significant. Two variables should emerge as significant by chance alone if 40 variables were examined, and so on. As a consequence, if a consultant identifies a couple of variables as significant predictors, the attorney should cautiously note how many factors were originally examined.

Another problem that can affect scientific jury selection is a lack of reliability in survey responses. Reliability refers to whether respondents would provide consistent responses if additional related (or identical) measurements were taken. There are several techniques that researchers can use to help ensure the reliability of the survey. The *alternate forms reliability check* refers to the use of slightly different forms of the same instrument to determine if the responses are similar. For example, a jury selection consultant might measure attitudes in slightly different ways and compare responses. The *split-half reliability check*, in which related items on a measure are split into two groups and compared, can also be used. Further, if a questionnaire contains multiple items to measure a single concept, such as multiple questions regarding attitudes toward tort reform, responses to those measures should be related to each other.

In some cases, attorneys may want information about how prospective jurors would respond to specific opening and closing arguments. If the attorney wants the consultant to provide this additional service and the consultant chooses to use a mock jury (see chap. 9) in addition to the broad community survey, the criterion validity of a measure can be assessed. Criterion validity refers to whether a measure has high predictive value. Thus, on the basis of responses to a pretrial survey, a consultant should be able to predict the behavior of mock jurors shown a more extensive summary of the evidence (for an example of a mock jury validation of survey data in an actual case, see Frederick, 1984).

It is important in the long term for jury selection consultants to provide validation for their methodology, because there is reason to believe that verdict prediction in actual cases will be even worse than the results of mock jury studies discussed in this book (which typically show less than 10%–15% of verdict variance accounted for by demographic and personality factors) because of situational factors associated with voir dire. When empirical research studies are conducted, investigators have the luxury of including entire scales to measure concepts such as authoritarianism, locus of control, and just world beliefs, or extensive questions regarding topics such as tort reform or death penalty sentiments. However, judges will often limit voir dire questions to those that appear clearly relevant to a case and to conform to a preset time limit. Similar restrictions apply to the use of in-court questionnaires. For example, although attitudes toward the death penalty indicate conviction proneness in general, the judge will likely prohibit death penalty related questions in all but trials where capital punishment is an option. In addition, even when judges are willing to ask additional questions submitted by the attorney, the judge may reword them, reducing their predictive ability (Diamond, 1990). The result is that jury selection consultants may be forced to use measures whose psychometric properties have never been validated and techniques that have not been standardized (Kovera et al., 2003; Lecci, Snowden, & Morris, 2004).

Combining the Information

At some point between the conclusion of voir dire questioning and the exercise of peremptory challenges, consultants and attorneys must work together to combine all of the available information to rank order prospective jurors in terms of desirability. When information is combined, a more complete picture of prospective jurors should be available. For example, in the trial of Joan Little, a woman accused of murdering a jailer while she was in custody, McConahay, Mullin, and Frederick (1977; see also Frederick, 1984) measured levels of anxiety expressed by prospective jurors using five variables (body orientation, body posture, body movement, hand movement, and eye contact) and two paralinguistic measures (vocal intonation and vocal hesitancy). These factors were observed during voir dire by multiple raters, and the ratings of each observer were combined to form a final rating indicating the juror's attitudes toward the defense. The ratings were then correlated with scores on an authoritarianism measure, revealing a negative correlation between the two scales, so high authoritarianism was associated with low nonverbal ratings for the defense. By combining the approaches of verbal and nonverbal responses, attorneys were able to have a better understanding of juror attitudes than if they had relied on only one assessment technique.

A critical job for the consultant then becomes determining exactly how to combine the different sources of information at their disposal. For example, should nonverbal responses be given more, less, or equal weight to background characteristics identified as predictive factors? Unfortunately, one limitation of the published research on systematic approaches to jury selection is that the research has looked at the approaches independently. That is, much research exists on the effects of background factors, and research exists on the general effectiveness of using nonverbal behavior to detect deception, but there have not been discussions in the literature of how data based on these different methodological techniques may be systematically combined in a mathematical prediction equation.

If a clear mathematical model for combining all sources of information is not used, then consultants will not be able to provide a purely statistical approach to selecting jurors. Rather, juror profiles based on the analysis of survey responses produce a statistically derived guideline for identifying potentially biased jurors. Profiles are typically combined with experientially oriented clinical judgments of attorneys based on their years of experience and possibly on nonverbal observations (see chap. 7), which are less reliant on statistical-based predictions. It would be useful to have empirical research conducted comparing the effectiveness of (a) a purely actuarial approach to jury selection (based only on predictions derived from survey data), with (b) the predictions based on nonverbal observations, with (c) attorneys' reliance on their own hunches, and with (d) the combination of these approaches.

The use of a mathematical model may also expedite the analysis and interpretation of data. The judge may only allow a limited time between the end of voir dire questioning and the execution of peremptory challenges. As a result, the attorneys may have to quickly integrate information provided by several consultants who specialize in a different area of jury selection (e.g., a nonverbal behavior expert and a community survey expert). When all members of the legal team are in agreement as to whether a juror is favorable, the process should proceed relatively smoothly and quickly. However, when there is disagreement among members of the team, the leader must be careful to allow each member to fully articulate the logic behind their position to avoid important information being lost.

> For example, if the person representing the survey was more argumentative and articulate than the person representing the juror investigations,

then the former type of information tends to determine close decisions more often than the latter. Thus, potentially valuable information from less vocal and less assertive group members is often disregarded. (Hafemeister, Sales, & Suggs, 1984, p. 150)

Further, when there is pressure to make quick decisions, individuals are more likely to rely on gut-level instincts, hunches, and stereotypes (e.g., Kruglanski & Freund, 1983). If attorneys fall back on simplistic decision schemes because of time pressure imposed by the judge, it can negate the effort associated with scientific jury selection.

When consultants and attorneys consider the multiple sources of information available to them, the dynamic interactions among jurors of different personality types should also be considered. For example, a group of 12 aggressive, task-oriented individuals may not function effectively as a group. Groups typically have leaders and followers, and it may be useful to attempt to seat a jury with a balance of "dominant, passive and flexible personalities" (Covington, 1985, p. 595). As noted in chapter 7, nonverbal behavior may be useful at identifying leaders and followers.

Hastie, Penrod, and Pennington (1983) reported that persuasiveness can be thought of as an individual personality trait, and that highly persuasive jurors were likely to speak more and provide more information about facts and issues than less persuasive jurors. Presumably, such information should have an effect on jury selection decisions. It has been noted that it is dangerous to have a persuasive individual remain on the jury if his or her predisposition to the parties involved is unknown or unfavorable. It is better to allow unfavorably disposed individuals who are persuadable followers to remain on the jury, rather than persuasive individuals whose dispositions are unknown (Hafemeister et al., 1984; Sage, 1973).

Demographic, personality, and attitudinal characteristics may also be important indicators of which jurors are likely to pair off into subgroups. There is much social science research that has shown that similar people are attracted to each other. Jurors who possess similar characteristics should be drawn to each other and are likely to become members of a specific subgroup. As a consequence, there are a variety of competing issues and sources of data that should be considered when making peremptory challenge decisions. Future research should be directed at determining how attorneys make peremptory challenge decisions during voir dire when scientific jury selection information is available to them, and how that process can be improved.

CAN MINIMALLY IMPROVED PREDICTIVE ABILITY BE USEFUL?

As noted in this chapter's introduction, it is important when attempting to determine the ultimate utility of the scientific jury selection approach to compare it with the effectiveness of the alternative approach, whereby an attorney simply relies on his or her best guesses to eliminate prospective jurors. If one assumes that attorneys' selection techniques operate at a chance (50%) level (Fulero & Penrod, 1990; Kovera et al., 2003; Olczak, Kaplan, & Penrod, 1991; Zeisel & Diamond, 1978; see chap. 3), then scientific jury selection

> could improve the accuracy of predicting a venire person's verdict inclination to about 65% provided that there were predictors with an approximate correlation of $r = .30$ with verdicts. Alternatively, if one assumes that an average correlation between attitudes . . . and verdict inclination of roughly $r = .20$, then predictive accuracy rises from 50% to 60%. (Moran et al., 1994, p. 328)

Of course, if an attorney is highly skilled at selecting biased jurors his or her accuracy rate should be greater than 50%, and the additional benefit of scientific jury selection is, of course, minimized. However, an attorney must actually be able to identify biased jurors above a chance level, not falsely perceive such success.

As previously noted, several authors have argued that scientific jury selection does not work in all cases (Diamond, 1990; Moran et al., 1994), such as when the weight of the evidence is so strong (or weak) that a particular verdict is almost certain. However, there is almost always a majority and minority created on the first vote of the jury during deliberations because in most cases there is not clearly overwhelming evidence one way or another (Kalven & Zeisel, 1966). Moran et al. (1994) noted that "[scientific jury selection] predictors have been shown to explain 30% (as opposed to 10%) of the variance if the evidence is not overwhelming" (p. 328). Thus, in a good number of cases, it may be useful to pursue scientific jury selection approaches if sufficient resources exist.

Moreover, although the general conclusion many social science studies have reached is that background characteristics of jurors typically account for less than about 15% of verdict variance, it is important to remember that those figures represent the average variance accounted for across all jurors in a given study. However, during voir dire, attorneys are not interested in excluding all jurors. Rather, they are interested in excluding the jurors who are most unfavorable to their side (Frederick, 1984). Scientific jury selection techniques may be more useful at identifying extreme jurors who hold strong biases, rather than predicting the behavior of average jurors who do not possess strong case-relevant attitudes.

How successful does scientific jury selection need to be at identifying and eliminating biased jurors to justify its use? The answer is entirely a subjective determination that will vary from case to case. Although there are a number of reasons to believe that factors identified in the process of scientific jury selection will have only a small impact on verdict in most cases, the impact may be significant enough to sway a jury's decision. It may be that identifying one additional biased juror may be enough to have an impact on a jury's verdict, if the identified juror is a person who will hold a great deal of influence over the jury's final verdict or if unanimity is required in the verdict. As noted by Moran et al. (1994), "the validity of [scientific jury selection] is demonstrated by the degree to which case relevant attitudes relate to juror prejudice" (p. 327). Minimal increases in predictive power provided by scientific jury selection techniques may be of significant value to attorneys and their clients if key variables can be identified as predictive of verdict in the specific case at hand.

CONCLUSION

Determining the effectiveness of scientific jury selection is difficult because there are not many published studies that have directly examined the technique; the studies that do exist are methodologically flawed in a variety of ways. Despite the limited direct research, there has been considerable criticism of the approach in the academic community. Much of that criticism has been based on research examining the general (weak) relationship between demographics, personality and attitudinal factors, and behavior. However, it may be possible to somewhat improve the utility of the scientific jury selection approach through the application of social psychological principles identified in attitudinal research. Furthermore, other lines of research have consistently indicated that actuarial-based predictors of human behavior are superior to intuitively based judgments, creating a theoretical reason why scientific jury selection may be superior to traditional jury selection strategies used by attorneys, particularly in cases in which the evidence is closely matched. If scientific jury selection creates even minimal improvement in an attorney's ability to identify and eliminate a biased juror, then the use of this approach can be worthwhile.

Even if the case-relevant attitudes that are identified during scientific jury selection activities do not ultimately predict juror verdicts in a particular case, it is unlikely that the consultant's activities will harm an attorney's case, aside from the time the attorney spends with the consultant and the costs that will be passed to the litigant (Treger, 1992). The attorney's client may be reassured if he or she believes all tools have been used to ensure an unbiased jury is seated (Moran, 2001).

Finally, scientific jury selection can be used to obtain a change of venue when damaging pretrial publicity exists and to argue for expanded voir dire. It can also be used to identify key issues and themes to be addressed in opening statements and trial strategy, with these strategies being refined through the consultant's use of mock juries, focus groups, or similar techniques (Vidmar, 1999). Using selection consultants in this way can result in identifying the types of prospective jurors who will be most or least favorable to a litigant's claim. We therefore discuss these additional services in the next chapter.

9

ADDITIONAL TRIAL CONSULTING TECHNIQUES THAT AID JURY SELECTION

In prior chapters we reviewed a variety of scientific jury selection strategies for evaluating jurors on the basis of identifying demographic factors, personality and attitudinal characteristics, or using nonverbal observation to detect hidden biases. As previously discussed, the influence of these factors is often outweighed by the strength of the trial evidence. However, juror characteristics and evidentiary factors should not be thought of as fundamentally distinct from each other. Rather, the types of jurors that are desirable to a particular party will depend on the evidence in the case and on how the attorney intends to present the evidence to the jurors. Thus, an important part of the scientific jury selection process is identifying how jurors will respond to key themes that attorneys use to structure cases. In addition, pretrial community surveys may identify commonsense notions of justice (Finkel, 1995) individuals possess about legal issues relevant to the case (e.g., conceptions of insanity) that may affect adherence to legal instructions and verdict choice.

In this chapter we discuss how community survey data can be complemented with additional trial consultant techniques (i.e., mock juries and focus groups) that provide mechanisms for the identification of case-relevant commonsense notions of justice and for the development of case themes that can be targeted to specific types of jurors. In addition, we discuss several other trial consulting services (e.g., shadow juries and posttrial juror interviews) that can be used for validating scientific jury selection strategies.

COMMONSENSE JUSTICE

Commonsense justice refers to the "intuitive notions jurors bring with them to the jury box when judging both a defendant and the law. It is what ordinary people think the law ought to be" (Finkel, 1995, p. 2) and reflects the combination of moral and psychological influences that can affect the accuracy with which people perceive the law and legal issues. As a consequence, these beliefs may substantially differ from the *black-letter law* conveyed in the jury instructions and may impact the outcome of a case in a variety of ways. For example, jurors' commonsense justice notions may lead them to intentionally nullify the law or inadvertently render a verdict inconsistent with the law because these notions interfere with the jurors' ability to follow jury instructions.

Finkel and Handel (1988, 1989), for example, concluded that preexisting schemas may affect jury decisions regarding insanity. Mock jurors given instructions on how to base a not guilty by reason of insanity verdict were no more likely to convict or acquit than those who were told to rely on their own commonsense beliefs (Finkel & Handel, 1988). The authors maintain this is the result of jurors having preconceived constructs or beliefs about sanity and insanity, and that these constructs are likely to be very strong and more powerful than those put forth in jury instructions (Finkel & Handel, 1988, 1989).[1]

Scientific jury selection can be used to identify the types of jurors who are more likely to hold specific types of constructs. For example, jurors who live in inner cities and frequently take subways may have repeated experiences with homeless people who have severe forms of mental illness and go into the subway system for warmth in winter and air conditioning in summer. These repeated experiences with homeless individuals with mental illnesses may create a preconceived construct that people who have a wild, dirty appearance are severely mentally ill and likely to qualify for the insanity defense. However, suburban jurors (who may be less likely to take innercity mass transportation) may have fewer interactions with homeless people with mental illnesses and as a result have different beliefs about the appearance and behavior of "insane" people.

---

[1]Finkel and Groscup (1997) have also found that individuals hold multiple commonsense justice prototypes for many different types of crimes.

This is important because Smith (1991) has argued that preexisting mental representations of legal issues may affect the verdict decision. She suggests that poor comprehension on the part of jurors is not simply the result of badly written instructions, but rather is the result of prior knowledge of the law interfering with those instructions. It is assumed that jurors have no knowledge of the law and will simply rely on judicial instructions when forming a verdict. However, Smith demonstrated that jurors have preexisting mental representations of the elements of different crimes. Unfortunately, their concepts do not include the correct legal definitions of those crime categories. For example, when participants were asked to list "all the features and attributes they felt were common to, or characteristic of" (p. 860) the crime of robbery, the most common responses were "something of value is taken," "perpetrator is armed," "money is taken," and "occurs in a home–apartment," rather than the specific criteria defined by law—that a "[d]efendant takes property from victim by force or threat of force" (p. 861). These preexisting prototypes are not discarded when conflicting judicial instructions are presented to them. As a result, Smith maintains that jurors must be informed that the way they may want to make a decision is improper.

In addition, when jurors are faced with incomprehensible instructions (many studies found comprehension rates in the 50%–60% range; Lieberman & Sales, 1997), they may be forced to rely on their commonsense notions of what the law is or should be. Reliance on such beliefs may lead to unpredictable verdicts. As a result, attorneys should ascertain a general level of comprehension for key instructions in the case prior to voir dire, along with commonsense notions of legal issues relevant to the case. If instruction comprehension is low and commonsense notions regarding specific legal issues are clear and strong, there may be a high likelihood of jurors relying on their commonsense beliefs during evidence presentation and decision making.

COMMONSENSE JUSTICE, CASE THEMES, AND SCIENTIFIC JURY SELECTION

Commonsense beliefs can provide a heuristic for organizing the trial evidence. This is important because a tremendous amount of information may be presented at trial, and it may become difficult for jurors to process and retain all relevant information without relying on commonsense stories. Attorneys may try to build on this effect by presenting case themes; that is, providing jurors with framing references or "thematic anchors" (Vinson, 1993, p. 166; see also Mauet, 1992) for organizing critical information. For example, in a wrongful death case, a plaintiff's attorney might develop a theme of loneliness to characterize the surviving spouse, such as " as we grow older, the thing we fear most is being alone' or 'this case is about loneliness'" (Mauet,

1992, p. 382). Each theme should be simple enough that it can be conveyed in a single sentence (Gross & Webber, 2003). It has been recommended that case themes be emotionally compelling and focus on universally admired principles, such as "David and Goliath" if an individual is litigating against a large corporation, or "fighting city hall" if an attorney represents a person who is the victim of inflexible policies resulting from government bureaucracies (Tanford, 1993, p. 158).

One important product of themes is that they may help jurors form stories as they integrate the evidence presented during the trial. Research indicates that trial information is often organized by jurors in a story structure, and that jurors are more likely to favor a party that presented evidence in a story format, as opposed to an unstructured format (Pennington & Hastie, 1993; see chap. 11 for a review). The stories that jurors construct are composed of both trial evidence and extralegal factors that jurors enter the courtroom with, such as their beliefs about characteristics of similar crimes or stereotypes about individuals with backgrounds similar to the defendants. Extralegal factors can produce a variety of inferences regarding the facts in a case, which can then be used to produce a completed story structure when there are missing pieces in the presentation of evidence.

Community surveys conducted as part of scientific jury selection can identify the types of individuals who are most likely to hold beliefs (commonsense justice notions) or produce specific types of stories that are congruent with or responsive to the attorney's themes. This information can be used during the jury selection process to strike jurors who are likely to be least responsive to the attorney's themes and arguments. For example, consider a homicide case in which eyewitnesses report they saw the defendant and victim get into a verbal altercation and trade insults early in the evening. The facts also show that the victim was much larger and more physically intimidating than the defendant, and that the eyewitnesses later saw the defendant stab the victim. To decide the case, jurors will have to determine what the defendant's motivations were. Perhaps the defendant acted out of anger or of fear. Such attributions could lead to quite different verdicts. If self-defense is a possible reason for a not guilty verdict, jurors must place themselves in the mind of the defendant and ask what a reasonable person would do under similar circumstances. Jurors with different backgrounds may produce different stories, which may result in different verdict choices. An aggressive juror may believe that the defendant stabbed the victim because of the need to maintain pride after having been publicly insulted. A more timid individual may feel that fear would have been his or her overwhelming reaction to an argument with a larger and stronger person.

A community survey may reveal that a variety of themes are appealing to prospective jurors. For example, "[i]n a contraception product liability case . . . issues relating to God, children, femininity, sexuality, motherhood, family, abortion, and death may be infinitely more important in verdict determination than testimony involving epidemiology, biochemistry, or arcane aspects of medical science" (Vinson, 1993, pp. 166–167). It may be found that some of these issues are more powerful for a specific group of jurors (e.g., women). Thus, community surveys may be useful at identifying how strongly different themes affect potential jurors and may allow a bridge to be developed among case evidence, juror backgrounds, and jury selection decisions. However, if too many or complicated themes are used, theme effectiveness will be diminished because it will become difficult for jurors to integrate information in a clear and consistent manner. As a result, an attorney may need to reduce the number of potentially relevant themes.

In conclusion, community surveys provide an initial opportunity to identify and refine key themes in a case (Vinson, 1993) and the types of jurors who will be most amenable to specific themes. The jury selection process can be an important component in case planning and strategizing; unfortunately, there is no published research on this selection strategy.[2]

MOCK JURIES AND SCIENTIFIC JURY SELECTION

Asking survey respondents about the importance of key issues may not produce the strong effects that might be obtained if respondents were presented with a well-crafted opening statement built around relevant case themes. Thus, an alternative approach to exclusive reliance on community surveys is to supplement survey responses regarding potentially important case themes with mock jurors' reactions to expanded arguments and testimony.

Mock juries comprise groups of individuals, recruited by jury selection consultants, who fit specific criteria of interest. For example, mock jurors may be recruited to create a sample of individuals that match the general stratification of the venire population. Each mock jury is brought to a facility, presented with some type of case information, and observed as the mock jurors respond to that information.

Mock juries are used for a number of purposes, including verifying information obtained in pretrial surveys; refining the presentation of information to jurors, including opening or closing arguments and trial evidence; developing overall trial strategies; and determining which types of jurors will respond most or least favorably to different adversarial tactics. As a result, mock juries are an important tool in scientific jury selection. Mock juries are used in a similar manner as telephone surveys, in that reactions to aspects of a case can be gathered before the jury is selected and the case is presented to the actual trial jury. However, mock juries allow respondents to be presented

---

[2]However, there is research on the effects of using a story-like presentation to deliver evidence. This line of work on the story model of juror decision making (Pennington & Hastie, 1990, 1993) is discussed in chapter 11.

with far more information in a realistic manner and questioned far more extensively than is possible during a telephone survey.

As with community surveys, mock juries are often conducted in the community where a trial will be held, with selection consultants running a number of mock juries separated by such factors as participants' races, ages, and occupations (Farrell & Bunch, 1999). This ensures that information can be gathered on the relationship between evidence and juror characteristics, with this information used in jury selection. There are two main approaches to mock juries—exploratory mock juries (or focus groups) and simulated trial mock juries.

Exploratory Mock Juries–Focus Groups

The mock jury may be structured in a relatively informal way as a focus group. This type of mock jury is used to explore general reactions to the likely evidence and trial participants. This allows an attorney to practice opening statements and present general descriptions of evidence to mock jurors, rather than specific testimony from witnesses (Abbott, 1999b). As a result, there is minimal trial realism.

Exploratory mock juries, however, may be useful for uncovering jurors' commonsense beliefs regarding legal issues and for exploring reactions to case themes. For example, the scientific jury selection consultant could have mock jurors articulate their expectations about the behavior and characteristics of an insane person. A free-flowing discussion among mock jurors may produce a more detailed picture of beliefs about characteristics of insanity than could be assessed with phone surveys. However, social psychologists have long been cognizant of conformity pressures that arise when individuals are put into groups (e.g., Asch, 1955, 1956), which may cause mock jurors to agree with others, even though the responses do not accurately characterize their beliefs. It is probably best to have exploratory mock jury participants record their responses to key issues in written form prior to group discussion, to identify and minimize conformity influences.

Although general feedback can be obtained from exploratory mock juries, they are not very useful for obtaining reliable evidence or allowing for statistical analysis of the evidence. Attorneys often can only obtain general narratives of mock jurors' discussions and conclusions unless the jurors are videotaped or attorneys view the mock jury sessions.

Although there are definite limitations in terms of the quality of information provided by exploratory mock juries–focus groups, the one advantage over alternative mock jury approaches is that of cost. The mock jury session may be completed in less than one or two hours, minimizing the cost of financially compensating participants. In addition, the preparation time for attorneys is minimal compared with the more elaborate simulated trial mock jury discussed in the next section (Abbott, 1999b).

Exploratory mock juries can be a useful component of scientific jury selection because they allow for a relatively quick, but crude, identification of reactions to evidence or statements, particularly when responses are consistent. For example, Toobin (1996; see chap. 1, this volume) reports that in mock jury focus groups conducted by Donald Vinson for the prosecution in the O.J. Simpson criminal trial, there was great consistency among African American mock jurors in terms of negative reactions to the lead prosecutor, Marcia Clark. This information could, and probably should, have been used as a guide in jury selection. However, in the absence of such consistent responses and if financial resources permit, more sophisticated simulated mock jury trials should be used.

Simulated Mock Jury Trials

Mock juries can also be conducted with a structured process that provides greater realism and more closely matches that of the actual trial experience, assuming the mock jurors were selected to closely match actual jurors in a trial. For example, in this type of simulation mock jurors can be presented with opening statements, simulated witness testimony and exhibits, and potential arguments from the opposing side. A complete mock jury simulation should contain all these elements, condensed down to key issues and evidence. For example, the case may be reduced to a few issues or the testimony of three or four primary witnesses. Simulated mock jurors may also be allowed to deliberate. The lead attorney in the case should conduct the direct examination and a colleague should conduct the cross-examination (Covington, 1985). By enhancing the realism of the experience, the trial consultant can increase the validity of mock juror responses. Of course, this approach does not perfectly replicate the actual courtroom experience, and it requires attorneys and trial consultants to guess at the approach the opposing side will take. However, simulated mock juries are more informative than exploratory mock juries because of the greater realism and specificity associated with the technique.

In addition, simulated mock juries, which are chosen because of their representativeness to the venire and not actual jurors, are useful for validating pretrial survey research, identifying underlying cognitive processes and connections, refining the presentation of evidence that will be most effective with specific types of jurors, and ultimately refining the jury selection decisions. We consider these separate benefits in the following sections.

Validating Pretrial Survey Research

Mock juries allow for the validation of pretrial survey conclusions. That is, if a pretrial community survey is preformed and the survey identifies a number of key demographic or attitudinal factors that are predictive of verdicts based on the summary of trial information presented in the survey, those factors can be confirmed in a follow-up study with mock jurors (see, e.g., Frederick, 1984). Presumably, if reliable factors have been identified it should be possible to predict the verdicts of mock jurors exposed to more extensive evidence. If the survey-based predictors are not able to predict mock juror verdicts, then the predictors may be unreliable and attorneys should be cautious about relying on them in jury selection (Diamond, 1990).

Identifying Underlying Cognitive Processes and Constructions

An additional benefit of mock jury research is that it affords jurors an opportunity to discuss their thought processes when rendering a verdict. This is particularly valuable because it may be difficult to accurately identify the complexity of respondents' thoughts in a survey. However, in both simulated and exploratory mock jury settings, discussions can be held with jurors regarding scenarios they may construct as to how and why a crime (or other behavior in civil trials) was committed. Thus, attorneys can assess the elements of stories jurors have constructed to organize the evidence and identify the type of story associated with the most desirable verdict. When attorneys want greater detail about the specific thoughts of specific types of mock jurors (e.g., African Americans), attorneys can also have mock jurors provide ongoing verbal reactions to the information presented to them (see, e.g., Ericsson & Simon, 1993). These ongoing verbal descriptions of a mock juror's thoughts can give attorneys greater insight into prospective juror cognitions about important aspects of the case, thereby aiding the scientific jury selection process.

Refining the Presentation of Information to Jurors

Simulated mock juries help attorneys determine the effectiveness of trial strategies before the strategies are presented to the actual jury and determine how different strategies will affect different types of jurors. As the information presented to mock juries is more extensive than that included in a telephone survey, the responses should provide more accurate estimates of prospective jurors' responses to critical aspects of a trial and of their ultimate verdict. This approach allows the attorneys to determine if there will be differences in processing case information among different types of jurors, thereby facilitating the accuracy of scientific jury selection decisions. For example, mock juries can be used to identify for specific types of jurors which evidence is most likely to be attended to, which evidence will most likely be ignored, what types of messages will be most clear, which case themes will be most plausible, what types of testimony will be most likely convincing or unconvincing, and if missing information will be troubling.

Moreover, simulated mock juries allow for multiple versions of trial information to be presented (Diamond, 1990). For example, jury decision-making research has shown that the timing and content of opening statements has an important effect on verdicts because opening statements may provide a cognitive structure that guides how jurors process information during a trial (Pyszczynski & Wrightsman, 1981). Consultants can use mock trials to present different versions of the opening statement to determine the most persuasive approach to take during the actual trial, given specific configurations of the jury. As different types of mock jurors may react in different ways to alternate versions of the opening statement, the scientific jury selection consultant can aid the attorney in selecting a jury that will be most receptive to the opening statements, as well as help to modify the opening statement to reflect the composition of the jury finally selected.

In addition to examining different strategies for opening arguments, simulated mock juries can help identify jurors' receptivity to case strategies and tactics. For example, an attorney may be concerned with how best to present scientific or statistically oriented evidence, particularly if pretrial research indicates that most people living in a particular community from which jurors are likely to be selected are not well-educated and are not likely to follow complex, mathematically oriented testimony. When presenting DNA evidence, for example, there are different ways of conveying match probability estimates (i.e., the likelihood that a sample of DNA recovered from the crime scene or victim matches a sample of DNA drawn from the defendant; Lieberman & Miethe, 2006). Research has shown that match statistics presented in the language of probability (e.g., 0.1%) are more influential than statistics presented in the form of frequencies (e.g., 1 in 1,000; Koehler, 2001). Rather than providing specific matching probabilities, attorneys may want to take advantage of FBI lab policy that now allows examiners to simply state that an individual is the source of the DNA sample with "a reasonable degree of scientific certainty" (Hart, 1998). Such personal opinion-oriented testimony has been shown to be more effective than statistically based (actuarial) testimony (Krauss, Lieberman, & Olson, 2004; Krauss & Sales, 2001). Pretrial mock jury research could determine if these findings hold true for individuals with backgrounds similar to those likely to be drawn for the venire, or if highly educated people respond negatively to attempts at dumbing down trial testimony. This information, once again, can aid in scientific jury selection decisions and in case preparation, in light of the resultant juror composition.

Trial consultants with a background in psychology or communications may also assist attorneys by analyzing case strategy according to a variety of psychological principles. For example, an attorney may be inclined to use emotional language or vivid, emotion-arousing exhibits during the trial. However, emotional processing may produce unintended side effects, such as increasing jurors' reliance on extralegal cues (Lieberman, 2002). Thus, in these situations it may be especially important to use mock juries to identify extralegal biases or cues held by specific types of jurors, which in turn can alter the jury selection strategy. Psychological assessment instruments exist that can identify individuals as either highly rational–cognitively oriented or more inclined to rely on emotions, gut-level instincts, and heuristic cues (Cacioppo & Petty, 1982; Pacini & Epstein, 1999). Items from these instruments could identify these types of individuals through community and pretrial questionnaires. It may be useful to assess how both types of individuals respond to emotionally oriented testimony and exhibits and use the findings to guide jury selection. Assessing whether or not individuals are highly cognitively oriented may also have important implications for the degree to which jurors are likely to closely follow complex and lengthy testimony. Thus, the development of trial strategy should be done with an adequate understanding of the effects of different approaches on different types of potential jurors.

Finally, mock jury techniques allow consultants to work with attorneys to develop the best order of evidence presentation given a particular composition of the jury. For example, the attorney may be undecided as to whether critical evidence should be presented first to set a strong tone for the case and capitalize on primacy effects, in which initial information is better remembered, or to present evidence last so it is fresh in jurors' minds when they make their decisions and thus is more influential (i.e., with a recency effect). Trial consultants can evaluate attorneys' interaction style as well. The interaction distance between an attorney and prospective jurors may influence the amount of information jurors are willing to disclose during voir dire (Suggs & Sales, 1981). Issues such as these, as well as others involving attorney appearance and demeanor, can be examined with mock juries prior to voir dire and jury selection.

Conclusions Regarding the Use of Mock Juries and Scientific Jury Selection

If the scientific jury selection consultant has analyzed the results of the community survey prior to initiating the mock jury research, and if the mock jurors match the demographic characteristics predictive of the most and least favorable prospective jurors, then results of the mock jury manipulations on the different types of jurors can be assessed. For example, it may be that juror type X is least favorable to Trial Strategy 1, but extremely favorable to Trial Strategy 2. This knowledge adds important value when attorneys exercise their peremptory challenges at the outset of the case. They would be aware of the effectiveness of their alternate trial strategies with different types of jurors.

Conducting Mock Juries

In conducting a mock jury trial, consultants need to consider a variety of issues, such as how to select a sample of participants; whether to use an experimental design and if so, the specific type of design to use; where to conduct the mock trial; how to observe mock deliberations; and how to collect data. These factors will have a large impact on the quality and usefulness of the information obtained.

Sampling Issues

In selecting participants to serve as mock jurors, either probability or nonprobability sampling may be used. Probability sampling is ideal because it allows every member of a population a chance to be selected. This minimizes potential differences in characteristics between the sample and the population from which the sample is drawn and, in turn, reduces potential error in estimates of how others in the population will behave. However, consultants often recruit participants from such sources as employment agencies, newspaper ads, and telephone interviews (Abbott, 1999c). As a result, many members of the population will not have a chance to be included in the sample and nonprobability sampling must be used.

Nonprobability sampling is used when all members of a population do not have an equal chance of being selected in a sample. A variety of nonprobability techniques exist, such as availability–convenience sampling (using respondents who are most easily accessible), quota sampling (selecting participants to match population characteristics), purposive sampling (selecting individuals with specific backgrounds of interest), and snowball sampling (asking participants to refer people they know who may be useful to include in the sample). Quota sampling typically is the method that allows a sample to best represent the characteristics of the population; however, other factors, such as the need to conduct a study quickly or to find individuals who have unusual backgrounds, may create a need to use alternate nonprobability sampling approaches.

Ultimately, the most appropriate sampling procedure is likely to depend on the specific goals of the mock jury study and specific restrictions and complications that may exist (see Babbie, 1998, for a thorough review of these sampling techniques). For example, if an attorney needs a mock jury study conducted in a brief period of time, it may be impossible to use an elaborate quota sampling procedure. The trial consultant may have to rely on an availability–convenience sampling procedure instead.

When participants are selected it is best to refrain from informing them which side has hired them, as that knowledge may lead to biased responses (Blue, 2001). For example, jurors might provide unnaturally favorable responses to attorneys who were financially compensating them or view the retaining party as manipulative and provide dishonest responses as a result. However, no published research addresses this issue.

Experimental Design

If the goal of the mock jury study is to test the effects of different ways of presenting information to jurors or to test the effects of information on different types of jurors, various experimental and quasi-experimental designs will be used (Campbell & Stanley, 1963). A true experimental design requires participants to be randomly assigned to either an experimental group that receives some type of treatment (e.g., the presentation of a computer generated reenactment of an accident or crime scene), a control group that does not receive a treatment (e.g., no reenactment presented), or a comparison group that receives an alternate treatment (e.g., the presentation of a diagram instead of the computer reenactment). By randomly assigning participants to conditions, a researcher can be confident that differences among the groups are due to the manipulation of interest, not to individual differences in members of the groups.

True experimental designs are ideal for testing hypotheses. However, in many situations it may be impossible to have random assignment; as a result, quasi-experimental designs must be used. *Quasi-experimental designs* refer to studies in which a comparison is made between two or more groups (with a treatment given to the experimental group), but random assignment to the groups is impossible. For example, volunteers from two social clubs might be used as mock jurors to test the effects of two different trial presentation approaches, with a different approach presented to each group (Abbott, 1999c). Quasi-experimental designs require additional observations prior to delivering the manipulation of interest to be made (e.g., pretest measures to ensure that participants in the two groups are comparable) to ensure that group differences are due to the manipulated factors and not the result of having different types of individuals in each group (Babbie, 1998).

There are a wide variety of decisions that must be made in terms of the specific experimental design used with mock juries. For example, if an attorney and consultant are trying to decide which of two case themes is best to present in trial, these themes may be tested with a simulated mock jury study. However, the consultant will have to decide whether one group of mock jurors should be presented with both themes and asked to respond to each (i.e., a *within-group* design), or whether a comparison of the two themes should be made between separate groups, with each presented with only one theme (i.e., a *between-groups* design). Advantages and disadvantages exist for each of these techniques (such as cost and confidence in findings; see Babbie, 1998; Campbell & Stanley, 1963). Thus, it is critical that the trial consultant is skilled in experimental research to most effectively conduct mock juries that involve simulated trials.

Mock Trial Location

Mock trials can be held in a wide variety of locations, including: real courtrooms, mock courtrooms, law firm conference rooms, classrooms, hotel meeting rooms, and market research focus group studios (Abbott, 1999c). As a general rule, it is best to have the trial location at a site as similar to an actual courtroom as possible. An unused real courtroom (e.g., used over the weekend) certainly allows for the greatest realism. However, it may not be possible to get courtroom access when needed, and an actual courtroom may not provide the best location for observing jurors (e.g., no two-way mirrors;

National Jury Project, 2004) or for splitting mock jurors into multiple small groups for independent discussions or deliberations (Abbott, 1999c). Mock courtrooms in law schools may provide good alternatives to actual courtrooms, although cost and location may be important factors in location selection. Despite the logic of these recommendations, no published empirical research has studied the effect of different locales on jurors in mock trial studies.

Observing and Collecting Data

The goal of mock jury trials is to replicate the actual courtroom experience as much as possible. However, an important exception to that goal is in the observation and collection of data. Actual juries deliberate in private and render a single, final verdict for the entire group. Mock juries could be conducted in an identical manner and provide only a single verdict. However, this approach has two drawbacks. It would provide almost no data for statistical analysis unless a large number of simulated trials were conducted. By only asking for a verdict (e.g., guilty vs. innocent), substantial information about the jurors' and jury's reasoning in reaching that verdict will be lost. To maximize the value of mock juries, it is important to gather as much information as possible from jurors. As a result, it is useful to observe and record any juror deliberations and to have the mock jurors complete questionnaires about their decision-making process independently to identify specific predilections of different types of jurors. Attorneys may directly watch mock jurors as they deliberate, or sit in on focus groups run by the trial consultant. Alternatively, the trial consultant may provide attorneys with transcripts or videos of jurors' responses in focus groups or deliberations if a mock trial is held, as well as provide reports of mock juror questionnaire responses.

It will often be useful to have mock jurors provide multiple measures of their verdict inclinations or attitudes toward evidence and trial participants throughout the presentation of information. These observations can be made using repeated written responses or electronic technology. For example, jurors can turn dials back and forth during witness testimony or opening argument presentation to indicate positive, neutral, or negative affect. One important advantage of continuous monitoring is that it allows data to be obtained in response to specific arguments or phrases in testimony. Thus, one could see how both males and females react to the phrase *wife beater* as opposed to the phrase *domestic abuser* to characterize a defendant in an opening statement; this information could be used to develop case themes and identify characteristics of jurors most responsive to specific language used to characterize the themes. In addition, the approach of collecting multiple measures is useful because it allows for a *trend analysis* to be conducted.

A trend analysis allows for the examination of changes to a critical variable over time. For example, mock jurors' ratings of attorney credibility or the likelihood of a defendant's guilt could be measured during the beginning and end of opening statements, during presentation of prosecution and defense witnesses, and during the beginning and end of closing statements. By comparing the response trends of multiple groups (e.g., men vs. women, Whites vs. non-Whites, high vs. low income level) during a mock trial, it can be determined if a specific group has an important reaction to a particular element in the case. That is, identification can be made regarding the specific part of the trial where groups begin to differ in their perceptions of the case. Attorneys can then use voir dire to exclude those types of jurors who have reacted negatively to a critical aspect of the case or can adjust the presentation of that specific evidence if it is not possible to use voir dire to exclude all potentially problematic jurors. Abbott (1999c) argued that the "trend analysis is the most important of the forms of statistical analysis because it shows the dynamics of the trial" (p. 12).

Limitations of Mock Juries

Most attorneys find mock juries useful because it is often difficult for attorneys to get direct feedback about the success of their persuasive approaches, aside from verdicts and occasional posttrial questioning (Diamond, 1990). Despite the value of using a mock jury technique to refine jury selection and case presentation strategies in light of potential jury composition, there are a number of disadvantages associated with its use.

First, getting enough mock jurors of specific types to confirm and expand on the pretrial survey information may cost far more than alternative scientific jury selection techniques, such as community telephone surveys, in terms of time and expenses. Telephone surveys can be done fairly cheaply and quickly, with the major cost incurred by paying telephone interviewers to ask a series of predetermined questions. However, mock juries require respondents to travel to the research facility and to participate in activities that may take several hours. As a result, to increase motivation to participate and to obtain an adequate number of mock jurors, participants in mock trials are usually paid. In addition, the process of gathering information takes much longer in a mock trial because more extensive evidence is presented, and jurors may deliberate or engage in some other form of group discussion, rather than simply providing individual responses. Finally, instead of using relatively inexpensive telephone interviewers, mock juries often require that experienced, senior level consultants interact with the respondents because of the need to conduct structured discussions. Using experienced people will increase the cost to the client; however, the issue of cost will not be of concern to some clients, particularly in large scale civil litigation.

Second, mock juries may be less representative of the population of interest than what is desirable or achievable with other techniques, such as telephone surveys. As the time commitment for participation is significant, many people may decline to participate in mock juries. The sample of mock jurors will likely underrepresent high-income individuals who may not be motivated by the financial compensation offered and individuals who work in demanding occupations or have demanding lifestyles and little free time (e.g., mothers of small children). Further, if the testing location is in an area with minimal or no public transportation, it may be difficult, if not impossible, for lower-income or inner-city respondents to get to the facility (Diamond, 1990). Thus, the mock jury may underrepresent groups that make up a large portion of jury rolls.

Third, unless the client has deep financial resources, the significant financial compensation required may lead to a less than desirable number of mock jurors that can be used. A small sample for analysis may make it difficult to stratify the sample on key characteristics (such as race, economic status, educational level, etc.). A general rule of social science research is that larger samples are more representative of a population than smaller samples.

A fourth limitation is that the attorney and trial consultant must guess how the opposing attorney will present his or her arguments and conduct direct and redirect examinations. The guesses are then presented in terms of opening arguments, examinations, and cross-examinations of witnesses for the other side. If the opposing counsel uses an unforeseen strategy at the trial, the mock jurors will not have been exposed to a sufficiently close approximation of the trial, and their responses will be inaccurate predictors of the behavior of the actual jurors.

Fifth, the simulated nature of the mock jury experience may cause mock jurors to behave differently than they would if they were jurors in the actual trial. For example, mock jurors may exert less effort in attending to information presented to them or may less vigorously argue their verdict preferences during deliberations. However, a number of research studies have addressed this issue, yielding empirical evidence that mock jurors behave in a similar manner to actual jurors. For example, Zeisel and Diamond (1978) compared the deliberations of actual jurors with shadow jurors (discussed in the next section) exposed to the same trial evidence. The average deliberation time among actual jurors in 12 trials was 2 hours, 38 minutes. The deliberation time among experimental juries asked to act as shadow juries and sit through the same trial before deliberating about a nonbinding verdict was very similar, at 2 hours, 12 minutes. An analysis of tape recordings of the experimental juries' deliberations indicated that discussions were often heated and heavily focused on evidence and questions raised during the trial. Zeisel and Diamond did find that actual jurors were less punitive than mock jurors, but other research by Hastie, Penrod, and Pennington (1983), which examined the verdicts of a larger sample of 69 mock juries that had viewed a murder trial, found that mock jury verdicts were typically the same as the verdict of an actual jury presented with the same trial.

If the process of simulating court proceedings has an effect on verdict outcome, we would expect that the method of simulating the trial (presenting videotaped testimony vs. testimony in a written transcript) would have a strong effect on the responses of mock jurors. However, research has found that the method of presenting case information (trial summary vs. written transcript vs. audiotaped transcript vs. videotaped transcript) has little or no impact on juror decisions (Bornstein, 1999). Thus, the simulated nature of a mock jury does not appear to be cause for serious concern. Future research would be appropriate to validate this conclusion. One way to pursue this line of research is to validate the results of community surveys with mock jury studies. The validity of the mock jury technique can then be easily assessed by comparing the responses and behavior of mock jurors to those of actual jurors and individuals presented with actual case evidence, particularly when posttrial interviews and shadow juries are used.

ADDITIONAL TECHNIQUES FOR SUPPLEMENTING JURY SELECTION INFORMATION

Consultants can provide a variety of additional services, such as monitoring the progress of the trial (with shadow juries) and conducting posttrial interviews to determine the case factors that jurors felt were important to their final decision. Although these activities are generally beyond the scope of this book because they focus on trial consulting rather than jury selection consulting, both shadow juries and posttrial interviews do provide a means of validating jury selection strategies, which can influence scientific jury selection strategies in future cases. Thus, we briefly review both techniques in the following sections.

Shadow Juries

Shadow juries (sometimes known as *trial-monitoring mock juries*) consist of a group of individuals who are selected to match the characteristics of the members of the actual jury. Shadow jurors sit in the actual courtroom during the trial, listen to the testimony, and report their reactions to the consultants at the end of each day. As a result, the shadow jury is exposed to the same evidence, arguments, exhibits, objections, and other aspects of the case that the real jury is exposed to. The advantage of shadow juries is that the jurors can provide an online report of their reactions to the actual trial, as opposed to mock jurors who can only provide their impressions of evidence that an attorney expects to be presented in court. A shadow jury, therefore, allows an attorney to make adjustments in case presentation if the shadow jury members indicate that problems exist. Not surprising, shadow juries provide useful information and have been used with success in major litigation

(Loh, 1984). As with mock juries, it is best to avoid informing shadow jurors who is sponsoring the trial research, to prevent any response bias.

The chief disadvantage with this approach is that if an attorney has done a particularly poor job of examining a witness or extremely damaging information has been presented, the actual jurors may have already been irreparably influenced by the trial information, and the shadow juries' reactions may come too late to be useful. However, if this does occur, it is beneficial for the attorney to have objective feedback regarding the case so the damaging factors can either be addressed by later witnesses or in closing statements or a settlement can be pursued. One other disadvantage is that if the public becomes aware of a shadow jury operating during a trial, it may spark considerable controversy and negative attention (Loh, 1984).

Shadow juries provide an opportunity to validate pretrial jury selection strategies by providing a mechanism for monitoring at which point in the trial shadow jurors begin to adhere to strong pretrial verdict inclinations or are persuaded to ignore them. For example, as the trial progresses, shadow jurors can be asked to provide their verdict inclination and their confidence in that verdict. Thus, as jurors are exposed to prosecution or plaintiff evidence before defense evidence, shadow jurors who are identified using criteria developed during scientific jury selection as being favorable to the prosecution or plaintiff should commit to verdicts before defense-oriented jurors. However, if shadow jurors who were identified as favorable to the defense are the first to commit to verdicts supporting the prosecution–plaintiff, then the attorney may not want to depend on the information gathered through scientific jury selection and may need to revise his or her case strategy and tactics.

Ultimately, the shadow jury approach can be validated by comparing the actual jury decision to the verdict rendered by the shadow jury. In addition, after the trial, actual jurors can be interviewed (in a posttrial juror interview), and their responses can be compared with those of the shadow jurors. It is unfortunate that there is no published research on the accuracy of shadow juries.

Posttrial Juror Interviews

On the basis of community survey or mock jury responses, attorneys should be armed with information regarding whether particular jurors are likely to be favorably or unfavorably inclined to their case. A posttrial interview with jurors allows this information to be substantiated. Presumably, a juror who has been identified as favorable should provide voir dire responses that support this prediction, such as that they were convinced early on or that they took an active role in persuading other jurors to adopt their verdict choice, particularly if pretrial research had identified them as having strong leadership characteristics. Of course, it is impossible to predict the behavior of every juror, so one would not expect 100% accuracy. However, there should be a relatively strong correlation between pretrial predictions and posttrial responses.

In addition, a systematic recording of posttrial interview responses may be useful for preparing pretrial motions for expanded voir dire in future trials (Fargo, 1999). For example, Lilley (1994) reports that 87% of jurors interviewed after they had rendered a verdict indicated that they thought attorneys had failed to learn something important about them or another member of the jury. In addition, 73% indicated that they served with someone who probably should have been excluded from serving on the jury, and 32% felt the attitudes of jurors who should have been excluded from service (in their opinion) affected the jury's verdict.

As the information gained by such interviews may be useful if the case needs to be retried or for future cases, it is probably worth the relatively small expense associated with this technique. It is, of course, important to be aware of any legal restrictions on contacting jurors following the conclusion of a trial. It may be helpful to request that the judge instruct jurors that they are allowed to talk about the trial after it is concluded (Fargo, 1999). Finally, the interviews can be conducted either immediately following a trial or at a later date. Jurors may be eager to escape the confines of the court after a long trial, so scheduling an interview for a later date may be preferable.

CONCLUSION

Research has shown that background characteristics of jurors generally account for limited amounts of verdict variance. However, when background factors that are more specifically relevant to trial evidence are used, predictive ability is increased. Community surveys provide an opportunity to achieve specificity by examining how individuals drawn from the specific area where a trial will be held respond to descriptions of issues and evidence directly related to the case. Mock juries allow specificity to be increased further, by presenting jurors with specific opening statements, exhibits, and testimony that are likely to be presented in court, to determine how specific types of individuals will respond to such information.

Even if scientific jury selection approaches reveal weak relationships between background characteristics and verdict inclinations in a specific case, mock juries can be used to refine evidentiary and adversarial choices in light of the possible jury selection decisions. To this end, mock juries allow information to be gathered regarding the commonsense beliefs jurors have for legal issues that may affect verdict choice. In addition, information can be gathered from mock jurors about the types of stories specific types of jurors are likely to construct based on the evidence they are presented with and on extralegal biases they hold (that may be identifiable for actual jurors in voir dire). As a result, more effective case themes can be developed for specific types of jurors that will hear the case. Additional trial consulting techniques, such as shadow juries and posttrial interviews, allow for a determination of whether themes identified in mock jury research were successful and allow for a general validation of scientific jury selection strategies. The attorney should find this information useful when deciding whether to use the same consultant, or scientific jury selection in general, in future cases.

Unfortunately, almost no empirical research has been published on the effectiveness of the trial consulting techniques discussed in this chapter. For example, do shadow juries produce reports that are different from attorneys' perceptions of how the case is developing? Are trial consultants able to extract more useful information in posttrial interviews than attorneys would be able to produce by themselves? Does the formal nature of simulated trial mock juries produce discussions and verdicts that are substantially different from exploratory mock juries? These are unanswered questions that should be addressed in future research. However, there are additional questions regarding ethical and professional concerns surrounding scientific jury selection that we address in the next chapter.

10

ETHICAL AND PROFESSIONAL ISSUES IN SCIENTIFIC JURY SELECTION

Scientific jury selection techniques allow information to be gathered for a variety of purposes, including: determining the nature and extent of community bias (which may be useful for establishing grounds for a change of venue), allowing predictions to be made about prospective jurors' verdict inclinations, and identifying important issues for the development of case themes that are tailored to the specific types of jurors who will hear a case. The potential utility of these services has contributed to dramatic growth in the consulting field during the past 30 years. During that time, however, the practice has been criticized on the grounds that it creates an unfair advantage for parties that employ scientific jury selection consultants, who in most cases will be financially well-off clients.

In this chapter we discuss the ethical and professional issues that emerge from scientific jury selection and consider a variety of proposed reforms that may mitigate potential injustices created by the practice. Our analysis and discussion is divided into two sections. We first consider the ethical and professional issues related to scientific jury selection: fairness, affordability, and standards for scientific jury selection consulting. We then consider the reforms that have been proposed to address these concerns: licensure of scientific jury selection consultants, allowing for discovery of scientific jury selection information, use of court-appointed consultants, provision of pro bono services, lowering the cost of consulting by using academic researchers or directly hiring survey firms, and restricting the application of scientific jury selection information.

ETHICAL AND PROFESSIONAL CONCERNS

Since the beginning of the use of scientific jury selection, ethical and professional concerns about the use of the procedure have been raised (e.g., Etzioni, 1974; Saks, 1976). For example, Etzioni (1974) argued that

> The impartiality of the jury is threatened because defense attorneys have recently discovered that they can manipulate the composition of the jury by the use of social science techniques, so as to significantly increase the likelihood that the defendants will be acquitted. (p. 28)

In addition to the concern that scientific jury selection will create an unbalanced group of jurors and potentially violate the constitutional right to trial by an impartial jury, critics have also argued that the procedure is so expensive that it is only available to a small portion of the population and that social scientists cannot accurately predict verdicts on the basis of juror characteristics, so the practice of scientific jury selection is deceptive (Herbsleb, Sales, & Berman, 1979; Saks, 1976; Wiener & Stolle, 1997).

Fairness

Does scientific jury selection violate the constitutional right to a trial by an impartial jury if one party uses the technique and the other does not? Scientific jury selection is based on the principle of identifying characteristics of individuals who are likely to possess favorable or unfavorable attitudes toward parties and issues involved in the case. Prospective jurors may then be excluded during voir dire following these predetermined criteria. The process of systematically excluding certain types of individuals may conflict with the objective of having the jury represent a cross section of community values (*Taylor v. Louisiana*, 1975). In addition, it may conflict with limitations placed on the use of peremptory challenges regarding race (*Batson v. Kentucky*, 1986; *Miller-El v. Dretke*, 2005) and gender (*J.E.B. v. Alabama*, 1994) when these factors are identified as important characteristics (Abramsom, 1994; Bonazzoli, 1998; "Development in the Law," 1997).

Proponents of scientific jury selection could attempt to refute this point by maintaining that the technique simply allows for an identification of biased jurors who may appropriately be excluded. Although it is true that biased jurors should be excluded, there is no evidence that attorneys use the technique simply to eliminate jurors who are biased against their side. Rather, attorneys may attempt to exclude as many jurors as possible who are not favorably predisposed to their side, including impartial jurors.

However, for scientific jury selection to create a competitive imbalance in the courtroom, it would require that the number of peremptory challenges be substantial enough to affect the jury composition. For example, even a lawyer who is highly skilled at identifying biased jurors, if given three peremptory challenges, is likely to have less an effect on the final jury composition than if given nine challenges. Whether even nine peremptory challenges are sufficient to avoid a biased jury is unknown. To create the competitive imbalance, we have to assume that the jury selection approach is effective enough to dramatically affect the outcome of cases on a routine basis. To date, as we discuss throughout this book, that has not been shown to be the case, with background characteristics typically accounting for less than 15% of verdict variance. Thus, the debate over the ethical implications of scientific jury selection is premature because social scientists have not improved the practice to an extent that it has more than a small effect (although as noted earlier, perhaps a significant effect in some cases) on predictive validity and trial outcome (Hepburn, 1980).

Although scientific jury selection has not been shown to be effective enough to create a serious imbalance that threatens constitutional rights, it may create a public perception of unfairness. Such a perception could contribute to dissatisfaction with jury verdicts in cases in which scientific jury selection was used, which can in turn detract "from the legitimacy juries bring to the administration of justice—for the appearance of justice is undeniably as important as the reality to preserve and maintain public support for an instrument or an institution of justice" (Strier, 1999, p. 104).

There is an argument that would support an opposite conclusion, however. Concerns about perceptions of fairness in the trial process are related to general procedural justice issues (Lind & Tyler, 1988; Thibault & Walker, 1975). When individuals have greater control over the process of a procedure, they are more likely to view the outcome as fair. Presumably, the presence of a jury selection consultant should increase perceptions that the party who employs him or her has greater control over the proceedings. Thus, from a procedural justice perspective, both the litigant who retains the consultant and neutral observers may think that the trial procedure is more, rather than less, fair when scientific jury selection is used.

Stolle, Robbennolt, and Wiener (1996) investigated the perceived fairness of trials in which consultants were used to aid jury selection. Participants in the study were presented with cases (both civil and criminal) in which consultants were either used or not used by the prosecution–plaintiff and the defense. In addition, trial outcome was manipulated so that one side or the other won the case. Participants indicated their perceptions of fairness by responding to a series of 22 procedural justice related questions about the trial. Stolle et al. (1996) found that the use of scientific jury selection by itself did not lead to a perception that the trial was unfair. Rather, the trial was viewed as more fair when both sides either had or did not have assistance from a consultant than when only one side had a consultant. Thus, if only one side is aided by a consultant, Strier's (1999) concern is supported.

Despite this concern, proponents of scientific jury selection argue that the procedure is simply an extension of what lawyers have always done: relying on their instincts about what types of individuals are likely to be favorable or unfavorable jurors. Further, it is a lawyer's duty to represent his or her client to the best of his or her ability, and scientific jury selection simply provides a legitimate tool for accomplishing that duty ("Development in the Law," 1997). Thus, the issue of fairness does not appear to be a significant limitation from the legal system's perspective, although it can raise concerns about the perceived legitimacy of the trial process in the minds of neutral observers.

Affordability

In order for the adversarial system to work, both sides must be matched relatively equally in terms of skills and preparation. If only one party at trial uses scientific jury selection, a small but potentially meaningful advantage may be created. Hans and Vidmar (1986) have noted that "the major problem with social science in the courtroom is not the techniques themselves but rather the fact that in our society the condition for equality of resources is most often not met" (p. 94).

It is not clear how frequently financial disparities between parties at trial lead to only one side using a scientific jury selection consultant. It has become more common for jury selection consulting to occur in large scale civil litigations, such as securities fraud and antitrust cases, rather than in criminal litigation (Ellis, 2005). In such large scale corporate litigation, both sides may be able to afford consultants. In criminal trials, consultants may be used primarily in high-profile trials of celebrities or other wealthy individuals (e.g., Michael Jackson, Martha Stewart, William Kennedy Smith, and O.J. Simpson). In such cases, the budget for the prosecution may be increased to cover consulting services, or consultants may offer their services pro bono. Pro bono consultant services may also be offered to defendants without deep financial resources when they are accused of committing crimes that have captured the public's attention at a national level.

What is clear, however, is that disparities can occur in the use of scientific jury selection consultants. As a result, it has been argued that the advantage wealthy individuals and corporations have by being able to afford top legal counsel, investigators, and expert witnesses is further increased when they use scientific jury selection (Strier, 1999). However, the abilities and resources of counsel are never perfectly equal. Eliminating scientific jury selection would not eliminate disparities that already exist in our adversarial system of justice.

Standards for Scientific Jury Selection Consulting

Concerns have been raised regarding standards to which scientific jury selection consultants adhere. In contrast to such fields as law, medicine, and accounting, which impose some form of regulation on practitioners, there is no regulation imposed on these or other trial consultants. Whereas a number of other fields require licensing or certification to identify oneself as a professional, anyone can call him- or herself a consultant and can register with the American Society of Trial Consultants. This lack of regulation is apparent in the wide diversity of educational backgrounds of trial consultants, with approximately 50% possessing a doctor of philosophy degree and 8% having a bachelor's degree or less as their highest obtained degree (Strier & Shestowsky, 1999).

The American Society of Trial Consultants does have a code of professional standards (see http://www.astcweb.org/content.php?page=aboutus_code). However, these standards have been described as being "rather anemic . . . and not nearly as rigorous as those of the American Psychological Association" (Strier, 1999, p. 107). In addition, because there is no state licensure for trial consultants, there are no continuing education requirements for individuals who engage in jury selection. As a result, there is no assurance that consultants are aware of current findings in the field, new statistical techniques, revised standards for the ethical treatment of human participants, or other related information.

Thus, the lack of regulation may lead to two fundamental problems related to professional practice. First, attorneys may hire consultants who do not have sufficient methodological and statistical training to produce accurate information. As a result, the consultant may not truly be able to use science when offering "scientific" jury selection research consultation services. Given that it is a challenge for well-trained social scientists to account for small amounts of variance when using juror characteristics to predict verdicts from research data, one would expect a consultant with questionable qualifications to produce little or no useful information. For example, if appropriate sampling procedures are not followed, and the sample does not proportionally represent the diversity of a population that the jury will be drawn from, one would expect substantial error in the conclusions based on the data.

It is possible that over time unqualified consultants would work on enough cases with unsuccessful outcomes that they would no longer be used. Thus, consultants who are able to remain in the marketplace should be of high quality and effective (Moran, 2001; Shartel, 1994; Stolle et al., 1996), regardless of their educational background. This has led some to argue that the regulation of consultants is unnecessary, because the free market will weed out the less competent ones (Moran, 2001).

Although the free-market solution has some merit, it does not address a second problem related to professional practices—the treatment of human participants in research. Scientific jury selection consultants engage in research when they collect data in community surveys, mock jury studies, focus groups, or posttrial surveys. The American Psychological Association (APA) has clear standards regarding the ethical treatment of individuals who participate in research studies, standards that require informed consent from participants. The APA "Ethical Principles of Psychologists and Code of Conduct" (American Psychological Association, 2002) guidelines state that psychologists must inform participants about the following:

> (1) the purpose of the research, expected duration, and procedures; (2) their right to decline to participate and to withdraw from the research once participation has begun; (3) the foreseeable consequences of declining or withdrawing; (4) reasonably foreseeable factors that may be expected to influence their willingness to participate such as potential risks, discomfort, or adverse effects; (5) any prospective research benefits; (6) limits of confidentiality; (7) incentives for participation; and whom to contact for questions about the research and research participants' rights. (Section 8.02, p. 11)

Further, the APA ethics code also contains a provision about the recording of voices and images in research. Psychologists should

> obtain informed consent from research participants prior to recording their voices or images for data collection unless (1) the research consists solely of naturalistic observations in public places, and it is not anticipated that the recording will be used in a manner that could cause personal identification or harm, or (2) the research design includes deception, and consent for the use of the recording is obtained during debriefing. (Section 8.03, p. 11)

The issue of confidentiality outlined in the APA ethics code is particularly important because research participants may be asked about personal information such as their attitudes and life experiences that may be relevant to the case at hand. Further, their behavior may be videotaped or recorded by other means. Without some form of continuing education requirement as part of general regulations on practitioners, it is unlikely consultants can keep up with constantly changing guidelines for ethical behavior involving research with human participants.

Thus far, the discussion of confidentiality has focused on protecting individuals who participate in scientific jury selection studies from having personal information revealed to third parties. However, the need to enforce confidentiality agreements is also relevant to protecting the interests of the parties who hire scientific jury selection consultants, which would argue for researchers obtaining confidentiality agreements from research participants. Whenever individuals participate in pretrial research conducted by consultants they will be exposed to information regarding how a party plans on presenting a case. This is especially true when mock jurors are used and are presented with opening statements, witness testimony, or exhibits. Although attorneys may take steps to prevent mock jurors from knowing which side has hired them, it may be possible for the jurors to deduce such information. A rogue juror may decide to capitalize on the knowledge gained during the scientific jury selection process by contacting the opposing side for financial gain or because he or she is hostile to the other party (Stolle, 2005). This may be especially likely in cases that have been surrounded by considerable pretrial publicity. The revelation of such information may create a tactical advantage for the other side.

PROPOSED REFORMS

A variety of solutions to the problems created by the ethical and professional issues discussed have been proposed. These include requiring licensure of consultants, allowing discovery of scientific jury selection information, requiring disclosure of the use of scientific jury selection, using court appointed consultants, providing pro bono services, lowering the cost of consulting by using academic researchers, and restricting voir dire questioning and peremptory challenges (Barber, 1994; Herbsleb et al., 1979; Serio, 2004; Stolle et al., 1996; Strier, 1999).

Licensure of Scientific Jury Selection Consultants

As noted previously, there are no requirements for certification or licensure of scientific jury selection consultants. Requiring licensure would provide guarantees of minimal academic backgrounds (or certification of training), protection against false advertising, and sanctions against practitioners who violate professional conduct standards put forth by the licensing body. In addition, a requirement of licensure could be participation in some form of continuing education to assure that practitioners remain current with recent research, methodological and statistical innovations, and ethical standards (Strier, 1999).

Strier and Shestowsky (1999) reported that the majority of trial consultants are not in favor of requiring state licensing. Fifty-five percent of trial consultants surveyed disagreed with the statement "Trial consultants should be licensed by the state" (p. 493), with 38% of those indicating strong disagreement. Less than one third (29.2%) expressed support for licensure, and 15.5% were uncertain. One survey respondent who opposed licensure asked why consultants should be licensed when expert witnesses are not, perhaps reflecting a sentiment held by many opponents of licensure. However, Strier and Shestowsky noted that

> [l]egitimate reasons justify discriminating against the two services. . . . Unlike trial consultants, expert witnesses do not work covertly. They are identified to the court as witnesses for one of the litigants. Moreover, expert witnesses are subject to cross-examination—perhaps the single greatest due process protection offered by the adversary system—and to the scrutiny of the factfinder. (p. 493)

In addition, expert witnesses do not reflect a single class of professionals but are composed of professionals from many fields, some of which do require licensing.

Several additional arguments have been made against licensure of consultants. Moran (2001) contends that if licensure is required, qualified unlicensed professionals may be unfairly excluded from serving as consultants. As evidence for this possibility, Moran reports that "[i]n Illinois, clinical psychologists, not necessarily renowned psychometricians, exclude—via licensure—industrial/organizational psychologists (I/O) from employment testing. Clinicians routinely rig competitions for screening police applicants by excluding unlicensed, but more expert, I/O psychologists" (p. 83). In addition, Moran maintains that licensed professionals may rely on dubious methodologies that are damaging to clients and notes that licensure of psychologists and other mental health professionals did not protect against the false memory debate that took place during the 1990s. Finally, he points out that licensure in many fields, such as law and medicine, requires the completion of a specific technical education. However, there are no formal education programs offered anywhere in the country that are specifically designed to train scientific jury selection consultants.

An alternative to licensing consultants is to prohibit consulting by nonlawyers (Etzioni, 1974; Hanna & O'Brien, 1995; Strier, 1999). However, as attorneys are not trained in scientifically studying human behavior, there is no reason to believe that any advantage would be gained by this prohibition. Instead, the product might well be less reliable, with less valid information applied to voir dire decisions. Inferior information could be quite damaging in cases in which strong community bias existed against parties involved with a case. As a result, it makes more sense to focus on solutions that improve the quality of consultants' work.

Allowing for Discovery of Scientific Jury Selection Information

The ethical problems that may arise when one side has used a consultant and the other has not could be largely overcome by allowing for discovery of scientific jury selection information (Barber, 1994; Herbsleb et al., 1979; Strier, 1999). Discovery is a procedure in which adversarial parties are required to disclose certain evidence prior to the commencement of a trial. Its purpose is to promote the search for truth by eliminating the element of surprise. Allowing discovery of scientific jury selection information would promote the goal of selecting an impartial jury (Herbsleb et al., 1979; Strier, 1998–1999).

However, scientific jury selection information has been protected by the attorney work product rule. As noted by the U.S. Supreme Court in *United States v. Nobles* (1975),

> The interests of society and the accused in obtaining a fair and accurate resolution of the question of guilt or innocence demand that adequate safeguards assure the thorough preparation and presentation of each side of the case. . . . At its core, the work-product doctrine shelters the mental processes of the attorney, providing a privileged area within which he can analyze and prepare his client's case. But the doctrine is an intensely practical one, grounded in the realities of litigation in our adversary system. One of those realities is that attorneys often must rely on the assistance of investigators and other agents in the compilation of materials in preparation for trial. It is therefore necessary that the doctrine protect material prepared by agents for the attorney as well as those prepared by the attorney himself. (pp. 238–239)

This broad protection explains why there is no contravening law requiring the disclosure of the information scientific jury selection consultants bring to the hiring attorney in preparation for a case.

An exception to this rule is laid out in Rule 26(B)(3) of the *Federal Rules of Civil Procedure* which deals with the scope and limits of discovery.

> [A] party may obtain discovery of documents and tangible things . . . prepared in anticipation of litigation or for trial by or for another party or by or for that other party's representative (including the other party's . . . consultant . . .) only upon a showing that the party seeking discovery has substantial need of the materials in the preparation of the party's case and that the party is unable without undue hardship to obtain the substantial equivalent of the materials by other means. In ordering discovery of such materials when the required showing has been made, the court shall protect against disclosure of the mental impressions, conclusions, opinions, or legal theories of an attorney or other representative of a party concerning the litigation.

This provision and related state law allows the community survey, mock jury studies, et cetera, and their results to be sought after in discovery, but not the consultant's conclusions and opinions based on those results. For the motion for discovery to be successful, however, two conditions must be met: The party seeking discovery must have a substantial need for the materials, and that party could not obtain those materials without undue hardship. Other than in the case of an indigent defendant in a criminal case, it is hard to imagine the undue hardship criterion being satisfied; even in this situation, we know of no case where the request for discovery has been made or won.[1]

Edwards, Goldstein, Handler, and Wentzel (2004) argued that it is possible that a jury selection consultant's work could be discovered if it was relevant to a hearing on a *Batson* (or related) challenge. Under such a challenge, the attorney may be required to justify his or her logic for advancing the peremptory challenge in question. If the challenge was based on a jury selection consultant's recommendation, the consultant's data and notes in question may have to be produced to satisfy the court that the basis for the challenge was not impermissible under *Batson v. Kentucky* (1986). However, we know of no case in which this has occurred.

If discovery were allowed, it would create a special ethical obligation for the consultant conducting the jury research. Section 4.02 of the APA ethics code requires that researchers discuss with their research participants both the limits of confidentiality and the foreseeable uses of the information gathered during the research. This provision also stipulates that this discussion take place before the study begins and "thereafter as new circumstances may warrant." If discovery of the data were granted to the opposing party, the consultant would lose control over it. In that case, it would become imperative that consultants inform the research participants (e.g., respondents in the community survey) that their responses would not be kept confidential. It might be useful in such a scenario for the hiring attorney to request that the court require the opposing party to maintain the confidentiality of the information, vis-à-vis persons and entities that were not part of the litigation, under a contempt of court sanction if confidentiality is breeched (Herbsleb et al., 1979).

Court-Appointed Consultants

An alternative to allowing discovery of scientific jury selection data is the use of a court-appointed consultant. The Federal Criminal Justice Act of 1964 allows indigents to request expert services that are "necessary for an adequate defense" (Strier, 1999). Despite this foundation for making a request, state courts have generally been reluctant to pay for scientific jury selection or other trial consultants (Stolle et al., 1996). This reluctance may be due to budget limitations or skepticism regarding the importance of appointing a consultant, given the debate that exists within the social science community regarding the potential effectiveness of scientific jury selection method. However, not all requests have been unsuccessful. For example, in

---

[1]We are only referring to the situation in which the jury selection consultant is not testifying as an expert in the trial nor providing information for a testifying expert to rely on. Discovery in these two situations becomes almost routine.

the well-publicized trial of two men accused of attempted murder in the beating of Reginald Denny during the Rodney King riots, a consultant from Litigation Sciences (see chap. 1) was appointed by the Los Angeles Superior Court. To determine the cases in which it may be appropriate to appoint a consultant, it may be necessary to require parties to disclose if they have hired a consultant to assist with a case (Strier, 1999).

In addition to the financial needs of a defendant, the seriousness of charges brought against a defendant provides a criterion that could be used for determining whether courts should grant requests for court-appointed scientific jury selection consultants. Serio (2004) contended that in capital trials the uniqueness of death as punishment enhances due process needs because of the severity of punishment and the dual responsibilities of jurors. That is, jurors are not only required to make a determination of guilt, but are also required to make a sentencing determination of life in prison or death. The need for greater scrutiny of juror backgrounds in capital cases is evident in the development of specific legal standards for excluding biased jurors. For example, in *Wainwright v. Witt* (1985) and *Lockhart v. McCree* (1986), the Supreme Court held that jurors can be excluded if their views regarding the death penalty would prevent or substantially impair the performance of their duties. Serio concluded that given the importance of jury selection in capital cases, it is appropriate for courts to appoint consultants to assist in eliminating biased jurors during voir dire. The same logic could be applied to other types of cases, but the question becomes, what criteria should courts use to determine whether a case is sufficiently serious to justify the need for the appointment of a consultant?

Answering this question is beyond the scope of this book. But if a court appointed a consultant for an indigent defendant in a case in which strong community bias was suspected, or in a case in which the defendant was charged with a capital crime, an inequity could be created unless the prosecution was also provided with a court-appointed consultant. As a consequence, additional financial burdens could be placed on the court. A possible solution might be the appointment of a single consultant who would report information based on data collected using scientific jury selection approaches to both parties.

> At its discretion, the court could order a community survey by a neutral party, such as a court-appointed master or other expert under the Federal Rules of Evidence, . . . the Federal Rules of Civil Procedure, . . . or comparable state statutes. (Strier, 1998–1999, p. 708)

Although it may be difficult for courts to pay fees typically charged by consultants, it is possible to reduce (or eliminate) the cost of scientific jury selection by having consultants providing pro bono services, by appointing academic researchers as consultants, or by hiring survey research firms (discussed in the next two sections).

Pro Bono Services

It may be possible to provide scientific jury selection services to attorneys via a set percentage of pro bono work on the part of consultants. However, as already noted, there is no binding code of ethics or other regulatory mechanisms in place for all scientific jury selection consultants. Perhaps the implementation of pro bono requirements will be addressed as the field continues to evolve and considers issues such as the licensing of consultants and the implementation of a binding code of ethics. However, obligating nonlawyers to provide free services to the legal system is unlikely; at least we know of no precedent or compelling logic for such an ethically or legally derived rule.

Lowering the Cost of Consulting by Using Academic Researchers or Directly Hiring Survey Firms

In lieu of pro bono services, there are a number of ways to make consulting more affordable for parties with limited financial resources. First, academic researchers may provide a less expensive alternative to full-time professional consultants. Many universities have professors who specialize in the psychology of law and their social science backgrounds may make them ideal consultants. They may be more familiar with cutting-edge statistical techniques or jury decision-making research than individuals in private corporations who have been away from the academic environment for some time and are thus unaware of recent material presented in academic journals and textbooks. Of course, the attorney must be careful to select an academic consultant who is familiar with the type of research needed in a given case. A professor may have great strengths in survey research or content analysis but minimal experience with conducting experiments. Second, academics may be able to use graduate or undergraduate research assistants to conduct surveys, mock jury research, or content analysis. The costs of using student workers may be far less than interviewers provided by private corporations.[2] However, it is essential to know that student interviewers used by a professor are reliable. If a professor were to ask students in a research methods class to conduct a phone survey for extra credit, there must be some system to check whether the students actually made the calls, and that they conducted the surveys according to the specific directions provided by the academic researcher. A limitation to the academic researcher approach is that large consulting firms may be able to provide additional services beyond what can be provided by an individual academic consultant. For example, although a so-

---

[2]Student workers will likely have the same confidentiality protection as their professor–consultant because the attorney would be hiring both the professor–consultant and her or his staff (i.e., the student assistants).

cial scientist at a university may be able to conduct a pretrial survey as well as, if not better than, a professional consultant, he or she may not be able to produce sophisticated materials for presentations in a trial (e.g., effective graphic presentations of evidence).

Third, an attorney can also try to lower the cost of obtaining some aspects of scientific jury selection data by directly hiring survey firms to conduct pretrial community surveys in the city where the trial is held. Consultants often subcontract interviews to local survey firms who will obtain jury eligible respondents based on the criteria dictated by the consultant. These same subcontractors could also put together a group of individuals who are similar to the actual jurors, so that an attorney could try out an opening statement ahead of time (Diamond, 1990). Of course, survey firms will be unable to provide additional consultant services such as conducting mock juries, making nonverbal in-court observations, or including relevant attitudinal or personality scales based on psychological principles in the survey. However, the limited information provided by survey firms may be preferable to having no scientific jury selection data available at all if financial resources are limited.

Restricting the Application of Scientific Jury Selection Information

A final solution to the problems raised by an inequitable distribution of resources, which allows only one party to hire a consultant to perform scientific jury selection, is for the courts to restrict the application of the information by limiting voir dire questioning by attorneys, or by reducing–eliminating peremptory challenges (Barber, 1994; Strier, 1999).

As discussed in chapter 6, depending on jurisdiction, attorneys can be restricted from asking questions directly during voir dire, with questioning carried out instead by the judge. Even when attorney-conducted voir dire takes place, restrictions can be placed on the scope of the questioning. Restricted questioning should reduce or eliminate the opportunity to apply scientific jury selection information beyond basic demographic characteristics (e.g., gender, race, and occupation) and observable nonverbal behaviors. However, as we previously discussed, this is not a desirable approach because biased jurors are more likely to be identified when attorneys rather than the judge conduct voir dire questioning, and when questioning is expanded rather than restricted (Jones, 1987; Moran, Cutler, & Loftus, 1990; Nietzel & Dillehay, 1982; Nietzel, Dillehay, & Himelein, 1987; Suggs & Sales, 1981).

A more drastic alternative to restricting the application of scientific jury selection information is to reduce or eliminate peremptory challenges altogether. Despite a long history of debate over this issue, the constitutional guarantee of the right to trial by an impartial jury should ensure that peremptory challenges remain in the foreseeable future. Peremptory challenges are necessary for eliminating biased jurors who have not clearly articulated their biases and thus cannot be excused under a challenge for cause. If the goal of voir dire is to eliminate biased prospective jurors, it is important to retain peremptory challenges and to improve the accuracy and availability of scientific jury selection.

CONCLUSION

Ethical and professional concerns regarding the fairness of scientific jury selection have long been voiced. It has been argued that when attorneys use consultants to aid in jury selection they are creating a competitive imbalance in the courtroom, particularly because consultant services are primarily used by clients with deep financial resources. It has also been argued that scientific jury selection raises ethical and professional concerns because there are no clear standards or requirements for consultants. As a result, some consultants may have insufficient methodological and statistical training to produce useful data for attorneys, or consultants may violate basic ethical principles when conducting research on human participants.

A variety of potential solutions have been proposed to address these concerns, including requiring licensure of consultants, allowing discovery of scientific jury selection information, requiring disclosure of the use of scientific jury selection, using court-appointed consultants, providing pro bono services, lowering the cost of consulting by using academic researchers, and restricting voir dire questioning and peremptory challenges. Although some of these solutions, such as restricting voir dire questioning and peremptory challenges, are not likely to be supported by attorneys or adopted by the courts, other solutions such as the requirement for licensure or the use of court-appointed consultants may be worthy of serious consideration.

It should be noted that the practice of hiring consultants is legally permissible, and one could even argue inherently important for attorneys to do, if they are going to represent clients to the best of their abilities by using all the tools at their disposal. Any imbalance in the courtroom created by the disparate wealth between individuals or corporations involved in litigation would be present regardless of whether jury selection consultants were used. Indeed, as fairness is an important component of trials, it is worth considering steps that can be taken to increase the availability of scientific jury selection to a greater number of people or small businesses. In addition, because scientific jury selection is ultimately based on the principle of identifying potentially biased individuals and excluding them from jury service, it is important to advance the field so the techniques used by jury selection consultants can be improved. Chapter 11 discusses a number of potential future directions for growth and improvement of the scientific jury selection field.

11

FUTURE DIRECTIONS FOR SCIENTIFIC JURY SELECTION

The practice of scientific jury selection has produced a wide variety of reactions since its inception, ranging from criticism regarding its effectiveness and potential injustice to a perception that it can have a dramatic effect on a case, leading to its glamorization in popular films, such as *Runaway Jury* (Downer & Fleder, 2003). As we discuss earlier in this volume, because the amount of verdict variance accounted for by background factors is relatively small, it appears that the perception of scientific jury selection as an overwhelmingly powerful tool is not accurate. However, scientific jury selection does not appear to be as ineffective as some critics have maintained. In some cases (such as when the evidence for opposing sides is particularly evenly matched), the small effect of background factors may be meaningful. Further, as scientific jury selection continues to evolve and as psychological researchers advance the understanding of human behavior, it may be possible to increase the amount of verdict variance that can be accounted for using scientific jury selection techniques, thereby increasing the practical utility of this approach for attorneys.

Some strides have already been made in terms of improving the predictive ability of scientific jury selection, such as identifying the need for increasing the specificity of correspondence between an attitude and behavior. When increased specificity is combined with other techniques, such as making nonverbal in-court observations or conducting mock juries, the ability to predict juror behavior may be enhanced. In this chapter, we conclude the book by discussing a number of strategies for the further improvement of scientific jury selection. These strategies include developing broader theories of juror behavior, applying innovative statistical techniques to analyzing research on juror behavior, developing approaches for measuring personality and attitudes that have greater practical utility in the courtroom, and improving collaboration between consultants and academic researchers.

DEVELOPING BROADER THEORIES OF JUROR BEHAVIOR

As discussed in chapter 8, evidence strength has been shown to be a more powerful predictor of verdicts than background characteristics of jurors. However, when jurors walk into a jury room, they are usually not unanimous in their verdict preferences (Ellsworth, 1993; Kalven & Zeisel, 1966). Thus, evidence strength cannot be the only factor in juror decisions. Individual differences must also be considered. The influence of individual differences may be small, but they are powerful enough to lead to differential interpretations of evidence strength. For the field of scientific jury selection to continue to advance it must develop theoretical models that better explain the relationship between personality factors, evidence strength, and other relevant influences produced by courtroom experiences, rather than developing microlevel theories that explain behavioral reactions to specific elements of the trial.

For example, the application of the just world theory (see chap. 5) to the voir dire process allows a researcher to identify individuals as high or low in just world beliefs and to classify them in separate groups. Verdict preferences are then compared between the groups. Although this classification may go beyond simply using personality characteristics by taking into account evidentiary factors (such as whether the victim did anything to precipitate the incident), many other relevant factors are still ignored. Relevant factors may include: the type of case, the strength of the evidence, the background of the witnesses, the style of the testimony (e.g., conclusions based on the application of actuarial instruments or clinical judgments, highly emotional descriptions of events, complicated statistical testimony), jury instructions (i.e., both the elements contained in the instructions and the writing style), the composition of the jury (e.g., are there dynamic leaders, tight-knit subgroups, or other jurors with similar backgrounds), and relevant events that occur outside the courtroom prior to the trial, just to name a few. Over the past 3 decades, researchers have made some strides in developing broad theories to explain the interaction between different types of relevant factors that affect juror decisions. A prime example of a broad theory that has significantly advanced the field is the story model (Pennington & Hastie, 1990, 1993).

Story Model

As discussed in chapter 9, the story model indicates that jurors use a story structure to integrate trial evidence with prior real world knowledge about similar events. The result of this process is the development of a story (or stories) for events, such as those events that surrounded the commission of a crime. Constructed stories are then compared with beliefs regarding potential verdict categories that consist of both formal judicial instructions on the law and prior ideas about crime categories. According to this empirically supported model, jurors ultimately render a verdict that best fits with the most plausible story that has been constructed (Pennington & Hastie, 1990, 1993).

The strength of the story model is that it allows for mediating factors, including important background factors, to come between the evidence and the verdict, which in turn may allow for greater precision in scientific jury selection. For example, in research on juror verdicts in a murder trial, Pennington and Hastie (1990) reported that social class was related to the harshness of the verdicts. Jurors from wealthier suburbs typically inferred that the defendant intended to injure or kill the victim because he was carrying a knife at the time of the crime. However, jurors sampled from poorer neighborhoods were not surprised that the defendant possessed a weapon and were more likely to accept the defense's claim that the defendant carried the knife either out of habit or for general protection.

The incorporation of mediating factors related to juror backgrounds is an advantage over earlier mathematical models of juror decision making (for a review see Hastie, 1993; Pennington & Hastie, 1981) that depicted how evidentiary factors would be combined in a rational way according to Bayesian norms or other mathematical weightings, in a typically linear manner (MacCoun, 1989; Pennington & Hastie, 1981, 1993). In these mathematical models, juror judgments regarding perceptions of evidence strength are compared with a decision threshold that corresponds to a standard of proof, such as reasonable doubt. These models do not assume that jurors actually make computations in their heads. Rather, the formulas are used to make clear predictions regarding the impact of different evidentiary elements of a case. As a result, mathematical models can be seen as complementing the story model (Lopes, 1993). We hope future theoretical developments and refinements will focus on the integration of these complementary theories. In addition, improvements in the predictive ability of background factors on verdict decisions may come from the application of innovative theories that examine the interaction between individual differences and external influences on behavior. Terror management theory (Greenberg, Solomon, & Pyszczynski, 1997) provides an example of such an interaction.

Terror Management Theory

A recent line of research on terror management theory (TMT) has explored the relationship between awareness of death and jury decisions (Arndt, Lieberman, Cook, & Solomon, 2005) and has identified important interactions between individual differences and external influences. TMT maintains that the unique human capacity for self-awareness and self-reflection, coupled with an innate animal instinct for self-preservation, produces an intense fear of death in humans. To manage the anxiety that is produced by this mortality salience, individuals invest in and defend a *cultural worldview*. Cultural worldviews are fragile social constructions that require validation from cultural supporters (i.e., others who share our belief system). However, one must periodically confront others who threaten our beliefs and values.

From a TMT perspective lawbreakers represent worldview threats, because criminal behavior reflects a rejection of the accepted rules of society. Initial research in TMT (Rosenblatt, Greenberg, Solomon, Pyszczynski, & Lyon, 1989, Study 1) demonstrated that municipal court judges reminded of their own mortality were more punitive to a lawbreaker (a prostitute) than judges who were not asked to contemplate their death. However, a second study revealed that mortality salience effects emerged only when subjects held negative beliefs about prostitution (Rosenblatt et al., 1989, Study 2). Thus, individual differences regarding attitudes toward prostitution exerted a powerful influence in this context. Individual differences regarding self-esteem are also highly relevant to mortality salience effects because self-esteem has been shown to serve as a buffer against the anxiety produced by mortality salience (Greenberg et al., 1997). Selecting jurors with high levels of self-esteem would theoretically make them less likely to be influenced by personal biases toward the parties involved (namely the defendant) in cases in which mortality is salient (e.g., death penalty cases or wrongful death civil suits).

As a consequence, the main finding that emerges is that mortality salience will activate personality attributes and individual biases that have important interactive effects with case factors, judicial instructions, and external events. For example, mortality salience can lead jurors to be more likely to adhere to judicial instructions to ignore inadmissible evidence if beliefs regarding procedural fairness are highly important to them (Cook, Arndt, & Lieberman, 2004). As a result, scientific jury selection consultants and attorneys may want to carefully consider the influence of those factors when death is a salient feature of a trial, such as in a homicide case or in a personal injury trial about a fatality. The impact of external reminders of death on jurors has not escaped the notice of consultants. For example, one trial consultant speculated that mortality salience caused by the September 11th terrorist attacks may have had an impact on juror decisions in criminal and civil cases tried immediately after the attacks (Rowland, 2002). In the future, scientific jury selection consultants should attempt to apply other broad theories of human behavior that may be able to account for the interaction of various key factors present during a trial.

APPLYING INNOVATIVE STATISTICAL APPROACHES

In addition to developing improved theoretical models, it is important to explore new statistical techniques that may improve the science behind scientific jury selection. For example, new statistical techniques may be useful not only in predicting the behavior of jurors but also for examining the conditions in which scientific jury selection has succeeded or failed. A newly developed statistical technique known as qualitative comparative analysis (QCA) may be useful in analyzing the multitude of variables present in successful and unsuccessful applications of scientific jury selection. QCA has been increasingly used in the past decade to model comparative data (for a review see Ragin, 1987; Miethe & Drass, 1999). QCA could be used to provide a descriptive profile of the particular combinations of case and evidentiary factors that are (a) uniquely observed among "successful" applications of scientific jury selection, (b) uniquely observed among "failures" (e.g., unsuccessful trial outcomes where scientific jury selection has been used), and (c) common among both successes and failures. This method is often used on small samples so it is an appropriate technique to use to examine the success patterns within a consulting firm or law firm. By empirically modeling the particular conditions under which scientific jury selection is successfully used, in the future consultants and attorneys would have clearer knowledge of the particular case and evidentiary attributes that may determine whether scientific jury selection is worthwhile, or whether the evidentiary factors (e.g., the presence of a DNA sample in a rape case) are so strong that the case should be disposed of through a criminal trial, plea negotiation, or pretrial dismissal.

DEVELOPMENT OF MORE PRACTICAL
PREDICTORS OF BEHAVIOR

When jury decision-making studies that focus on the influence of personality factors are conducted in academic environments, researchers often ask participants to complete lengthy scales. For example, scales measuring authoritarianism, juror bias, or just world beliefs frequently contain as many as 20 to 30 questions (see chap. 5). From the standpoint of creating a strong empirical test of the influence of these factors, using scales with many questions is necessary to increase the reliability of the scale. Unfortunately, during jury selection the practical utility of this approach is limited. It will almost certainly be impossible for attorneys to ask all the questions on any of these scales, or to include entire scales in pretrial questionnaires given to the venire members. In many cases, judges simply will not allow it. As a result, it will be useful to develop more concise scales or clearly identify critical questions that produce the strongest relationships between responses and behavior. However, when the opportunity arises, attorneys should assess personality characteristics using as many questions as the judge will allow, as multiple measures of a concept are generally superior to single measures (Babbie, 1998).

IMPROVE COLLABORATION BETWEEN CONSULTANTS AND ACADEMIC RESEARCHERS

Greater collaboration between consultants and academic researchers is critical to advance the field of scientific jury selection and will likely be beneficial to the attorneys, their clients, and the courts. For example, greater collaboration should allow for better tests of the effectiveness of the scientific jury selection approach. Despite the fact that scientific jury selection has been used for over 3 decades, relatively few studies have directly evaluated the effectiveness of the technique. One direct test was conducted by Horowitz (1980), who compared the effectiveness of scientific jury selection with traditional selection methods (see chap. 8). However, Horowitz's methodology was highly artificial, as individuals in the scientific jury selection condition were law students who had been given brief training in this approach and presented with profiles of jurors ranging from "most friendly" to "least friendly." Other examinations of the effectiveness of scientific jury selection have reported the results of the approach in only one or two cases or by using hypothetical computer modeling (Frederick, 1984; Tindale & Nagao, 1986; Zeisel & Diamond, 1976).

Thus, better research is needed regarding the effectiveness of scientific jury selection. Perhaps the strongest test would be to use Horowitz's mock jury approach but with the participation of practicing attorneys, an actual judge, and a full-size venire of prospective jurors who accurately represent the characteristics of the juror pool. This process should be conducted with a series of different trials (both criminal and civil). Ideally, each attorney who participated would select jurors in multiple trials. That would allow participating attorneys to conduct voir dire in a traditional approach, and with the aid of a consultant at least once. Conducting such a study would certainly be expensive. However, the cost would be trivial compared with the total amount of money that attorneys (through their clients) spend on consultants each year in the absence of certainty regarding the effectiveness of this approach.

A more valid test of the effectiveness of scientific jury selection may be useful for courts as well. If it can be clearly demonstrated that scientific jury selection can identify biased jurors more effectively than traditional selection approaches and that trial outcome is affected by failure to exclude biased jurors via traditional selection decisions, it bolsters the argument that courts should grant requests for court-appointed consultants in certain cases.

In addition, jury decision making researchers frequently use simulated mock jury procedures that lack the dynamics of an actual courtroom experience because of a need to conduct the study in highly controlled conditions and financial constraints on research. Researchers would greatly benefit from an opportunity to replicate findings obtained in their studies in an actual courtroom environment. Consultants could facilitate this process and in turn be exposed to current research findings and trends. This would be particularly beneficial to consultants, as no continuing education requirements currently exist.

Academic researchers would also benefit from having access to consultants' data, as it may facilitate the investigation of a wide variety of interesting issues. For example, providing information regarding the characteristics of trials in which scientific jury selection has been successfully or unsuccessfully used may provide a better understanding of conditions that must be present for a successful application. Further, it has been noted that attorneys who have hired jury selection and other trial consultants use the information drawn from scientific jury selection as a supplement to their own intuitions, rather than as a substitute for them (Treger, 1992). In light of this, it would be useful to know the specific conditions that determine when attorneys will and will not rely on scientific jury selection guidelines. For example, as discussed in chapter 1, Marcia Clark, the lead prosecutor in the O.J. Simpson case, decided against following the advice of Donald Vinson, the trial consultant working for her side. It is not uncommon for individuals to rely on personal beliefs over statistical information (Pacini & Epstein, 1999). Perhaps attorneys are more likely to do so when they have less investment in using the consultant. In Marcia Clark's case, Vinson was working pro bono, so Clark's investment of resources was minimal. This analysis is purely speculative; it may be useful for academics to conduct empirical research in this area with the aid of consultants to try to identify the conditions under which attorneys are likely to go against useful statistical information and potentially make errors in judgments.

Consultants may also benefit from partnerships with academics. Time and financial constraints hinder the ability of consultants to run large-scale studies to test pretrial predictions. As a result, mock jury studies run by consultants are methodologically limited in a number of ways, including having small sample sizes, not holding stimulus materials constant across conditions (e.g., having witnesses with different qualifications present different material to jurors, so that any identified effects of testimony on verdict preferences are naturally confounded by witness background characteristics), and infrequently using control groups (Ellis, 2005). It may be useful for consultants to periodically work with academic researchers to examine jury selection strategy recommendations in a methodologically sound manner. For example, a consultant may benefit from conducting a confirmatory study regarding juror behavior predictions they have made to determine whether the strategy was truly successful. To make this determination, basic information regarding juror characteristic predictions could be presented to an academic researcher, along with a trial transcript of the case. The academic researcher could conduct carefully controlled experimental studies to test the relevant hypotheses generated by pretrial predictions. The use of undergraduate participants would allow confirmatory research to be conducted in a cost-effective manner. The results would allow consultants to verify the effectiveness of their recommendations or look for causes of failure, so revisions could be made in future cases.

Finally, greater collaboration between academics and professional consultants may lead to better education and training, which should improve the overall effectiveness of scientific jury selection. If those who conduct scientific jury selection are not well-trained in social scientific methodology, there is no reason to believe the data they collect will be particularly useful. As previously noted, currently there are no formal educational programs for scientific jury selection and other trial consultants (Moran, 2001). As a result, those interested in becoming consultants are often forced to create their own educational programs on a piecemeal basis in which they take a number of classes they think might someday be useful and work with their adviser in some relevant, but limited, area of research. Many quality doctoral programs are built on a strong mentoring approach to education in which students work closely with an adviser and are trained in the adviser's theoretical and methodological orientation. For example, social science students (particularly those in psychology) typically are trained in either survey methodology or in experimental research (critical for conducting quality mock jury studies), but not both. This approach is useful if the student wants to continue in his or her adviser's line of research in an academic setting. However, it does not necessarily work well if the goal is to produce a well-rounded consultant capable of conducting projects that use the different scientific jury selection techniques. That is, both survey research and experimental methodology skills are highly important to scientific jury selection; the ability to make skilled nonverbal observations might be a critical skill as well. A program that provides strong education in all these areas would be quite useful. Thus, academics are critical to producing well-trained consultants. Academic programs would benefit from input from consultants in terms of providing the marketplace with graduates who are trained in highly desirable skills. For example, would it be useful to consulting firms for students to graduate with a background in psychophysiology so more direct measurements can be made of emotional arousal during mock jury studies? Collaboration, or at least improved communication, is necessary to convey an issue such as this to educators. Collaborative efforts between academics and consultants may also lead to expanded internship opportunities, which could provide valuable experience for students and potentially lower the cost of consulting activities and services, as the cost to pay interns for their activities is relatively small.

CONCLUSION

It is important that new approaches be developed for the field of scientific jury selection to continue to evolve. There will certainly be advancements in the field of psychology that will give a better understanding of factors that influence human behavior. The practical applications of these advancements are likely to improve the utility of scientific jury selection, particularly if advancements are accompanied by improved academic training.

It is also important to get a better sense of exactly how effective scientific jury selection currently is. Because there are a paucity of studies that directly examined the effectiveness of scientific jury selection and those that have been conducted have been methodologically limited, we do not yet have a complete understanding regarding the effectiveness of this approach. For the most part, the studies that cast doubt on the effectiveness of scientific jury selection have typically focused on the influence of background characteristics and ignored supplemental techniques such as nonverbal behavior observations and mock jury trials. Therefore, it cannot be accurately claimed that scientific jury selection is not beneficial to the parties that choose to use it.

Finally, improved collaboration between academic researchers, professional consultants, and attorneys is critical to producing high quality evaluation studies and facilitating the development of the next generation of research. Thus, we are hopeful that researchers' interest in scientific jury selection will continue and that as predictive ability based on scientific jury selection data is increased, the proposed reforms discussed in chapter 10 will be considered, so there can be wider and more equitable use of scientific jury selection. The ultimate product of such advancements and reforms should be an increase in the elimination of biased jurors and a more fair process for *all* parties involved in trials.

REFERENCES

Abbott, W. F. (1987). *Analytic juror rater*. Philadelphia: American Law Institute.

Abbott, W. F. (1999a). The analytic juror rater: Toward an unobtrusive technique. In W. F. Abbott & J. Batt (Eds.), *Handbook of jury research* (pp. 15-1–15-81). Philadelphia: American Law Institute–American Bar Association.

Abbott, W. F. (1999b). Step 1–Diagnostics: The scope of the planning conference. In W. F. Abbott & J. Batt (Eds.), *Handbook of jury research* (pp. 26-1–26-12). Philadelphia: American Law Institute–American Bar Association.

Abbott, W. F. (1999c). Step 3–Designing and implementing mock trials: A checklist. In W. F. Abbott & J. Batt (Eds.), *Handbook of jury research* (pp. 28-1–28-40). Philadelphia: American Law Institute–American Bar Association.

Abramsom, J. (1994). *We, the jury: The jury system and the ideal of democracy*. New York: Basic Books.

Adkins, J. C. (1968–1969, December). Jury selection: An art? A science? Or luck? *Trial, 5*, 37–39.

Adler, F. (1973). Socioeconomic factors influencing juror verdicts. *New York University Review of Law and Social Change, 3*, 1–10.

Adorno, T., Frenkel-Brunswik, E., Levinson, D., & Sanford, N. (1950). *The authoritarian personality*. New York: Harper.

Ajzen, I., & Fishbein, M. (1977). Attitude–behavior relations: A theoretical analysis and review of empirical literature. *Psychological Bulletin, 84*, 888–918.

Allport, G. W., & Vernon, P. E. (1933). *Studies in expressive movement*. New York: Macmillan.

Altemeyer, B. (1988). *Enemies of freedom*. San Francisco: Jossey-Bass.

American Bar Association. (1983). *Model rules of professional conduct*. Chicago: Author.

American Psychological Association. (2002). *Ethical principles of psychologists and code of conduct*. Retrieved May 2, 2005, from http://www.apa.org/ethics/

American Society of Trial Consultants. (2004). *ASTC president says professionally conducted surveys yield reliable data for trial decisions* [Electronic version]. Retrieved December 5, 2005, from http://www.astcweb.org/aboutus/newspr.php

Anderson, C. A., Lepper, M. R., & Ross, L. (1980). Perseverance of social theories: The role of explanation in the persistence of discredited information. *Journal of Personality and Social Psychology, 39*, 1037–1049.

Appleman, J. (1952). *Successful jury trials: A symposium*. Indianapolis, IN: Bobbs-Merrill.

Arndt, J., Lieberman, J. D., Cook, A., & Solomon, S. (2005). Terror in the courtroom: Exploring the effects of mortality salience on legal decision-making. *Psychology, Public Policy, and Law, 11*, 407–438.

Arnold, S., & Gold, A. (1978–1979). The use of a public opinion poll on a change of venue application. *Criminal Law Quarterly, 21*, 445–464.

Asch, S. E. (1955, November). Opinions and social pressure. *Scientific American, 193*, 31–35.

Asch, S. E. (1956). Studies of independence and conformity: I. A minority of one against a unanimous majority. *Psychological Monographs, 70*, 1–70.

Babbie, E. (1998). *The practice of social research.* Belmont, CA: Wadsworth.

Bailey, F. L. (1974). *Fundamentals of criminal advocacy.* Rochester, NY: Lawyers Co-operative.

Bailey, F. L., & Rothblatt, H. B. (1971). *Successful techniques for criminal trials.* Rochester, NY: Lawyers Cooperative.

Bailey, F. L., & Rothblatt, H. B. (1985). *Successful techniques for criminal trials* (2nd ed.). Rochester, NY: Lawyers Cooperative.

Bal Theatre Corporation v. Paramount Film Distributing Corporation, 206 F. Supp. 708 (1962).

Balch, R. W., Griffiths, C. T., Hall, E. L., & Winfree, L. T. (1976). The socialization of jurors: The voir dire as a rite of passage. *Journal of Criminal Justice, 4*, 271–283.

Baldus, D. C., Woodworth, G., & Pulaski, C. A., Jr. (1990). *Equal justice and the death penalty: A legal and empirical analysis.* Boston: Northeastern University Press.

Baldus, D. C., Woodworth, G., Zuckerman, D., Weiner, N. A., & Broffitt, B. (2001). The use of peremptory challenges in capital murder trials: A legal and empirical analysis. *University of Pennsylvania Journal of Constitutional Law, 3*, 1–172.

Baldwin, J., & McConville, M. (1980). Does the composition of an English jury affect its verdict? *Judicature, 64*, 133–139.

Bales, R. F. (1958). Task roles and social roles in problem solving groups. In E. E. Maccoby, T. M. Newcomb, & E. L. Hartley (Eds.), *Readings in social psychology* (pp. 437–447). New York: Holt, Rinehart & Winston.

Barber, J. W. (1994). The jury is still out: The role of science in the modern American courtroom. *American Criminal Law Review, 31*, 1225–1252.

Bar-Hillel, M., & Ben-Shakhar, G. (2000). The a priori case against graphology: Methodological and conceptual bases. In T. Connolly & H. R. Arkes (Eds.), *Judgment and decision making: An interdisciplinary reader* (2nd ed., pp. 556–569). New York: Cambridge University Press.

Batson v. Kentucky, 476 U.S. 79 (1986).

Beaman, A. L., Klentz, B., Diener, E., & Svanum, S. (1979). Self-awareness and transgression in children: Two field studies. *Journal of Personality and Social Psychology, 77*, 525–537.

Belli, M. (1982). *Modern trials.* St. Paul, MN: West Publishing.

Ben-Shakhar, G., Bar-Hillel, M., Bilu, Y., Ben-Abba, E., & Flug, A. (1986). Can graphology predict occupational success? Two empirical studies and some methodological ruminations. *Journal of Applied Psychology, 71*, 645–652.

Berg, K., & Vidmar, N. (1975). Authoritarianism and recall of evidence about criminal behavior. *Journal of Research in Personality, 9,* 147–157.

Berman, J., & Sales, B. D. (1977). A critical evaluation of the systematic approach to jury selection. *Criminal Justice and Behavior, 4,* 219–239.

Bermant, G. (1977). *Conduct of the voir dire examination: Practices and opinions of federal district judges.* Washington, DC: Federal Judicial Center.

Bermant, G. (1985). Issues in trial management: Conducting the voir dire examination. In S. M. Katzin & L. S. Wrightsman (Eds.), *The psychology of evidence and trial procedure* (pp. 298–322). Beverly Hills, CA: Sage.

Biskind, E. L. (1954). *How to prepare a case for trial.* Englewood Cliffs, NJ: Prentice Hall.

Blue, L. A. (2001, February). *Identifying and addressing juror bias-voir dire* . Reference materials presented at the American Trial Lawyers Winter Convention, Nashville, TN.

Bodenhausen, G. V. (1990). Stereotypes as judgmental heuristics: Evidence of circadian variations in discrimination. *Psychological Science, 1,* 319–322.

Bodenhausen, G. V., & Lichtenstein, M. (1987). Social stereotypes and information-processing strategies: The impact of task complexity. *Journal of Personality and Social Psychology, 52,* 871–880.

Boehm, V. R. (1968). Mr. Prejudice, Miss Sympathy, and the authoritarian personality: An application of psychological measuring techniques to the problem of jury bias. *Wisconsin Law Review, 1968,* 734–750.

Bonazzoli, M. J. (1998). Jury selection and bias: Debunking invidious stereotypes through science. *Quinnipiac Law Review, 18,* 247–305.

Bond, C. F., Jr., Kahler, K. N., & Paolicelli, L. M. (1985). The miscommunication of deception: An adaptive perspective. *Journal of Experimental Social Psychology, 21,* 331–345.

Bond, C. F., Jr., Omar, A., Pitre, U., Lashley, B. R., Skaggs, L. M., & Kirk, C. T. (1992). Fishy-looking liars: Deception judgment from expectancy violation. *Journal of Personality and Social Psychology, 63,* 969–977.

Bornstein, B. H. (1999). The ecological validity of jury simulations: Is the jury still out? *Law and Human Behavior, 23,* 75–91.

Bornstein, B. H., & Rajki, M. (1994). Extra-legal factors and product liability: The influence of mock jurors' demographic characteristics and intuitions about the cause of an injury. *Behavioral Sciences & the Law, 12,* 127–147.

Bornstein, B. H., Whisenhunt, B. L., Nemeth, R. J., & Dunaway, D. L. (2002). Pretrial publicity and civil cases: A two-way street? *Law and Human Behavior, 26,* 3–17.

Bottoms, B. L., & Goodman, G. S. (1994). Perceptions of children's credibility in sexual assault cases. *Journal of Applied Social Psychology, 24,* 702–732.

Boyll, J. R. (1991). Psychological, cognitive, personality and interpersonal factors in jury verdicts. *Law & Psychology Review, 15,* 163–184.

Bray, R. M., & Noble, A. M. (1978). Authoritarianism and decisions of mock juries: Evidence of jury bias and group polarization. *Journal of Personality and Social Psychology, 36,* 1424–1430.

Brekke, N., & Borgida, E. (1988). Expert psychological testimony in rape trials: A social–cognitive analysis. *Journal of Personality and Social Psychology, 36,* 1424–1430.

Brenner, S. (1989). Voir dire and jury selection. In S. Allen, I. Rosen, D. Winston, & L. Belfiore (Eds.), *Criminal defense techniques* (pp. 21–136). New York: Matthew Bender.

Bridgeman, D. L., & Marlowe, D. (1979). Jury decision making: An empirical study based on actual felony trials. *Journal of Applied Psychology, 64,* 91–98.

Broeder, D. W. (1959). The University of Chicago jury project. *Nebraska Law Review, 38,* 744–761.

Broeder, D. W. (1965). Voir dire examinations: An empirical study. *Southern California Law Review, 38,* 503–528.

Bronson, E. J. (1970). On the conviction proneness and representativeness of the death-qualified jury: An empirical study of Colorado veniremen. *University of Colorado Law Review, 42,* 1–32.

Brooks v. Zahn, 170 Ariz. 545 (Ariz. App., 1991).

Bruner, J. S., & Tagiuri, R. (1954). Person perception. In G. Lindzey (Ed.), *Handbook of social psychology* (Vol. 2, pp. 634–654). Reading, MA: Addison-Wesley.

Bryan, W. J. (1971). *The chosen ones.* New York: Vantage Press.

Buckhout, R., Baker, E., Perlman, M., & Spiegel, R. (1977). Jury attitudes and the death penalty. *Social Action and the Law, 3,* 80–81.

Buckhout, R., Licker, J., Alexander, M., Gambardella, J., Eugenio, P., & Kakoullis, B. (1979). Discretion in jury selection. In L. E. Abt & I. R. Stuart (Eds.), *Social psychology and discretionary law* (pp. 176–196). New York: Van Nostrand Reinhold.

Buller, D. B., Comstock, J., Aune, R. K, & Strzyzewski, K. (1989). The effect of probing on deceivers and truthtellers. *Journal of Nonverbal Behavior, 13,* 155–169.

Buller, D. B., Strzyzewski, K., & Comstock, J. (1991). Interpersonal deception I: Deceivers' reactions to receivers' suspicions and probing. *Communications Monographs, 58,* 1–24.

Bureau of Justice Statistics. (1998). *State court organization.* Washington, DC: U.S. Department of Justice.

Burgoon, J. K., Buller, D. B., Dillman, L., & Walther, J. B. (1995). Interpersonal deception IV: Effects of suspicion on perceived communication and nonverbal behavior dynamics. *Human Communication Research, 22,* 163–196.

Byrne, D., & Kelley, K. (1981). *An introduction to personality* (3rd ed.). Englewood Cliffs, NJ: Prentice-Hall.

Cacioppo, J. T., & Petty, R. E. (1982). The need for cognition. *Journal of Personality and Social Psychology, 42,* 116–131.

Calder, B., & Ross, M. (1973). *Attitudes and behavior*. Morristown, NJ: General Learning Press.

Campbell, D. T., & Stanley, J. C. (1963). *Experimental and quasi-experimental designs for research*. Boston: Houghton Mifflin.

Cartwright, R. E. (1977). Jury selection. *Trial, 13*, 29–31.

Carver, C. S., & Scheier, M. F. (1978). Self-focusing effects of dispositional self-consciousness, mirror presence, and audience presence. *Journal of Personality and Social Psychology, 36*, 324–332.

Carver, C. S., & Scheier, M. F. (1981). Attention and self-regulation. New York: Springer-Verlag.

Cecil, J. S., Lind, E. A., & Bermant, G. (1987). *Jury service in lengthy civil trials*. Washington, DC: Federal Justice Center.

Chawkins, S. (2005, February 13). Attorneys wary of 'stealth jurors' in Jackson's trial. *Los Angeles Times* [Electronic version]. Retrieved March 10, 2005, from http://www.latimes.com/news/local/la-me-stealth13feb13,1,2228258.story?ctrack=1&cset=true

Chiang, H. (2002, November 20). Chronicle profile: Madelyn Chaber godmother of tobacco suits bay area lawyer won first multimillion-dollar verdict for a smoker. *SFGate.com*. Retrieved February 24, 2006, from http://www.sfgate.com/cgi-bin/article.cgi?file=/chronicle/archive/2002/11/20/MN217741.DTL

Christie, R. (1976). Probability v. precedence: The social psychology of jury selection. In G. Bermant, C. Nemeth, & N. Vidmar (Eds.), *Psychology and the law* (pp. 265–281). Lexington, MA: Lexington Books.

Christie, R. (1991). Authoritarianism and related constructs. In J. P. Robinson, P. R. Shaver, & L. S. Wrightsman (Eds.), *Measures of personality and social psychological attitudes* (pp. 501–571). San Diego, CA: Academic Press.

Christie, R., & Geis, F. L. (1970). *Studies in Machiavellianism*. New York: Academic Press.

Consedine, N. S., & Magai, C. (2002). The uncharted waters of emotion: Ethnicity, trait emotion, and emotion expression in older adults. *Journal of Cross-Cultural Gerontology, 17*, 71–100.

Constanti, E., & King, J. (1980). The partial juror: Correlates and causes of prejudgment. *Law & Society Review, 15*, 9–40.

Cook, A., Arndt, J., & Lieberman, J. D. (2004). The effects of mortality salience on reactions to inadmissible evidence. *Law and Human Behavior, 28*, 389–410.

Corboy, P. H. (1980). Opening statement. *Litigation, 6*, 1–2, 67.

Cornelius, A. L. (1932). *Trial tactics*. New York: Matthew Bender.

Cotsirilos, J. G., & Philipsborn, J. T. (1986, July). A change of venue roadmap. *The Champion*, 8–15.

Covington, M. (1985). Jury selection: Innovative approaches to both civil and criminal litigation. *St. Mary's Law Journal, 16*, 575–598.

Cowan, C. L., Thompson, W. C., & Ellsworth, P. C. (1984). The effects of death qualification on jurors' predisposition to convict and on the quality of deliberation. *Law and Human Behavior, 8*, 53–79.

Cox, M., & Tanford, S. (1989). Effects of evidence and instructions in civil trials: An experimental investigation of rules of admissibility. *Social Behaviour, 4*, 31–55.

Crowne, D. P., & Marlowe, D. (1960). A new scale of social desirability independent of psychopathology. *Journal of Consulting Psychology, 24*, 349–354.

Cutler, B. L., Moran, G., & Narby, D. J. (1992). Jury selection in insanity cases. *Journal of Research in Personality, 26*, 165–182.

Cutrow, R. J., Parks, A., Lucas, N., & Thomas, K. (1972). The objective use of multiple physiological indices in the detection of deception. *Psychophysiology, 9*, 578–588.

Daniels, S. (1991). Tracing the shadow of the law: Jury verdicts in medical malpractice cases. *Defense Law Journal, 40*, 415–449.

Darden, W. R., DeConinck, J. B., Babin, B. J., & Griffin, M. (1991). The role of consumer sympathy in product liability suits. *Journal of Business Research, 22*, 65–89.

Darrow, C. (1936, May). Attorney for the defense. *Esquire, 5*, 36.

Davidson, A. R., & Jaccard, J. J. (1979). Variables that moderate the attitude behavior relation: Results of a longitudinal survey. *Journal of Personality and Social Psychology, 37*, 1364–1376.

Dearen, J. (2004, May 27). Peterson jury to be seated today. *Marin Independent Journal.* Available from LexisNexis Web site, http://web.lexis-nexis.com/universe

DecisionQuest. (1997). *When- and when-not to use a jury questionnaire.* Retrieved December 5, 2005, from http://www.decisionquest.com/litigation_library.php?NewsID=237

Deitz, S. R., Blackwell, K. T., Daley, P. C., & Bentley, B. J. (1982). Measurement of empathy toward rape victims and rapists. *Journal of Personality and Social Psychology, 43*, 372–384.

Deitz, S. R., Littman, M., & Bentley, B. J. (1984). Attribution of responsibility for rape: The influence of observer empathy, victim resistance, and victim attractiveness. *Sex Roles, 10*, 261–280.

Denove, C. F., & Imwinkelried, E. J. (1995). Jury selection: An empirical investigation of demographic bias. *American Journal of Trial Advocacy, 19*, 285–336.

DePaulo, B. M., & Pfeifer, R. L. (1986). On-the-job experience and skill in detecting deception. *Journal of Applied Social Psychology, 16*, 249–267.

DePaulo, B. M., Stone, J. L., & Lassiter, G. D. (1985). Deceiving and detecting deceit. In B. R. Schlenker (Ed.), *The self and social life* (pp. 323–370). New York: McGraw-Hill.

deTurck, M., & Miller, G. R. (1985). Deception and arousal: Isolating the behavioral correlates of deception. *Human Communication Research, 12*, 181–202.

Development in the law: Jury selection and composition. (1997). *Harvard Law Review, 110,* 1443–1466.

Dexter, H. R., Cutler, B. L., & Moran, G. (1992). A test of voir dire as a remedy for the prejudicial effects of pretrial publicity. *Journal of Applied Social Psychology, 22,* 819–832.

Diamond, S. S. (1990). Scientific jury selection: What social scientists know and do not know. *Judicature, 73,* 178–183.

Diamond, S. S. (1997). Illuminations and shadows from jury simulations. *Law and Human Behavior, 21,* 561–571.

Diamond, S. S., Saks, M. J., & Landsman, S. (1998). Juror judgments about liability and damages: Sources of variability and ways to increase consistency. *DePaul Law Review, 48,* 301–325.

Diamond, S. S., & Zeisel, H. (1974). A courtroom experiment on juror selection and decision-making. *Personality and Social Psychology Bulletin, 1,* 276–277.

Dibner, A. S. (1956). Cue-counting: A measure of anxiety in interviews. *Journal of Consulting Psychology, 20,* 475–478.

Diener, E. (1980). Deindividuation: The absence of self-awareness and self-regulation in group members. In P. Paulus (Ed.), *The psychology of group influence* (pp. 1160–1171). Hillsdale, NJ: Erlbaum.

Dillman, D. A. (1993). *Mail and telephone surveys: The total design method.* New York: Wiley.

Dillman, D. A. (1999). *Mail and internet surveys: The tailored design method* (2nd ed.). New York: Wiley.

Dimitrius, J., & Mazzarella, M. (1999). *Reading people: How to understand people and predict their behavior—anytime, anyplace.* New York: Ballantine Books.

DiPerna, P. (1984). *Juries on trial.* New York: Dembner Books.

Downer, J. (Producer), & Fleder, G. (Director). (2003). *Runaway jury* [Motion picture]. United States: 20th Century Fox.

Driskell, J. E., & Mullen, B. (1990). Status, expectations, and behavior: A meta-analytic and test of the theory. *Personality and Social Psychology Bulletin, 16,* 541–553.

Duval, S., & Wicklund, R. A. (1972). *A theory of objective self-awareness.* New York: Academic Press.

Duval, T. S., Duval, V. H., & Mulilis, J. P. (1992). Effects of self-focus, discrepancy between self and standard, and outcome expectancy favorability on the tendency to match self to standard or to withdraw. *Journal of Personality and Social Psychology, 62,* 340–348.

Edmonson v. Leesville Concrete Co., Inc., 111 S. Ct. 2077 (1991).

Edwards, C. A., Goldstein, L. A., Handler, S. P., & Wentzel, D. F. (2004). Use of jury consultants: §64:21. Effective partnering strategies—Discoverability of the jury consultant's work. In R. L. Haig (Ed.), *Successful partnership between inside and outside counsel.* St. Paul, MN: West Group.

Edwards, K., & Bryan, T. S. (1997). Judgmental biases produced by instructions to disregard: The (paradoxical) case of emotional information. *Personality and Social Psychology Bulletin, 23*, 849–864.

Efran, J. S. (1968). Looking for approval: Effects on visual behavior of approbation from persons differing in importance. *Journal of Personality and Social Psychology, 10*, 21–25.

Ekman, P. (1973). Cross-cultural studies of facial expression. In P. Ekman (Ed.), *Darwin and facial expression* (pp. 169–222). New York: Academic Press.

Ekman, P., & Friesen, W. V. (1969). Nonverbal leakage and clues to deception. *Psychiatry, 32*, 88–106.

Ekman, P., & Friesen, W. V. (1972). Hand movements and deception. *Journal of Communication, 22*, 353–374.

Ekman, P., & Friesen, W. V. (1974). Detecting deception from the body or face. *Journal of Personality and Social Psychology, 29*, 288–298.

Ekman, P., Friesen, W. V., & Scherer, K. R. (1976). Body movement and voice pitch in deceptive interaction. *Semiotica, 16*, 23–27.

Ekman, P., & O'Sullivan, M. (1991). Who can catch a liar? *American Psychologist, 46*, 913–920.

Ekman, P., O'Sullivan, M., Friesen, W. V., & Scherer, K. R. (1991). Invited article: Face, voice, and body in detecting deceit. *Journal of Nonverbal Behavior, 2*, 125–135.

Ellis, L. (2005, March). *Bridging the gap between the lab and the courtroom: How researchers, consultants, and attorneys can work together to expand the understanding of jury decision-making.* Paper presented at the American Psychology–Law Society Conference, La Jolla, CA.

Ellsworth, P. C. (1993). Some steps between attitudes and verdicts. In R. Hastie (Ed.), *Inside the juror: The psychology of juror decision making* (pp. 42–64). New York: Cambridge University Press.

Ellsworth, P. C., Bukaty, R. M., Cowan, C. L., & Thompson, W. C. (1984). The death qualified jury and the defense of insanity. *Law and Human Behavior, 8*, 81–93.

English, P. W., & Sales, B. D. (2005). *More than the law: Behavioral and social facts in legal decision making.* Washington, DC: American Psychological Association.

Ericsson, K. A., & Simon, H. A. (1993). *Protocol analysis: Verbal reports as data.* Cambridge, MA: MIT Press.

Etzioni, A. (1974). Creating an imbalance. *Trial, 10*, 28–30.

Fargo, M. (1999). Postverdict juror interviews. In W. F. Abbott & J. Batt (Eds.), *Handbook of jury research* (pp. 25-1–25-18). Philadelphia: American Law Institute–American Bar Association.

Farrell, D., & Bunch, W. T., II (1999). Using social science methods to improve voir dire and jury selection. In W. F. Abbott & J. Batt (Eds.), *Handbook of jury research* (pp. 4-1–4-17). Philadelphia: American Law Institute–American Bar Association.

Fazio, R. H., (1986). How do attitudes guide behavior? In R. M. Sorrentino & E. T. Higgins (Eds.), *Handbook of motivation and cognition* (pp. 204–243). New York: Guilford Press.

Fazio, R. H., & Zanna, M. P. (1981). Direct experience and attitude–behavior consistency. In L. Berkowitz (Ed.), *Advances in experimental social psychology* (Vol. 14, pp. 162–202). New York: Academic Press.

Federal Criminal Justice Act of 1964, 18 U.S.C. sec. 3006 (e). (1993).

Field, H. S. (1978a). Juror background characteristics and attitudes toward rape: Correlates of jurors' decisions in rape trials. *Law and Human Behavior, 2,* 73–93.

Field, H. S. (1978b). Attitudes toward rape: A comparative analysis of police, rapists, crisis counselors, and citizens. *Journal of Personality and Social Psychology, 36,* 156–179.

Field, L. (1965). Voir dire examination—A neglected art. *University of Missouri at Kansas City Law Review, 33,* 171–187.

Finkel, N. J. (1995). *Commonsense justice: Jurors' notions of the law.* Cambridge, MA: Harvard University Press.

Finkel, N. J., & Groscup, J. L. (1997). Crime prototypes, objective versus subjective culpability, and a commonsense balance. *Law and Human Behavior, 21,* 209–230.

Finkel, N. J., & Handel, S. F. (1988). Jurors and insanity: Do test instructions instruct? *Forensic Reports, 1,* 65–79.

Finkel, N. J., & Handel, S. F. (1989). How jurors construe "insanity." *Law and Human Behavior, 13,* 41–59.

Finkelstein, M. O., & Levin, B. (1997). Clear choices and guesswork in peremptory challenges in federal criminal trials. *Journal of the Royal Statistical Society, Series A: Statistics in Society, 160,* 275–288.

Fishbein, M., & Ajzen, I. (1975). *Belief, attitude, intention, and behavior: An introduction to theory and research.* Reading, MA: Addison Wesley.

Fitzgerald, D. R., & Ellsworth, P. C. (1984). Due process vs. crime control: Death qualification and jury attitudes. *Law and Human Behavior, 8,* 31–51.

Flowers v. Flowers, 397 S.W. 2d 121 (Tex. Ct. of Civil App. 1965).

Frederick, J. T. (1984). Social science involvement in voir dire: Preliminary data on the effectiveness of "scientific jury selection." *Behavioral Sciences and the Law, 2,* 375–394.

Freedman, J. L., & Burke, T. M. (1996). The effect of pretrial publicity: The Bernaldo case. *Canadian Journal of Criminology, 38,* 253–270.

Freedman, J. L., Martin, C. K., & Mota, V. L. (1998). Pretrial publicity: Effects of admonitions and expressing pretrial opinions. *Legal and Criminological Psychology, 3,* 255–270.

Freedman, N., & Hoffman, S. P. (1967). Kinetic behavior in altered clinical states: An approach of objective analysis of motor behavior during clinical interviews. *Perceptual and Motor Skills, 24,* 527–539.

Fukurai, H., Butler, E. W., & Krooth, R. (1993). *Race and the jury*. New York: Plenum Press.

Fulero, S. M., & Penrod, S. D. (1990). Attorney jury selection folklore: What do they think and how can psychologists help? *Forensic Reports, 3,* 233–259.

Furnham, A. (1998). Measuring the beliefs in a just world. In L. Montada & M. J. Lerner (Eds.), *Responses to victimization and belief in a just world* (pp. 141–162). New York: Plenum Press.

Furnham, A., Chamorro-Premuzic, T., & Callahan, I. (2003). Does graphology predict personality and intelligence? *Individual Difference Research, 1,* 78–94.

Furnham, A., & Gunter, B. (1987). Graphology and personality: Another failure to validate graphological analysis. *Personality and Individual Differences, 8,* 433–435.

Garcia, L., & Griffitt, W. (1978). Evaluation and recall of evidence: Authoritarianism and the Patty Hearst case. *Journal of Research in Personality, 12,* 57–67.

Gerbasi, K. C., Zuckerman, M., & Reis, H. T. (1977). Justice needs a new blindfold: A review of mock jury research. *Psychological Bulletin, 84,* 323–345.

Gilbert, D. T., & Hixon, J. G. (1991). The trouble of thinking: Activation and application of stereotypic beliefs. *Journal of Personality and Social Psychology, 50,* 509–517.

Ginger, A. F. (1977). *Jury selection in criminal trials.* Tiburon, CA: Law Press Corporation.

Glick, P., Gottesman, D., & Jolton, J. (1989). The fault is not in the stars: Susceptibility of skeptics and believers in astrology to the Barnum effect. *Personality and Social Psychology Bulletin, 15,* 572–583.

Goldstein, I. (1935). *Trial technique.* Chicago: Callaghan.

Goodman, J., & Loftus, E. F. (1987). How to play to the jury you select. *Criminal Justice, 2,* 2–5, 42–43.

Goodman, J., Loftus, E. F., & Greene, E. L. (1990). Matters of money: Voir dire in civil cases. *Forensic Reports, 3,* 303–329.

Gosling, S. D., Vazire, S., Srivastava, S., & John, O. P. (2004). Should we trust Web-based studies? A comparative analysis of six preconceptions about Internet questionnaires. *American Psychologist, 59,* 93–104.

Graziano, S. J., Panter, A. T., & Tanaka, J. S. (1990). Individual differences in information processing strategies and their role in juror decision making and selection. *Forensic Reports, 3,* 279–301.

Green, E. (1968). The reasonable man: Legal fiction of psychosocial reality. *Law & Society Review, 2,* 241–257.

Greenberg, J., Solomon, S., & Pyszczynski, T. (1997). Terror management theory of self-esteem and social behavior: Empirical assessments and conceptual refinements. In M. P. Zanna (Ed.), *Advances in experimental social psychology* (Vol. 29, pp. 61–139). New York: Academic Press.

Grisham, J. (1996). *Runaway jury.* New York: Doubleday.

Gross, D. J. F., & Webber, C. F. (2003). *PTM: The power trial method.* Notre Dame, IN: National Institute for Trial Advocacy.

Grove, W., & Meehl, P. (1996). Comparative efficiency of informal (subjective, impressionistic) and formal (mechanical, algorithmic) prediction procedures: The clinical–statistical controversy. *Psychology, Public Policy, and Law, 2*, 293–323.

Hafemeister, T. L., Sales, B. D., & Suggs, D. L. (1984). Behavioral expertise in jury selection. In D. N. Weisstub (Ed.), *Law and mental health: International perspectives* (Vol. 1, pp. 123–161). New York: Pergamon Press.

Hagen, J. (1974). Extra-legal attributes and criminal sentencing: An assessment of a sociological viewpoint. *Law and Society, 8*, 357–383.

Hahn, P. W., & Clayton, S. D. (1996). The effects of attorney presentation style, attorney gender, and juror gender on juror decisions. *Law and Human Behavior, 20*, 533–554.

Hamilton, V. L. (1978). Obedience and responsibility: A jury simulation. *Journal of Personality and Social Psychology, 36*, 126–146.

Haney, C. (1984). On the selection of capital juries: The biasing effects of the death qualification process. *Law and Human Behavior, 8*, 121–132.

Haney, C., Hurtado, A., & Vega, L. (1994). "Modern" death qualification: New data on its biasing effects. *Law and Human Behavior, 18*, 619–633.

Hanna, J., & O'Brien, J. (1995, October 31). O.J. case leads Philip to make a case against consultants, *Chicago Tribune*, p. 3.

Hannaford-Agor, P. L., Hans, V. P., Mott, N. L., & Munsterman, G. T. (2002). *Are hung juries a problem? The National Center for State Courts—Report to the National Institute of Justice*. Williamsburg, VA: National Center for State Courts.

Hans, V. P., & Jehle, A. (2003). Avoid bald men and people with green socks? Other ways to improve the voir dire process in jury selection. *Chicago Kent Law Review, 78*, 1179–1201.

Hans, V. P., & Lofquist, W. S. (1992). Juror judgments of business liability in tort cases: Implications for the litigation explosion debate. *Law & Society Review, 26*, 85–115.

Hans, V. P., & Lofquist, W. S. (1994). Perceptions of civil justice: The litigation crisis attitudes of civil jurors. *Behavioral Sciences & the Law, 12*, 181–196.

Hans, V. P., & Vidmar, N. (1982). Jury selection. In N. L. Kerr & R. M. Bray (Eds.), *The psychology of the courtroom* (pp. 39–82). Orlando, FL: Academic Press.

Hans, V. P., & Vidmar, N. (1986). *Judging the jury*. New York: Plenum Press.

Harrington, D. C., & Dempsey, J. (1969). Psychological factors in jury selection. *Tennessee Law Review, 37*, 173–178.

Hart, A. (1998). New FBI policy revolutionizes DNA court testimony. *Silent Witness—American Prosecutors Research Institute Newsletter, 4*(1). Retrieved February 28, 2006, from http://www.ndaa.org/publications/newsletters/silent_witness_volume_4_number_1_1998.html

Hass, R. G., & Eisenstadt, D. (1990). The effects of self-focused attention on perspective-taking and anxiety. *Anxiety Research, 2*, 165–176.

Hastie, R. (1991). Is attorney conducted voir dire an effective procedure for the selection of impartial juries? *American University Law Review, 40,* 703–726.

Hastie, R. (Ed.). (1993). *Inside the juror: The psychology of juror decision making.* New York: Cambridge University Press.

Hastie, R., Penrod, S., & Pennington, N. (1983). *Inside the jury.* Cambridge, MA: Harvard University Press.

Hawrish, E., & Tate, E. (1974–1975). Determinants of jury selection. *Saskatchewan Law Review, 30,* 285–292.

Hayden, G., Senna, J., & Siegel, L. (1978). Prosecutorial discretion in peremptory challenges: An empirical investigation of information use in the Massachusetts jury selection process. *New England Law Review, 13,* 768–791.

Hazlewood, D. L., & Brigham, J. C. (1998). Effects for juror anonymity on jury verdicts. *Law and Human Behavior, 22,* 695–713.

Hepburn, J. R. (1980). The objective reality of evidence and the utility of systematic jury selection. *Law and Human Behavior, 4,* 89–102.

Herbsleb, J. D, Sales, B. D., & Berman, J. J. (1979). When psychologists aid in the voir dire: Legal and ethical considerations. In L. A. Abt & I. R. Stuart (Eds.), *Social psychology and discretionary law* (pp. 197–217). New York: Van Nostrand Reinhold.

Heyl, C. (1952). Selection of the jury. *Illinois Bar Journal, 40,* 328–341.

Hocking, J. E., Bauchner, J. E., Kaminski, E. P., & Miller, G. R. (1979). Detecting deceptive communications from verbal, visual, and paralinguistic cues. *Human Communication Research, 6,* 33–46.

Horowitz, I. A. (1980). Juror selection: A comparison of two methods in several criminal cases. *Journal of Applied Social Psychology, 10,* 86–99.

Hunt, M. (1982, November 28). Putting jurors on the couch. *The New York Times Magazine,* pp. 70–72, 78, 82, 85–86, 88.

Jacobs, S. K. (1983, December). Jury selection tips. *California Trial Lawyers Association Forum,* 344–355.

Jamieson, D. W., & Zanna, M. P. (1989). Need for structure in attitude formation and expression. In A. R. Pratkanis, S. J. Breckler, & A. G. Greenwald (Eds.), *Attitude structure and function* (pp. 383–406). Hillsdale, NJ: Erlbaum.

Janoff-Bullman, R., Timko, C., & Carli, L. L. (1985). Cognitive biases in blaming the victim. *Journal of Experimental Social Psychology, 21,* 161–177.

J.E.B. v. Alabama ex rel. T. B., 511 U.S. 127 (1994).

Johnson, C., & Haney, C. (1994). Felony voir dire: An exploratory study of its content and effect. *Law and Human Behavior, 18,* 487–504.

Johnson, J. D., Whitestone, E., Jackson, L. A., & Gatto, L. (1995). Justice is still not colorblind: Differential racial effects of exposure to inadmissible evidence. *Personality and Social Psychology Bulletin, 21,* 893–898.

Jones, C., & Aronson, E. (1973). Attribution of fault to a rape victim as a function of respectability of the victim. *Journal of Personality and Social Psychology, 26,* 415–419.

Jones, S. E. (1987). Judge- versus attorney-conducted voir dire. *Law and Human Behavior, 11*, 131–146.

Jordan, W. (1980). *Jury selection*. Colorado Springs, CO: Shepard's/McGraw-Hill.

Judge conducted voir dire as a time saving trial technique. (1970). *Rutgers–Camden Law Journal, 2*, 161–184.

Jurow, G. (1971). New data on the effect of a death qualified jury on the guilt determination process. *Harvard Law Review, 84*, 567–611.

Jury Selection and Service Act, 28 U.S.C.A. § 1861–1867 (1968).

Kahneman, D., & Tversky, A. (1982). The simulation heuristic. In D. Kahneman, P. Slovic, & A. Tversky (Eds.), *Judgment under uncertainty: Heuristics and biases* (pp. 201–208). New York: Cambridge University Press.

Kairys, D., Kadane, B., & Lehoczky, P. (1975). Jury representativeness: A mandate for multiple source lists. *California Law Review, 65*, 776–827.

Kairys, D., Schulman, J., & Harring, S. (Eds.). (1975). *The jury system: New methods for reducing prejudice*. Philadelphia: National Jury Project and the National Lawyers Guild.

Kalajian, D. (2004, February). Martha's jury: Eight women, four men. *Cox News Service*. Available from LexisNexis Web site, http://web.lexis-nexis.com/universe

Kalven, H., & Zeisel, H. (1966). *The American jury*. Boston: Little, Brown.

Kaplan, M. F., & Miller, L. E. (1978). Reducing the effects of juror bias. *Journal of Personality and Social Psychology, 36*, 1443–1455.

Kassin, S. M., & Garfield, D. A. (1991). Blood and guts: General and trial-specific effects of videotaped crime scenes on mock jurors. *Journal of Applied Social Psychology, 21*, 1459–1472.

Kassin, S. M., & Wrightsman, L. S. (1983). The construction and validation of a juror bias scale. *Journal of Research in Personality, 17*, 423–442.

Kassin, S. M., & Wrightsman, L. S. (1988). *The American jury on trial*. New York: Hemisphere Publishing.

Katz, L. S. (1968–1969, December–January). The twelve man jury. *Trial Magazine*, 39–42.

Kauffman, R. A., & Ryckman, R. M. (1979). Effects of locus of control, outcome security, and attitudinal similarity of defendant on attributions of criminal responsibility. *Personality and Social Psychology Bulletin, 5*, 340–343.

Kerr, N. L., Harmon, D. L., & Graves, J. K. (1982). Independence of multiple verdicts by jurors and juries. *Journal of Applied Social Psychology, 12*, 12–29.

Kerr, N. L., Hymes, R. W., Anderson, A. B., & Weathers, J. E. (1995). Defendant–juror similarity and mock juror judgments. *Law and Human Behavior, 19*, 545–567.

Kerwin, J., & Shaffer, D. R. (1991). The effects of jury dogmatism on reactions to jury nullification instructions. *Personality and Social Psychology Bulletin, 17*, 140–146.

Kerwin, J., & Shaffer, D. R. (1994). Mock jurors versus mock juries: The role of deliberations in reactions to inadmissible testimony. *Personality and Social Psychology Bulletin, 20,* 153–162.

Kiesler, C. A. (1971). *The psychology of commitment: Experiments linking behavior and belief.* New York: Academic Press.

King, N. J. (1993). Postconviction review of jury discrimination: Measuring the effects of juror race on jury decisions. *Michigan Law Review, 92,* 63–130.

Knapp, M. L., Hart, R. P., & Dennis, H. S. (1974). An exploration of deception as a communication construct. *Human Communication Research, 1,* 15–29.

Koehler, J. J. (2001). The psychology of numbers in the courtroom: How to make DNA-match statistics seem impressive or insufficient. *University of Southern California Law Review, 74,* 1275–1305.

Koehnken, G. (1987). Training police officers to detect deception. Does it work? *Social Behavior, 2,* 1–17.

Kovera, M. B., Dickinson, J. J., & Cutler, B. L. (2003). Voir dire and jury selection. In A. M. Goldstein (Ed.), *Handbook of psychology: Forensic psychology* (pp. 161–175). New York: Wiley.

Kovera, M. B., Gresham, A. W., Borgida, E., Gray, E., & Regan, P. C. (1997). Does expert testimony inform or influence juror decision-making? A social cognitive analysis. *Journal of Applied Psychology, 82,* 178–191.

Kovera, M. B., McAuliff, B. D., & Hebert, K. S. (1999). Reasoning about scientific evidence: Effects of juror gender and evidence quality on juror decisions in a hostile work environment case. *Journal of Applied Psychology, 84,* 362–375.

Kramer, G. P., Kerr, N. L., & Carroll, J. S. (1990). Pretrial publicity, judicial remedies, and jury bias. *Law and Human Behavior, 14,* 409–438.

Kraus, S. J. (1995). Attitudes and the prediction of behavior: A meta-analysis of the empirical literature. *Personality and Social Psychology Bulletin, 21,* 58–75.

Krauss, D. A., Lieberman, J. D., & Olson, J. (2004). The effects of rational and experiential information processing on expert testimony in death penalty cases. *Behavioral Sciences & the Law, 22,* 801–822.

Krauss, D. A., & Sales, B. D. (2001). The effects of clinical and scientific expert testimony on juror decision making in capital sentencing. *Psychology, Public Policy, and Law, 7,* 267–310.

Kraut, R., Olson, J., Banaji, M., Bruckman, A., Cohen, J., & Couper, M. (2004). Psychological research online: Report of the board of scientific affairs' advisory group on the conduct of research on the Internet. *American Psychologist, 59,* 105–117.

Kraut, R. E., & Poe, D. (1980). On the line: The deception judgments of customs inspectors and laymen. *Journal of Personality and Social Psychology, 39,* 784–798.

Kravitz, D. A., Cutler, B. L., & Brock, P. (1993). Reliability and validity of the original and revised legal attitudes questionnaire. *Law and Human Behavior, 17,* 661–667.

Kruglanski, A. W., & Freund, T. (1983). The freezing and unfreezing of lay-inferences: Effects on impressional primacy, ethnic stereotyping, and numerical anchoring. *Journal of Experimental Social Psychology, 19,* 448–468.

Lamberth, J., Kreiger, E., & Shay, S. (1982). Juror decision-making: A case of attitude change mediated by authoritarianism. *Journal of Research in Personality, 16,* 419–434.

Landry, K. L., & Brigham, J. C. (1992). The effect of training in criteria-based content analysis on the ability to detect deception in adults. *Law and Human Behavior, 16,* 663–676.

Lane, F. (1984). *Lane's Goldstein trial techniques* (3rd ed.). Wilmette, IL: Callaghan.

Lecci, L., & Myers, B. (2002). Examining the construct validity of the original and revised JBS: A cross-validation of sample and method. *Law and Human Behavior, 26,* 455–463.

Lecci, L., Snowden, J., & Morris, D. (2004). Using social science research to inform and evaluate the contributions of trial consultants in the voir dire. *Journal of Forensic Psychology Practice, 4,* 67–78.

Lerner, M. J. (1980). *The belief in a just world: A fundamental delusion.* New York: Plenum Press.

Levine, M. (2001). Persuasion in advocacy: Conditioning the jury in voir dire and opening statement. *Trial Lawyers Quarterly, 30,* 141–146.

Levit, W. H., Nelson, D. W., Ball, V. C., & Chernick, R. (1971). Expediting voir dire: An empirical study. *Southern California Law Review, 44,* 916–995.

Levy, P. S., & Lemeshow, S. (1999). *Sampling of populations: Methods and applications* (3rd ed.). New York: Wiley.

Lieberman, J. D. (2002). Head over the heart or heart over the head? Cognitive–experiential self-theory and extra-legal heuristics in juror decision-making. *Journal of Applied Social Psychology, 32,* 2526–2553.

Lieberman, J. D., & Arndt, J. (2000). Understanding the limits of limiting instructions: Social psychological explanations for the failures of instructions to disregard pretrial publicity and other inadmissible evidence. *Psychology, Public Policy, and Law, 6,* 677–711.

Lieberman, J. D., & Miethe, T. (2006). *DNA evidence and legal decisions.* Manuscript submitted for publication.

Lieberman, J. D., & Sales, B. D. (1997). What social science teaches us about the jury instruction process. *Psychology, Public Policy, and Law, 3,* 1–56.

Lilley, L. S. (1994). Techniques for targeting juror bias. *Trial, 74,* 75–79.

Lind, E. A., & Tyler, T. R. (1988). *The social psychology of procedural justice.* New York: Plenum Press.

Lockhart v. McCree, 466 U.S. 162 (1986).

Loh, W. D. (1984). *Social research in the judicial process.* New York: Russell Sage Foundation.

Lopes, L. (1993). Two conceptions of the juror. In R. Hastie (Ed.), *Inside the juror: The psychology of juror decision making* (pp. 255–262). New York: Cambridge University Press.

Lynch, M., & Haney, C. (2000). Discrimination and instruction comprehension: Guided discretion, racial bias, and the death penalty. *Law and Human Behavior, 24*, 337–358.

Lussier, R. J., Perlman, D., & Breen, L. J. (1977). Causal attributions, attitude similarity, and the punishment of drug offenders. *British Journal of Addiction, 72*, 357–364.

MacCoun, R. J. (1989, June 2). Experimental research on jury decision-making. *Science, 244*, 1046–1050.

MacCoun, R. J. (1993). Inside the black box: What empirical research tells us about decision making by civil juries. In R. E. Litan (Ed.), *Verdict: Assessing the civil jury system* (pp. 137–180). Washington, DC: The Brookings Institution.

MacGutman, S. (1972). The attorney conducted voir dire of jurors: A constitutional right. *Brooklyn Law Review, 39*, 290–329.

Marshall, L. L., & Smith, A. (1986). The effects of demand characteristics, evaluation anxiety, and expectancy on juror honesty during voir dire. *The Journal of Psychology, 120*, 205–217.

Matsumoto, D. (1993). Ethnic differences in affect intensity, emotion judgments, display rule attitudes, and self-reported emotional expression in an American sample. *Motivation & Emotion, 17*, 107–123.

Mauet, T. (1992). *Fundamentals of trial techniques.* Boston: Little, Brown.

Mazzella, R., & Feingold, A. (1994). The effects of physical attractiveness, race, socioeconomic status, and gender of defendants and victims on judgments of mock jurors: A meta-analysis. *Journal of Applied Social Psychology, 24*, 1315–1344.

McBride, L. K., & Moran, G. (1967). Double agreement as a function of item ambiguity and susceptibility to demand: Implications of the psychological situation. *Journal of Personality and Social Psychology, 6*, 110–118.

McConahay, J., Mullin, C., & Frederick, J. (1977). The uses of social science in trials with political and racial overtones: The trial of Joan Little. *Law and Contemporary Problems, 41*, 205–229.

McConatha, J. T., Lightner, E., & Deaner, S. L. (1994). Culture, age, and gender as variables in the expression of emotions. *Journal of Social Behavior and Personality, 9*, 481–488.

McGowen, R., & King, G. D. (1982). Effects of authoritarian, anti-authoritarian, and egalitarian legal attitudes on mock juror and jury decisions. *Psychological Reports, 51*, 1067–1074.

McGuire, W. J. (1985). Attitudes and attitude change. In G. Lindzey & E. Aronson (Eds.), *The handbook of social psychology* (3rd ed., Vol. 2, pp. 233–346). New York: Random House.

McNulty, M. J. (2000). Practical tips for effective voir dire. *Louisiana Bar Journal, 48*, 110–114.

Meehl, P. E. (1954). *Clinical vs. statistical prediction*. Minneapolis: University of Minnesota Press.

Mehrabian, A. (1969). Significance of posture and position in the communication of attitude and status relationships. *Psychological Bulletin, 71*, 359–372.

Mehrabian, A. (1971). Nonverbal communication. In J. Cole (Ed.), *Nebraska Symposium on Motivation* (Vol. 19, pp. 107–161). Lincoln: University of Nebraska Press.

Mehrabian, A., & Ferris, S. R. (1967). Inference of attitudes from nonverbal communication in two channels. *Journal of Consulting Psychology, 31*, 248–252.

Middendorf, K., & Luginbuhl, J. (1995). The value of a nondirective voir dire style in jury selection. *Criminal Justice and Behavior, 22*, 129–151.

Miethe, T. D., & Drass, K. A. (1999). Exploring the social context of instrumental and expressive homicides: An application of quantitative comparative analysis. *Quantitative Criminology, 15*, 1–21.

Milgram, S. (1974). *Obedience to authority*. New York: Harper & Row.

Miller, G. R., & Burgoon, J. K. (1982). Factors affecting assessments of witness credibility. In N. L. Kerr & R. M. Bray (Eds.), *Psychology of the courtroom* (pp. 169–194). New York: Academic Press.

Miller, M. G., & Tessler, A. (1989). The effects of affective–cognitive consistency and thought on the attitude–behavior relation. *Journal of Experimental Social Psychology, 25*, 189–202.

Miller-El v. Dretke, 125 S.Ct. 2317 (2005).

Mills, C. J., & Bohannon, W. E. (1980a). Juror characteristics: To what extent are they related to jury verdicts? *Judicature, 64*, 23–31.

Mills, C. J., & Bohannon, W. E. (1980b). Character structure and jury behavior: Conceptual and applied implications. *Journal of Personality and Social Psychology, 38*, 662–667.

Mitchell, H., & Byrne, D. (1973). The defendant's dilemma: Effects of jurors' attitudes and authoritarianism on judicial decision. *Journal of Personality and Social Psychology, 25*, 123–129.

Mize, G. E. (2003). Be cautious of the quiet ones. *Voir Dire, 10*, 1–4.

Mogill, K. M., & Nixon, W. R. (1986). Practical primer on jury selection. *Michigan Bar Journal, 65*, 52–57.

Montada, L. (1998). Belief in a just world: A hybrid of justice motive and self-interest. In L. Montada & M. J. Lerner (Eds.), *Responses to victimization and belief in a just world* (pp. 217–246). New York: Plenum Press.

Montada, L., & Lerner, M. J. (Eds.). (1998). *Responses to victimization and belief in a just world*. New York: Plenum Press.

Moran, G. (2001). Trial consultation: Why licensure is not necessary. *Journal of Forensic Psychology Practice, 1*, 77–85.

Moran, G., & Comfort, J. C. (1982). Scientific jury selection: Sex as a moderator of demographic and personality predictors of impaneled felony juror behavior. *Journal of Personality and Social Psychology, 43*, 1052–1063.

Moran, G., & Comfort, J. C. (1986). Neither "tentative" nor "fragmentary": Verdict preference of impaneled felony jurors as a function of attitude toward capital punishment. *Journal of Applied Psychology, 71*, 146–155.

Moran, G., & Cutler, B. L. (1991). The prejudicial impact of pretrial publicity. *Journal of Applied Social Psychology, 21*, 345–367.

Moran, G., & Cutler, B. L. (1997). Bogus publicity items and the contingency between awareness and media-induced pretrial prejudice. *Law and Human Behavior, 21*, 339–343.

Moran, G., Cutler, B. L., & De Lisa, A. (1994). Attitudes toward tort reform, scientific jury selection, and juror bias: Verdict inclination in criminal and civil trials. *Law & Psychology Review, 18*, 309–328.

Moran, G., Cutler, B. L., & Loftus, E. F. (1990). Jury selection in major controlled substance trials: The need for extended voir dire. *Forensic Reports, 3*, 331–348.

Moran, K. (1991, November 3). Consultant postpones chemotherapy to help Kennedy's nephew at his trial. *The Houston Chronicle*, p. A8.

Moscovici, S. (1985). Social influence and conformity. In G. Lindzey & E. Aronson (Eds.), *The handbook of social psychology* (3rd ed., pp. 347–412). Hillsdale, NJ: Erlbaum.

Mossman, K. (1973, May). Jury selection: An expert's view. *Psychology Today*, 78–79.

Murphy, D. E. (2005, March 16). Case stirs fight on Jews, juries and execution. *The New York Times*, p. A1.

Murphy v. Florida, 421 U. S. 794 (1975).

Myers, B., & Lecci, L. (1998). Revising the factor structure of the Juror Bias Scale: A method for the empirical evaluation of theoretical constructs. *Law and Human Behavior, 22*, 239–256.

Myers, D. G. (1999). *Social psychology* (6th ed.). New York: McGraw-Hill.

Narby, D. J., & Cutler, B. L. (1994). Effectiveness of voir dire as a safeguard in eyewitness cases. *Journal of Applied Psychology, 79*, 724–729.

Narby, D. J., Cutler, B. L., & Moran, G. (1993). A meta-analysis of the association between authoritarianism and jurors' perceptions of defendant culpability. *Journal of Applied Psychology, 78*, 34–42.

National Jury Project. (2004). *Jurywork: Systematic techniques*. New York: West.

Neises, M. L., & Dillehay, R. C. (1987). Death qualification and conviction proneness: Witt and Witherspoon compared. *Behavioral Sciences & the Law, 5*, 479–494.

Neter, E., & Ben-Shakhar, G. (1989). The predictive validity of graphological inferences: A meta-analytic approach. *Personality and Individual Differences, 10*, 737–745.

Nevo, B. (1988). Yes, graphology can predict occupational success: Rejoinder to Ben-Shakhar et al. *Perceptual and Motor Skills, 66*, 92–94.

Nevo, B. (1989). Validation of graphology through the use of a matching method based on ranking. *Perceptual and Motor Skills, 69*, 1331–1336.

Nickerson, S., Mayo, C., & Smith, A. (1986). Racism in the courtroom. In J. Dovidio & S. Gaertner (Eds.), *Prejudice, discrimination, and racism* (pp. 255–278). New York: Academic Press.

Nietzel, M. T., & Dillehay, R. C. (1982). The effects of variations in voir dire procedures in capital murder trials. *Law and Human Behavior, 6,* 1–13.

Nietzel, M. T., & Dillehay, R. C. (1983). Psychologists as consultants for change of venue: The use of public opinion surveys. *Law and Human Behavior, 7,* 309–335.

Nietzel, M. T., & Dillehay, R. C. (1986). *Psychological consultation in the courtroom.* New York: Pergamon Press.

Nietzel, M. T., Dillehay, R. C., & Abbott, W. F. (1999). Legal surveys. In W. F. Abbott & J. Batt (Eds.), *Handbook of jury research* (pp. 6-1–6-37). Philadelphia: American Law Institute–American Bar Association.

Nietzel, M. T., Dillehay, R. C., & Himelein, M. J. (1987). Effects of voir dire variations in capital trials: A replication and extension. *Behavioral Sciences and the Law, 5,* 467–477.

Nisbett, R., & Ross, L. (1980). *Human inference: Strategies and shortcomings of social judgment.* Englewood Cliffs, NJ: Prentice Hall.

Olczak, P. V., Kaplan, M. F., & Penrod, S. (1991). Attorney's lay psychology and its effectiveness in selecting jurors: Three empirical studies. *Journal of Social Behavior and Personality, 6,* 431–452.

Orive, R. (1984). Group similarity, public self-awareness, and opinion extremity: A social projection explanation of deindividuation effects. *Journal of Personality and Social Psychology, 47,* 727–737.

Orne, M. T. (1962). On the social psychology of the psychological experiment: With particular reference to demand characteristics and their implications. *American Psychologist, 17,* 776–783.

Orne, M. T. (1969). Demand characteristics and the concept of quasi-control. In R. Rosenthal & R. Rosnow (Eds.), *Artifact in behavioral research* (pp. 143–179). New York: Academic Press.

Osborne, Y. H., Rappaport, N. B., & Meyer, R. G. (1986). An investigation of persuasion and sentencing severity with mock juries. *Behavioral Sciences and the Law, 4,* 339–349.

Pacini, R., & Epstein, S. (1999). The relation of rational and experiential information processing styles to personality, basic beliefs, and the ratio-bias phenomenon. *Journal of Personality and Social Psychology, 76,* 972–987.

Padawer-Singer, A., Singer, A., & Singer, R. (1974). Voir dire by two lawyers: An essential safe-guard. *Judicature, 57,* 386–391.

Patterson, A. H., & Neufer, M. S. (1997, Fall). Removing juror bias by applying psychology to challenges for cause. *Cornell Journal of Law and Public Policy, 7,* 97–106.

Pennington, N., & Hastie, R. (1981). Juror decision making models: The generalization gap. *Psychological Bulletin, 89,* 246–287.

Pennington, N., & Hastie, R. (1990). Practical implications of psychological research on juror and jury decision making. *Personality and Social Psychology Bulletin, 16,* 90–105.

Pennington, N., & Hastie, R. (1993). The story model for juror decision making. In R. Hastie (Ed.), *Inside the juror: The psychology of juror decision making* (pp. 192–221). New York: Cambridge University Press.

Penrod, S. (1990). Predictors of jury decision making in criminal and civil cases: A field experiment. *Forensic Reports, 31,* 261–277.

Penrod, S., & Cutler, B. L. (1987). Assessing the competence of juries. In I. B. Weiner & A. K. Hess (Eds.), *Handbook of forensic psychology* (pp. 293–318). Oxford, England: Wiley.

Penrod, S., Groscup, J., & O'Neil, K. (2004, March). *Consulting issues in cases involving pretrial publicity.* Presented at the American Psychology–Law Society Conference, Scottsdale, AZ.

Penrod, S., & Linz, D. (1986). Voir dire: Uses and abuses. In M. Kaplan (Ed.), *The impact of social psychology on procedural justice* (pp. 135–166). Springfield, IL: Charles C Thomas.

People v. Lanter, 230 Ill. App. 3d 72 (1992).

People v. Love, 222 Ill. App. 3d 428, 431 (1991).

Phares, E. J., & Wilson, K. G. (1972). Responsibility attribution: Role of outcome severity, situational ambiguity, and internal-external control. *Journal of Personality, 40,* 392–406.

Pollock, A. (1977). The use of public opinion polls to obtain changes of venue and continuances in criminal trials. *Criminal Justice Journal, 1,* 269–289.

Porter, S., & Yuille, J. (1996). The language of deceit: An investigation of the verbal clues in the interrogation context. *Law and Human Behavior, 20,* 443–458.

Posey, A. J., & Dahl, L. M. (2002). Beyond pretrial publicity: Legal and ethical issues associated with change of venue surveys. *Law and Human Behavior, 26,* 107–125.

Pyszczynski, T., & Wrightsman, L. (1981). The effects of opening statements on mock jurors' verdicts in a simulated criminal trial. *Journal of Applied Social Psychology, 11,* 301–313.

Ragin, C. (1987). *The comparative method: Moving beyond strategies.* Berkeley, CA: University of California Press.

Reagh, J. D. (1992). Legal implications of graphology in the United States. In B. L. Beyerstain & D. F. Beyerstain (Eds.), *Write stuff: Evaluations of graphology, the study of handwriting analysis* (pp. 465–476). Amherst, NY: Prometheus Books.

Reed, J. (1965). Jury deliberation, voting, and verdict trends. *Southwest Social Science Quarterly, 45,* 361–370.

Regan, D. T., & Fazio, R. (1977). On the consistency between attitudes and behavior: Look to the method of attitude formation. *Journal of Experimental Social Psychology, 13,* 28–45.

Rideau v. Louisiana, 373 U. S. 723 (1963).

Rokeach, M. (1960). *The open door and the closed mind*. New York: Basic Books.

Rose, M. (1999). The peremptory challenge accused of race or gender discrimination? Some data from one county. *Law and Human Behavior, 23*, 695–702.

Rose, M. (2001). Expectations of privacy? Jurors' views of voir dire questions. *Judicature, 85*, 10–17, 43.

Rosenberg, M. J. (1960). A structural theory of attitude dynamics. *Public Opinion Quarterly, 24*, 319–341.

Rosenblatt, A., Greenberg, J., Solomon, S., Pyszczynski, T., & Lyon, D. (1989). Evidence for terror management theory I: The effects of mortality salience on reactions to those who violate or uphold cultural values. *Journal of Personality and Social Psychology, 57*, 681–690.

Rosenthal, R. (1969). Interpersonal expectations: Effects of the experimenter's hypothesis. In R. Rosenthal & R. Rosenthal (Eds.), *Artifact in behavioral research* (pp. 181–277). New York: Academic Press.

Rotter, J. B. (1966). Generalized expectancies for internal vs. external control of reinforcement. *Psychological Monographs, 80*(1, Whole No. 609).

Rowland, C. K. (2002). Psychological perspectives on juror reactions to the September 11 events. *Defense Counsel Journal, 69*, 180–184.

Rubin, Z. & Peplau, A. (1975). Who believes in a just world? *Journal of Social Issues, 29*, 73–93.

Sage, W. (1973). Psychology and the Angela Davis jury. *Human Behavior, 2*, 56–61.

Saks, M. (1976). The limits of scientific jury selection: Ethical and empirical. *Jurimetrics Journal, 17*, 3–22.

Sample, J., & Warland, R. (1973). Attitude and prediction of behavior. *Social Forces, 51*, 292–304.

Sannito, T., & McGovern, P. J. (1993). *Courtroom psychology for trial lawyers. 1993 cumulative supplement*. New York: Wiley.

Sayer, J. W. (1997). *Ghost dancing the law: The Wounded Knee trials*. Cambridge, MA: Harvard University Press.

Schneider, D. J. (1973). Implicit personality theory: A review. *Psychological Bulletin, 79*, 294–309.

Schuller, R. A., (1992). The impact of battered woman syndrome evidence on jury decision processes. *Law and Human Behavior, 16*, 597–520.

Schuller, R. A., & Hastings, P. A. (1996). Trials of battered women who kill: The impact of alternative forms of expert evidence. *Law and Human Behavior, 20*, 167–188.

Schulman, J. (1973). A systematic approach to successful jury selection. *Guild Notes, 2*, 13–19.

Schulman, J., Shaver, P., Colman, R., Emrich, B., & Christie, R. (1973, May). Recipe for a jury. *Psychology Today*, 37–44, 77–84.

Schwartz, S. H. (1978). Temporal instability as a moderator of the attitude–behavior relationship. *Journal of Personality and Social Psychology, 36*, 715–724.

Scollon, C. N., Diener, E., Oishi, S., & Biswas-Diener, R. (2004). Emotions across cultures and methods. *Journal of Cross-Cultural Psychology, 35,* 304–326.

Sedikides, C., & Anderson, C. A. (1994). Causal perceptions of intertrait relations: The glue that holds person types together. *Personality and Social Psychology Bulletin, 20,* 294–302.

Seltzer, R., Venuti, M. A., & Lopes, G. M. (1991). Juror honesty during the voir dire. *Journal of Criminal Justice, 19,* 451–462.

Serio, S. C. (2004). A process right due? Examining whether a capital defendant has a due process right to a jury selection expert. *American University Law Review, 53,* 1143–1186.

Shaffer, D. R., & Case, T. (1982). On the decision to testify in one's own behalf: Effects of withheld evidence, defendant's sexual preferences, and juror dogmatism on juridic decisions. *Journal of Personality and Social Psychology, 42,* 335–346.

Shaffer, D. R., Plummer, D., & Hammock, G. (1986). Hath he suffered enough? Effects of jury dogmatism, defendant similarity, and defendant's pretrial suffering on juridic decisions. *Journal of Personality and Social Psychology, 50,* 1059–1067.

Shaffer, D. R., & Wheatman, S. R. (2000). Does personality influence reactions to judicial instructions? Some preliminary findings and possible implications. *Psychology, Public Policy, and Law, 6,* 655–676.

Shapley, D. (1974, September, 20). Jury selection: Social scientists gamble in an already loaded game. *Science, 185,* 1033–1034, 1071.

Shartel, J. S. (1994). Litigators describe key factors in use of jury consultants. *Inside Litigation, 8,* 23–29.

Sheldon, W. H. (1949). *Varieties of delinquent youth: An introduction to constitutional psychiatry.* New York: Harper & Row.

Sheppard v. Maxwell, 384 U.S. 333 (1966).

Shutt, R. K. (2004). *Investigating the social world* (4th ed.). Thousand Oaks, CA: Pine Forge Press.

Silver, D. (1978). A case against the use of public opinion pools as an aid in jury selection. *Journal of Computers and Law, 6,* 177–195.

Simner, M. L., & Goffin, R. D. (2003). A position statement by the International Graphonomics Society on the use of graphology in personnel selection testing. *International Journal of Testing, 3,* 353–364.

Simon, R. J. (1967). *The jury and the defense of insanity.* Boston: Little, Brown.

Simon, R. J. (1980). *The jury: Its role in American society.* Lexington, MA: D.C. Heath.

Simon, R. J., & Eimermann, T. (1971). The jury finds not guilty: Another look at media influence on the jury. *Journalism Quarterly, 48,* 343–344.

Simpson defense hires trial consultant. (1994, August 11). *Los Angeles Times,* p. A10.

Smith, V. L. (1991). Prototypes in the courtroom: Lay representations of legal concepts. *Journal of Personality and Social Psychology, 61,* 857–872.

Snyder, M. (1987). *Public appearances—private realities: The psychology of self-monitoring*. New York: Freeman.

Snyder, M., & Gangestad, S. (1986). On the nature of self-monitoring: Matters of assessment, matters of validity. *Journal of Personality and Social Psychology, 51,* 125–139.

Sommers, S. R., & Ellsworth, P. C. (2000). Race in the courtroom: Perceptions of guilt and dispositional attributions. *Personality and Social Psychology Bulletin, 26,* 1367–1379.

Sommers, S. R., & Ellsworth, P. C. (2001). White juror bias. An investigation of prejudice against Black defendants in the American courtroom. *Psychology, Public Policy, and Law, 7,* 201–229.

Sosis, R. H. (1974). Internal-external control and the perception of responsibility of another for an accident. *Journal of Personality and Social Psychology, 30,* 393–399.

Starr, V. H., & McCormick, M. (2000). *Jury selection* (3rd ed.). New York: Aspen.

State ex rel. Martinez v. Third Judicial District Court, reprinted as an appendix in State v. Singleton, 130 N.M. 583 (App. 2001).

State v. McCollum, 422 S.E.2d 866 (1992).

Steblay, N. M., Besirevic, J., Fulero, S. M., & Jimenez-Lorente, B. (1999). The effects of pretrial publicity on juror verdicts: A meta-analytic review. *Law and Human Behavior, 23,* 219–235.

Stolle, D. P. (2005, March). *Lawyers' ethical and legal obligations when mock jurors breach confidentiality agreements.* Paper presented at the American Psychology–Law Society Conference, La Jolla, CA.

Stolle, D. P., Robbennolt, J. K., & Wiener, R. L. (1996). The perceived fairness of the psychologist trial consultant: An empirical investigation. *Law & Psychology Review, 20,* 139–173.

Strauder v. West Virginia, 100 U.S. 303 (1879).

Strier, F. (1998–1999). Paying the piper: Proposed reforms of the increasingly bountiful but controversial profession of trial consulting. *South Dakota Law Review, 44,* 699–713.

Strier, F. (1999). Whither trial consulting? Issues and projections. *Law and Human Behavior, 23,* 93–115.

Strier, F., & Shestowsky, D. (1999). Profiling the profilers: A study of the trial consulting profession, its impact on trial justice, and what, if anything to do about it. *Wisconsin Law Review, 1999,* 441–499.

Studebaker, C. A., & Penrod, S. D. (2005). Pretrial publicity and its influence in juror decision making. In N. Brewer & K. D. Williams (Eds.), *Psychology and law: An empirical perspective* (pp. 254–275). New York: Guilford Press.

Studebaker, C. A., Robbennolt, J. K., Pathak-Sharma, M. K., & Penrod, S. D. (2000). Assessing pretrial publicity effects: Integrating content analytic results. *Law and Human Behavior, 24,* 317–336.

Studebaker, C. A., Robbennolt, J. K., Penrod, S. D., Pathak-Sharma, M. K., Groscup, J. L., & Devenport, J. L. (2002). Studying pretrial publicity effects: New methods for improving ecological validity and testing external validity. *Law and Human Behavior, 26,* 19–41.

Suggs, D., & Sales, B. D. (1978a). The art and science of conducting the voir dire. *Professional Psychology, 9,* 367–388.

Suggs, D., & Sales, B. D. (1978b). Using communication cues to evaluate prospective jurors during the voir dire. *Arizona Law Review, 20,* 629–642.

Suggs, D., & Sales, B. D. (1981). Juror self-disclosure in the voir dire: A social science analysis. *Indiana Law Journal, 56,* 245–271.

Swain v. Alabama, 380 U.S. 202 (1965).

Swann, W. B., Jr., & Read, S. J. (1981). Acquiring self-knowledge: The search for feedback that fits. *Journal of Personality and Social Psychology, 41,* 1119–1128.

Tanford, J. A. (1993). *The trial process: Law, tactics and ethics* (2nd ed.). Charlottesville, VA: Mitchie.

Taylor v. Louisiana, 419 U. S. 522 (1975).

Taylor, M. S., & Sackheim, K. K. (1988). Graphology. *Personnel Administrator, 33,* 71–76.

Thibault, J., & Walker, L. (1975). *Procedural justice: A psychological analysis.* Hillsdale, NJ: Erlbaum.

Thompson, W. C. (1989). Death qualification after *Wainwright v. Witt* and *Lockhart v. McCree. Law and Human Behavior, 13,* 185–215.

Thompson, W. C., Cowan, C. L., Ellsworth, P. C., & Harrington, J. C. (1984). Death penalty attitudes and conviction proneness: The translation of attitudes into verdicts. *Law and Human Behavior, 8,* 95–113.

Tindale, R. S., & Nagao, D. H. (1986). An assessment of the potential utility of "scientific jury selection": A "thoughtful experiment" approach. *Organizational Behavior and Human Decision Processes, 37,* 409–425.

Toobin, J. (1996, September 9). The Marcia Clark verdict. *The New Yorker, 72,* 58–71.

Traits of the right juror; many factors will be weighed in picking panel in Bryant case. (2004, July 12). *Rocky Mountain News,* p. 6A.

Treger, T. L. (1992). One jury indivisible: A group dynamics approach to voir dire. *Chicago–Kent Law Review, 68,* 549–580.

Tversky, A., & Kahneman, D. (1974, September 27). Judgment under uncertainty: Heuristics and biases. *Science, 185,* 1124–1131.

Ugwuegbu, D. C. E. (1979). Racial and evidential factors in juror attribution of legal responsibility. *Journal of Experimental Social Psychology, 15,* 133–146.

United States v. Burr, 25 Fed. Cas. 49, no. 14,692b (C.C.D. Va., 1807). Retrieved February 28, 2008, from http://press-pubs.uchicago.edu/founders/documents/amendV-VI_criminal_process35.html

United States v. Dellinger, 472 F.2d 340 (7th Cir. 1972).

United States v. Nobles, 422 U.S. 225 (1975).

Vallacher, R. R., & Solodky, M. (1979). Objective self-awareness, standards of evaluation, and moral behavior. *Journal of Experimental Social Psychology, 15,* 254–262.

Van Dyke, J. (1976). Voir dire: How should it be conducted to ensure that our juries are representative and impartial? *Hastings Constitutional Law Quarterly, 3,* 65–97.

Van Dyke, J. (1977). *Jury selection procedures.* Cambridge, MA: Ballinger.

Vidmar, N. (1999, November 11). *The performance and functioning of juries in medical malpractice cases.* Course of study taught for American Law Institute–American Bar Association Continuing Legal Education, San Francisco, CA.

Vidmar, N., & Ellsworth, P. C. (1974). Public opinion and the death penalty. *Stanford Law Review, 26,* 1245–1270.

Vidmar, N., & Schuller, R. A. (1987). Individual differences and the pursuit of legal rights: A preliminary inquiry. *Law and Human Behavior, 11,* 299–317.

Vidmar, N. J., & Schuller, R. A. (1989). Juries and expert evidence: Social framework testimony. *Law and Contemporary Problems, 52,* 133–176.

Vinson, D. E. (1993). *Jury persuasion: Psychological strategies and trial techniques.* Englewood Cliffs, NJ: Prentice Hall.

Visher, C. (1987). Juror decision making: The importance of evidence. *Law and Human Behavior, 11,* 1–17.

Vrana, S. R., & Rollock, D. (2002). The role of ethnicity, emotional content, and contextual differences in physiological, expressive, and self-reported emotional responses to imagery. *Cognition & Emotion, 16,* 165–192.

Vrij, A. (2000). *Detecting lies and deceit: The psychology of lying and the implications for professional practice.* Chichester, England: Wiley.

Vrij, A., Edward, K., & Bull, R. (2001). Stereotypical verbal and nonverbal responses while deceiving others. *Personality and Social Psychology Bulletin, 27,* 899–909.

Wagner, W. (1989). *The art of advocacy: Jury selection.* New York: Matthew Bender.

Wagstaff, G. (1982). Attitudes toward rape. The "just world" strikes again? *Bulletin of the British Psychological Society, 35,* 277–279.

Wainwright v. Witt, 469 U.S. 412 (1985).

Walker, G. (1995, October 22). Lawyers must show restraint if our jury system is to survive. *Boston Herald,* p. 34.

Warland, R., & Sample, J. (1973). Response certainty as a moderator variable in attitude measurement. *Rural Sociology, 38,* 174–186.

Weaver, D. (1993). Voir dire: Bonding with the jury. *Trial Lawyers Quarterly, 23,* 28–33.

Weir, J. A., & Wrightsman, L. S. (1990). The determinants of mock jurors' verdicts in a rape case. *Journal of Applied Social Psychology, 20,* 901–919.

Whalen, D. H., & Blanchard, F. A. (1982). Effects of photographic evidence on mock juror judgment. *Journal of Applied Social Psychology, 12*, 30–41.

Wicker, A. (1969). Attitudes vs. actions: The relationship of verbal and overt behavioral responses to attitude objects. *Journal of Social Issues, 25*, 1–78.

Wicker, A. W., & Pomazal, R. J. (1971). The between attitudes and behavior as a function of specificity of attitude object and presence of a significant person during assessment conditions. *Representative Research in Social Psychology, 2*, 26–31.

Wicklund, R. A. (1975). Objective self-awareness. In L. Berkowitz (Ed.), *Advances in experimental social psychology* (Vol. 8, pp. 233–275). New York: Academic Press.

Wicklund, R. A., & Frey, D. (1980). Self-awareness theory: When the self makes a difference. In D. M. Wegner & R. R. Vallacher (Eds.), *The self in social psychology* (pp. 31–54). New York: Oxford University Press.

Wiener, R. L., & Stolle, D. P. (1997). Trial consulting: Jurors' and attorneys' perceptions of murder. *California Western Law Review, 34*, 226–243.

Wiley, D. (1997). Pre-voir dire, case-specific supplemental juror questionnaires. In W. F. Abbott & J. Batt (Eds.), *Handbook of jury research* (pp. 16-1–16-44). Philadelphia: American Law Institute–American Bar Association.

Williams, F. P., III, & McShane, M. D. (1990). Inclinations of prospective jurors in capital cases. *Sociology and Social Science Research, 74*, 85–94.

Wishman, S. (1986). *Anatomy of a jury. The system on trial.* New York: Times Books.

Wissler, R. L., Hart, A. J., & Saks, M. J. (1999). Decision making about general damages: A comparison of jurors, judges, and lawyers. *Michigan Law Review, 98*, 1751–826.

Witherspoon v. Illinois, 391 U.S. 510 (1968).

Wozniak, L. (1995, July 24). Trial consultants are on the case. *St. Petersburg Times*, p. 10E.

Wrightsman, L. S., Greene, E., Nietzel, M. T., & Fortune, W. H. (2002). *Psychology and the legal system.* Belmont, CA: Wadsworth.

Zaidel, S. F., & Mehrabian, A. (1969). The ability to communicate and infer positive and negative attitudes facially and vocally. *Journal of Experimental Research in Personality, 3*, 233–241.

Zeisel, H. (1968). *Some data on juror attitudes toward capital punishment.* Chicago: Center for Studies in Criminal Justice, University of Chicago Law School.

Zeisel, H., & Diamond, S. S. (1976). The jury selection in the Mitchell–Stans conspiracy trial. *American Bar Foundation Research Journal, 87*, 151–174.

Zeisel, H., & Diamond, S. S. (1978). The effect of peremptory challenges on jury and verdict: An experiment in a federal district court. *Stanford Law Review, 30*, 491–531.

Zuckerman, M., DePaulo, B. M., & Rosenthal, R. (1981). Verbal and nonverbal communication of deception. In L. Berkowitz (Ed.), *Advances in experimental social psychology* (Vol. 14, pp. 1–59). New York: Academic Press.

Zuckerman, M., & Driver, R. (1985). Telling lies: Verbal and nonverbal correlates of deception. In A. W. Seigman & S. Feldstein (Eds.), *Multichannel integration of nonverbal behavior* (pp. 129–147). Hillsdale, NJ: Erlbaum.

TABLE OF AUTHORITIES

AUTHOR INDEX

Fulero, S. M., 32, 35, 36, 44, 57, 58, 59, 61, 65, 76, 159, 164
Furnham, A., 91, 138

Gangestad, S., 156
Garcia, L., 81
Garfield, D. A., 73
Gatto, L., 71
Geis, F. L. 88
Gerbasi, K. C., 91, 92
Gilbert, D. T., 24, 156
Ginger, A. F., 118
Glick, P., 138
Goffin, R. D., 138
Gold, A., 47–48, 152
Goldstein, I., 68, 73
Goldstein, L. A., 196
Goodman, G. S., 66
Goodman, J., 58, 61, 63, 65, 67, 92–93, 93, 99, 108, 153
Gosling, S. D., 49
Gottesman, D., 138
Graves, J. K., 62
Gray, E., 66
Graziano, S. J., 80, 102
Green, E., 64, 67
Greenberg, J., 204
Greene, E. L., 19, 58
Gresham, A. W., 66
Griffin, M., 63
Griffiths, C. T., 33
Griffitt, W., 81
Grisham, J., 3
Groscup, J. L., 48, 168n
Gross, D. J. F., 170
Grove, W., 146
Gunter, B., 138

Hafemeister, T. L., 25, 27, 104, 112, 163
Hagen, J., 71
Hahn, P. W., 67
Hall, E. L., 33
Hamilton, V. L., 81
Hamock, G., 86
Handel, S. F., 168
Handler, S. P., 196
Haney, C., 32, 33, 34, 71, 96, 106, 107, 122
Hanna, J., 194
Hans, V. P., 5, 12, 19, 36, 64, 74, 92, 93, 94, 99, 100, 119, 120, 151, 190
Harmon, D. L., 62
Harring, S., 39, 144

Harrington, D. C., 63, 137
Harrington, J. C., 66
Hart, A. J., 76, 175
Hart, R. P., 127
Harvard Law Review, 20, 143n, 188, 190
Hass, R. G., 155
Hastie, R., 62, 63, 66, 75, 102, 106, 107, 140, 145, 163, 170, 171n, 181, 203
Hastings, P. A., 66
Hawrish, E., 36, 65
Hayden, G., 35, 59
Hazelwood, D. L., 155
Hebert, K. S., 66
Hepburn, J. R., 63, 64, 70, 74, 75, 78, 100, 101, 189
Herbsleb, J. D., 188, 193, 194, 195, 196
Heyl, C., 65
Himelein, M. J., 109
Hixon, J. G., 24, 156
Hocking, J. E., 130
Hoffman, S. P., 131
Horowitz, I. A., 147, 148, 206
Hunt, M., 37
Hurtado, A., 96
Hymes, R. W., 71

Imwinkelried, E. J., 61, 63, 64, 67

Jaccard, J. J., 152, 154
Jackson, L. A., 71
Jacobs, S. K., 60
Jamieson, D. W., 156
Janoff-Bullman, R., 92
Jehle, A., 119, 120
Jimenez-Lorente, B., 44
John, P., 49
Johnson, C., 32, 33, 34, 106, 107
Johnson, J. D., 71
Jolton, J., 138
Jones, C., 92
Jones, S. E., 105, 114n, 199
Jordan, W., 64
Jurow, G., 83, 96

Kadane, B., 5
Kahler, K. N., 133
Kahneman, D., 146
Kairys, D., 5, 39, 144
Kalajian, D., 8
Kalven, H., 28, 147, 164, 202
Kaminski, E. P., 130
Kaplan, M. F., 34, 158

Wicker, A. W., 152
Wicklund, R. A., 155
Wiener, R. L., 59, 63, 64, 66, 75, 77, 78, 99,
    143n, 188
Wiley, D., 119, 120, 121
Williams, F. P. III, 70
Wilson, K. G., 88, 89, 90
Winfree, L. T., 33
Wishman, S., 58, 136
Wissler, R. L., 76
Woodworth, G., 25, 70
Wozniak, L., 8

Wrightsman, L. S., 19, 23, 55, 62, 84, 97,
    99, 114, 140, 175

Yuille, J., 128

Zaidel, S. F., 129
Zanna, M. P., 154, 156
Zeisel, H., 6, 24, 26, 28, 30, 32, 36, 96, 147,
    164, 181, 202, 206
Zuckerman, D., 25
Zuckerman, M., 91, 92, 127, 135

SUBJECT INDEX

specificity in, 9
Davis, Angela, 5
Death penalty
     and appointment of consultants, 197
     attitudes toward, 95–97
          and political leanings, 75
Deception
     and nonverbal behavior studies, 134, 141
     of prospective jurors, 22
Decision making, actuarial vs. clinical, 146
Decision making by jury. *See* Jury decision making
DecisionQuest, 6
Defendant, physical appearance of
     and jurors' processing mode, 73
     and Web-based survey, 49
Defense attorneys, focus of peremptory strikes by, 31
Deindividuation, 155
Demand characteristics, in voir dire, 115–116
Demeanor of juror, as voir dire characteristic, 35
     accuracy of challenges based on, 30
Demographic factors, 25, 57–59, 75–76, 77–78, 79
     academic researchers on, 145
     age, 64–65
     and death-penalty attitudes, 96
     ethnicity/race, 68–73
     vs. evidence strength, 158
     and federal voir dire limits, 108
     gender, 35, 36, 65–68 (*see also* Gender)
     juror mythology on, 72, 76–77
     marital status, 74–75
     occupation, 25, 30, 34, 35, 36, 60–62
     parenting, 59
     and personality factors, 77, 78
     religion, 25, 73–74
     socioeconomic status/income/education, 36, 62–63
     and voir dire limits, 108
Denny, Reginald, 197
Dershowitz, Alan, 37
Dimitrius, Jo-Ellan, 7, 126, 133
Discovery of scientific jury selection information, as proposed reform, 194
Distribution pattern of attitudes, 113–114
Diversity, of jurors, 19–20
Dogmatism, 86–88
Dow Corning breast plant liltigation, 8
"Dream Team," 7

Drugs, attitudes toward, 99, 153

East Coast Conspiracy to Save Lives, 4
Economic orthodoxy, 110
Ectomorphs, 139
Education
     as selection factor, 62–63
     of trial consultants, 9
          formal program for proposed, 208–209
     as voir dire purpose, 27
Electronic surveys, 49
Emotional orientation, of jurors, 175–176
Emotional processing mode of jurors, 72, 73
Empathy, and jury decision making, 101–102
Endomorphs, 139
Equity, and just world beliefs, 90
Ethical and professional issues in scientific jury selection, 187–188, 200
     affordability, 190–191
          through use of academic researchers or direct hiring of survey firms, 198
     consulting standards, 191–193
     fairness, 188–190, 200
     reforms proposed for
          court appointed consultants, 196–197
          discovery allowed for, 194–196
          licensure of consultants, 193–194
          pro bono services, 198
          restricting application of information gained, 199–200
          use of academic researchers or direct hiring of research firms, 198–199
Ethnicity, as selection factor, 68–73
Evaluation anxiety, in voir dire, 115–116
Evidence strength and presentation
     as inadequate for total explanation, 202
     in jury decision making, 100–101, 158–159
Expectancy effects, 116
Experience
     attitudes based on, 154
     of consultant, 10
Experimental design, of mock jury study, 62, 177–178
Experimenter bias, 116
Expert witnesses, trial consultants distinguished from, 193–194
Exploratory mock juries, 172–173
External locus of control, 88

Eye contact, by prospective juror, 129
Eyewitnesses, and juror behavior, 100, 153–154
Eysenck Personality Questionnaire, 138

Face-to-face interviews, 48
    vs. self-administered questionnaire, 119, 121
Facial cues, by prospective juror, 129–130
Factor analysis, 55
Fairness
    as issue, 188–190, 200
    perceptions of in voir dire, 106–107
False memory debate, and licensure, 194
Federal Criminal Justice Act (1965), on indigents' requests, 196
Federal Rules of Civil Procedure, on limits of discovery, 195
Fillers, as juror role, 140–141
First Amendment, and pretrial publicity, 43
Focus groups
    and IBM case, 6
    mock juries as, 172–173
    and O.J. Simpson trial, 7
Folk-based assumptions, on jury behavior, 72
Followers, jurors as, 140
Forensic Technologies Incorporated, 7
Free association, in survey questionnaire, 48
Future directions, 202, 209
    broader theories of juror behavior, 202–205
    formal educational programs, 208–209
    improved collaboration between consultants and academic researchers, 206–209
    innovative statistical approaches, 205
    practical predictors of behavior, 205–206

Gainesville Eight trial, 5, 118
Garcetti, Gil, 6
Gender
    and death-penalty attitudes, 96
    as factor in verdicts, 61, 62
    and just world beliefs, 91
    and peremptory challenges, 24, 31, 188
    as selection factor, 35, 36, 65–68
        accuracy of challenges based on, 30
        and gender of attorney, 67
    See also Women
General Belief in Just World Scale, 92
General Social Survey (GSS), 110

Golde, Stanley, 73–74
Goldman, Ronald, 7
Grandstand play, in voir dire, 27
Graphic presentations of evidence, and academic researchers, 198–199
Graphology, 137–138
Grubman, Lizzie, 54

Hand movement, by prospective juror, 131
Handwriting analysis (graphology), 137138
Harrisburg Seven trial (1972), 3–5, 12
    and Analytic Juror Rating, 112
    community surveys in, 40–42
Heflin, Howell, 109–110
Herman, R. Dixon, 4
Heuristics, 24, 146
Hinckley, John, 97
Holdouts, jurors as, 141
Hoover, J. Edgar, 4
Human participants in research, 192–193

IBM case, 6
"I don't know," as anxiety indicator, 128
Impartiality, as voir dire purpose, 27–28
Implicit personality theories, 77
Income, as selection factor, 62–63
In-court questioning of prospective jurors. *See* Voir dire
Individual differences among jurors, 202
Indoctrination, as voir dire aim, 27, 33
Ingratiation, as voir dire purpose, 27, 107
Initial verdict opinions, 28
    in Mitchell-Stans case, 147
    unanimity lacking in, 24, 26, 28, 164, 202
Injury, severity of, as factor in jury decisions, 76
Inquisitional process, vs. adversarial process (voir dire), 107
Insanity cases
    and Black jurors, 70
    and legal authoritarianism, 97, 98
    and mock juror occupation and income, 63
Instructions by judges. *See* Judges' instructions
Intelligence, as voir dire characteristic, 34, 35
Interaction of trial variables, 99–100
Internal-External Locus of Control Scale, 88–89
Internet
    juror questionnaires on, 120

surveys over, 49
Interviewers, reliability of, 54

Jackson, Michael, 8, 190
Judges
    and challenge for cause, 21–22
    and expanded voir dire, 110
    removal *causa sua sponte*, 21
    voir dire conducted by, 104–18, 122
        and community surveys, 39
        nonverbal behavior observed during, 135
Judges' instructions, 20
    vs. commonsense justice, 14, 168, 169
    jurors' comprehension of, 27
    and jurors' public commitment, 28
    nullification instructions (dogmatic jurors), 87–88
    rate of comprehension of, 169
    and simulation studies, 151
Juror behavior. *See* Jury decision making
Juror Bias Scale, 84–86, 97, 98
Juror eligibility, and survey sample, 50
Juror exclusion, voir dire as, 21
Juror mythology, 76–77
Jurors
    broader theories of behavior of (future direction), 202–205
    charisma level of, 114n
    disagreement among, 24, 26, 28 , 164, 202
    individual differences among, 202
    interactions among, 109, 163
    leaders among, 10, 139, 139–140, 142
        and gender, 68
        and occupation, 62
    leadership style and gender of, 68
    preexisting mental representations of, 169
    presentation of information to (mock juries), 174–176
    as representative cross section, 19–20
    See also Initial verdict opinions
Jurors, prospective
    and constraints on voir dire, 104
    and death penalty, 95
    inaccuracies in self-disclosure by, 21–22, 33, 44, 117, 122
    as lying during voir dire, 22
        and death-penalty attitudes, 96
        in Harrisburg Seven trial, 42
        in Wounded Knee case, 5

    nonverbal behavior of, 14, 123, 125–126, 141–142
    and authoritarianism, 149
    body language and hidden biases, 23, 158
    empirically supported and theoretically-based observation on, 136–139
    and jury deliberation roles, 139–141
    leaders and followers identified through, 163
    logic underlying observation of, 126–131
    systematic observation of, 131–136
    pretrial questionnaires for, 118
    sequestering of during voir dire, 116–118
    silent, 22, 157–158
    as uncomfortable with questions, 116–117
    and voir dire conducted by attorneys vs. judges, 104, 105–106
    See also Voir dire
Jury, death-qualified, 95
Jury decision making
    by actual vs. mock or shadow jury, 181
    and background factors, 12–13 (*see also* Demographic factors; Personality and attitudes)
    and case type, 99–100
    development of broader theories of (future direction), 202–205
    development of more practical prediction of (future direction), 205–206
    evidence strength and presentation in, 100–101
    initial majority prevalent in, 147
    interaction of trial variables in, 99–100
    personality and attitudes in, 79–80, 93, 97, 99, 100, 101–102
    academic researchers on, 145
    attitudes toward death penalty, 75, 95–97
    attitudes toward drugs, 99, 153
    attitudes toward psychiatrists, 97–98, 153
    attitudes toward rape judgments, 98–99
    attitudes toward tort reform and legal claims, 93–95, 153
    authoritarianism, 80–82 (*see also* Authoritarianism)
    and demographics, 77, 78

ABOUT THE AUTHORS

Joel D. Lieberman, PhD, is associate professor and chair of the Criminal Justice Department at the University of Nevada, Las Vegas. His work focuses on the application of social psychological theories to criminal justice issues. His recent research has been in the areas of jury decision making, aggression, and intergroup conflict. This research has resulted in numerous published articles and book chapters on the psychological factors that explain why jurors have difficulty comprehending judicial instructions and rely on inadmissible evidence, defendant characteristics, and less reliable expert witness testimony in their decision making.

Bruce D. Sales, PhD, JD, is professor of psychology, sociology, psychiatry, and law at the University of Arizona, where he also directs its Psychology, Policy, and Law Program. Some of his recent books are *Criminal Profiling: Developing an Effective Science and Practice* (with S. J. Hicks; American Psychological Association [APA], 2006); *Experts in Court: Reconciling Law, Science, and Professional Knowledge* (with D. Shuman; APA, 2005); *More Than the Law: Behavioral and Social Facts in Legal Decision Making* (with P. W. English; APA, 2005); *Family Mediation: Facts, Myths, and Future Prospects* (with C. J. A. Beck; APA, 2001); and *Treating Adult and Juvenile Offenders With Special Needs* (coedited with J. B. Ashford & W. H. Reid; APA, 2001). Professor Sales, the first editor of the journals *Law and Human Behavior* and *Psychology, Public Policy, and Law,* is a fellow of the American Psychological Association and the American Psychological Society and an elected member of the American Law Institute. He twice served as president of the American Psychology–Law Society. He received the Award for Distinguished Contributions to Psychology and Law from the American Psychology–Law Society, the Award for Distinguished Professional Contributions to Public Service from the American Psychological Association, and an honorary Doctor of Science degree from the City University of New York for being the "founding father of forensic psychology as an academic discipline."